This book is a study of the capital transfers to the United States in the nineteenth and twentieth centuries and, for the latter decades of that period, of the transfers from the United States to the rest of the world – particularly Canada, the Caribbean, Mexico, and Central and South America. It provides quantitative estimates of the level and industrial composition of those transfers and qualitative descriptions of the sources and uses of those funds; and it attempts to assess the role of those foreign transfers on the economic development of the recepient economies. In the process, it provides an analysis of the symbiotic relationship between the New York and London stock exchanges and of the evolution of the American domestic capital market. The work explains the centrality of foreign capital's role in American economic development, despite the high level of domestic savings. Finally, it explores the issue of domestic political response to foreign investment, attempting to explain why, given the obvious benefits of such investment, the political reaction was so negative and so intense in Latin America and in the American West, but so positive in Canada and the eastern United States.

International capital markets
and American economic growth, 1820–1914

International capital markets and American economic growth, 1820–1914

LANCE E. DAVIS

California Institute of Technology   *US Department of Commerce*

Published by the Press Syndicate of the University of Cambridge
The Pitt Building, Trumpington Street, Cambridge CB2 1RP
40 West 20th Street, New York, NY 10011–4211, USA
10 Stamford Road, Oakleigh, Melbourne 3166, Australia

First published 1994

Printed in the United States of Amercia

A catalog record for this book is available from the British Library

ISBN 0–521–46054–9 hardback

Contents

Acknowledgments

Intellectually this book draws heavily on five sources, in fact, it could not have been written without them. The quantitative estimate of capital flows are rooted in the pioneering work of Charles J. Bullock, John H. Williams, and Rufus S. Tucker, but the estimates owe even more to the careful work of Douglass C. North and Matthew Simon. Both the quantitative estimates of foreign capital and the industrial distribution of foreign capital and of American overseas investment as well as a not insignificant part of the institutional detail is drawn from the monumental work of Cleona Lewis. Finally, much of the institutional detail is based on Mira Wilkins' excellent, carefully researched and far reaching study of foreign investment in the United States.

Financially, this work has been supported by the National Science Foundation Grant No. SES-9122436, the Sloan Foundation, and the Division of the Humanities and Social Sciences of the California Institute of Technology.

Administratively, the works owe much to Eloisa B. Imel who has supervised, typed, and organized more drafts than either Bob or I care to count. Finally we thank Mira Wilkins and Michael Edelstein for their careful reading of the manuscript and their very many useful suggestions and corrections. The remaining mistakes are, of course, ours.

1

The international flow of
finance: an overview

1. Introduction

Three-quarters of a century ago, the United States replaced Great Britain as the world's largest supplier of export capital. As early as the 1890s Americans had begun to invest heavily in Canada and Mexico; in the 1920s and 30s the American capital markets directed financial resources toward Central and South America; at the end of the Second World War both private and public monies helped rebuild war ravaged western Europe; and in the 60s and 70s the same partnership of board room and Oval room directed billions in American savings toward the underdeveloped countries of South America, Africa, and Asia, while continuing to expand the American financial presence in western Europe and the self governing portions of the British Commonwealth. The past decade, however, has seen a reversal of this nation's fortunes. Within that short time span, the world's largest creditor has become the planet's largest debtor.[1]

Over the last century, the United States was also the world's largest recipient of foreign investment, although, because of relatively high domestic savings, the figures did not present the economy with the same problems as the present half trillion debt. Unlike their great grandchildren, 19th century Americans displayed a high propensity to save. Although the evidence for the early years is sketchy, the share of net capital formation in net national product appears to have averaged about six and a half percent in the years between 1805 and 1840 and to have risen to almost twenty percent by the end of the century; and most of the resources that were diverted from consumption were domestic not foreign.[2]

Although the data are still somewhat speculative, it appears that net foreign investment accounted for just less than five percent of the almost $60 billion increase in the nation's capital stock that occurred between 1799 and 1900.[3] Thus, many modern economic historians appear to have accepted the conclusion that foreign capital played an insignificant role in American development. Simon Kuznets, for example, wrote, "Less widely recognized is the fact that neither the gross international indebtedness of this country nor the net . . . has been large, either in

1

comparison with the total pool of international capital investments, or in comparison with the total capital in this country owned by its residents . . ."[4]

At first glance, it appears difficult to rationalize that conclusion with the emphasis that traditional economic historians have placed on the role of foreign capital; however, both Jeffrey Williamson, in his careful study of *American Growth and the Balance of Payments*, and Raymond Goldsmith, in his estimates of the growth of reproducible wealth in the United States, have provided a ready solution to the apparent dilemma.[5] Although, in the aggregate, the transfers do not loom large, for some periods the infusions represented a much larger share of total investment; and, during those crucial decades, they almost certainly played a critical role in shaping American development (see Table 1.1) In the years 1815 to 1840, foreign investment accounted for as much as twenty percent of new capital formation, in the Civil War decade, perhaps three-quarters of that amount, and, even in the 1880s, more than eight percent. As late as the years 1903 to 1914, years when long-term American capital exports totaled more than three-quarters of a billion dollars, long-term foreign investment in the United States exceeded $1.2 billion, or, according to Williamson's estimates, two and a half percent of net capital formation.[6]

Moreover, given the initially primitive and only gradually developing state of the American capital markets, foreign capital, directed by more mature markets, provided finance for projects that could not raise capital domestically. As Goldsmith concluded, "If the United States had been limited to domestic saving, the growth of wealth would certainly have been slower until near the end of the nineteenth century . . . because these imports were concentrated in crucial areas of growth, and particularly because without them the development of the American railroad system, probably the main economic achievement of the second half of the nineteenth century, would have been slowed down considerably".[7] In general, however, Goldsmith tends to agree with Kuznets' assessment, concluding that international trade and mass immigration made a greater contribution to the nation's economic development than foreign investment.

Because of its potentially important contribution at some times and in some industries – the 1830s and 1880s were decades of rapid industrial and spatial transformation for the American economy – the subject of foreign investment is important to any understanding of this nation's growth. Moreover, between 1890 and 1914 the United States became a major exporter of foreign capital particularly to Canada and Latin America, and it is in these turn-of-the-century decades that the still strident accusations of Yankee dollar imperialism have their roots.

Table 1.1. *Relative importance of net capital imports in net capital formation, 1799–1900*

Years	Net foreign capital imports/net domestic capital formation (Gallman)	Net foreign capital imports/net national capital formation (Gallman)	Net foreign capital imports/net national capital formation (Williamson)
1799–1805	−.012	−.013	
1806–1815	.005	.005	
1816–1840	.220	.199	
1841–1850	−.008	−.009	
1851–1860	.027	.026	
1861–1870	.158	.136	
1871–1880	.055	.055	.045
1881–1890	.086	.082	.102
1891–1900	−.028	−.030	−.020
1799–1900	.049	.048	
1871–1900	.038	.036	.042

Source: for columns (1) and (2) new capital imports are from Historical Statistics Series U 18–25 and the capital stock series are from R. Gallman, *The United States Capital Stock in the Nineteenth Century* and R. Gallman, *American Economic Growth before the Civil War: The Testimony of the Capital Stock Estimates*. Column (3) is from J. Williamson, *American Growth*, p. 142.

This study attempts to describe the history of foreign investment in the United States and the beginnings of American capital exports in the period 1820–1914. Section 2 of Chapter 1 summarizes the net flows of capital. Section 1 of Chapter 2 provides quantitative estimates of the sources and of the industrial structure of foreign investment in the US; section 2 adduces additional qualitative material to flesh out that story, and section 3 narrows the focus to a detailed analysis of funds channeled through the London Stock Exchange between 1865 and 1914. Chapter 3 explores the response of both American and foreign investors to those capital transfers. Section 1 of Chapter 4 examines the American securities listed on the New York and London Stock Exchanges in some detail, and section 2 discusses the shortcomings in the American capital market that opened the doors to foreign, in particular British, capital infusions. Chapter 5 examines the export of American capital in the years before the outbreak of World War I, and finally, Chapter 6 reports some tentative conclusions.

There is one major caveat. There are no official estimates of international capital movements before 1919, and there are no estimates, official or otherwise, of gross capital movements before 1900. Prior to that latter date, the net movements are derived as a residual from estimates of the balance of payments, and, since the residual captures errors and omissions as well as capital flows, there is substantial room for error. For example, for the year 1900 when both the "residual based" and the "gross" estimates of the long term movements are available, there is a $78 million (thirty-seven percent) discrepancy between the two reported capital flow figures. While a part of that difference can be attributed to "errors and omissions" the largest part – probably more than four-fifths – reflects the absence of estimates of short term capital movements in the post 1900 series.[8] Although the new basic series on net capital flows represents a marked improvement over earlier estimates, there remains a substantial margin for potential error. The estimates of net flows employed here are the work of Douglass North for the years 1790 to 1860 and Matthew Simon for the years 1861 to 1900 as revised by the United States Office of Business Economics.[9] The gross estimates for the years 1900 to 1918 are based on the work of Paul D. Dickens, of C. J. Bullock, John H. Williams, and Rufus S. Tucker, and of the Department of Commerce's *Monthly Summary of Foreign Commerce* as revised by Raymond Goldsmith.[10] Both North and Simon recognize the potential sources of errors; and the editors of *Historical Statistics* warn that "the figures for 1790–1918 are from publications by private authors; therefore, they are unofficial figures."[11]

2. The net flows of capital

Since there are no direct estimates of international capital flows for the years before 1900, the aggregate data are indirect estimates obtained as a residual from the calculation of the balance of payments. Those estimates are reported in Table 1.2. There have been three major quantitative studies of the history of the American balance of payments; and, while their focus and conclusions are somewhat different, their reports on the timing and magnitude of net capital imports are similar.[12] All three agree that, between 1790 and 1813, net capital movements fluctuated around zero. The figures indicate that there were thirteen years of net capital imports and ten of net exports; and, taken together, they suggest a very modest net capital inflow of $125,000 a year.

That flow was, however, greatly magnified over the six years 1814 to 1819. All three studies agree that the foreign capital was primarily employed and was particularly important in financing the federal government, the Second Bank of the United States, and the nation's external trade. North goes on the say that, "the limited supply of savings and the

Table 1.2. *Net international capital movements, capital inflow into the US minus outflow*
(Millions of Dollars)

Year	Net Inflow	Year	Net Inflow	Year	Net Inflow	Long Term Only
1790	1	1832	7	1874	82	
1791	8	1833	14	1875	87	
1792	8	1834	19	1876	2	
1793	−2	1835	30	1877	−57	
1794	−9	1836	59	1878	−162	
1795	13	1837	22	1879	−160	
1796	4	1838	3	1880	30	
1797	11	1839	49	1881	−41	
1798	2	1840	−31	1882	110	
1799	−15	1841	8	1883	51	
1800	2	1842	−6	1884	105	
1801	−2	1843	−22	1885	34	
1802	−7	1844	−4	1886	137	
1803	3	1845	−4	1887	231	
1804	−12	1846	−1	1888	287	
1805	10	1847	−19	1889	202	
1806	7	1848	2	1890	194	
1807	5	1849	−3	1891	136	
1808	17	1850	29	1892	41	
1809	−12	1851	6	1893	146	
1810	−7	1852	16	1894	−66	
1811	−35	1853	56	1895	137	
1812	21	1854	42	1896	40	
1813	−15	1855	15	1897	−23	
1814	9	1856	12	1898	−279	
1815	15	1857	17	1899	−229	
1816	58	1858	−23	1900a	−296	
1817	11	1859	26	1900b	−321	−218
1818	25	1860	−7	1901	−273	−245
1819	15	1861	103	1902	−82	−135
1820	−1	1862	0	1903	−154	−21
1821	−5	1863	13	1904	−117	10
1822	8	1864	111	1905	−94	−83
1823	−2	1865	59	1906	22	68
1824	−1	1866	95	1907	35	71
1825	−7	1867	145	1908	−187	−46
1826	3	1868	73	1909	143	59
1827	−10	1869	176	1910	229	255
1828	11	1870	100	1911	40	48
1829	−2	1871	101	1912	36	23
1830	−2	1872	242	1913	−142	87
1831	−8	1873	167	1914	−72	−72

Note: 1900a comparable to earlier years, 1900b comparable to later years.
Source: Historical Statistics, Series U 18–25.

primitive state of the capital market made the foreign contribution more important than the absolute figures might indicate." Important it may have been, but the following twelve years saw a return to the pattern established in the years before 1814 – small annual flows fluctuating around zero – but, in this instance, they resulted in an average net outflow of about $1.3 million per year.

As every American economic history textbook notes, the 1830's were a period of very substantial foreign investment in the United States. Between 1832 and 1839 the nation received, net, no less than $189 million in foreign capital – more than $12 for every man, woman, and child in the country. Williamson, for example, approvingly cites North's conclusion that "relative to the size of the economy it was probably the most significant inflow of capital during the nineteenth century". All three studies agree that the lion's share of the inflow was contracted by state and local government and directed toward the financing of commercial banks and, even more importantly, the expansion of the transportation sector.[13] Stimulated by the success of the Erie Canal, states and cities competed aggressively for funds that would permit them to link into the burgeoning "national" market. In the words of Bullock and his coauthors,

"Although the United States by 1835 had completely paid off its public debt, the states had begun to finance banks and public improvements, and borrowed during the period $174,000,000, of which $147,835,000 was borrowed between 1830 and 1838. Part of this was simply a reinvestment of money previously invested in the federal debt; part was a reinvestment of interest on previous investment; part was owed to domestic creditors; but the greatest part was a fresh flow of capital from abroad, resulting in a large inflow of goods which were paid for only in obligations, some of which unfortunately were ultimately dishonored."[14]

Because of foreign reaction to those dishonored debts and to the delay in the payment of interest and principal on even those loans that were not ultimately dishonored, Americans encountered difficulties borrowing abroad.[15] In only two of the ten years 1840 through 1849 do the net figures show an inflow of capital, and, for the entire decade, capital exports exceeded imports by $60 million.

In the taxonomy of Bullock, Williams, and Tucker, the next episode in the history of the American balance of payments encompassed the years 1850 through 1873, although, from the point of view of capital transfers, the data suggest that they could have extended it through 1876. In twenty-five of those twenty-seven years the net capital flows were positive, in one year the flow was close to zero, and in only one year was there a measurable outflow of funds. Overall the net capital inflow probably exceeded $1.7 billion.

The inflow in the 1850s was about equal to what it had been two decades before, although, as both North and Williamson note, it must have represented a smaller fraction of total economic activity. It did, however, include a greater portion of portfolio transfers; and, within that portfolio, there appears to have been a greater proportion of private – mostly railroad – issues. In 1853 the Secretary of the Treasury estimated that foreign investments in the United States totaled $222.2 million, but that figure excluded commercial and bank debts as well as direct ownership of land and business enterprises. Three years later, the figure for bank loans and commercial credit was put at $155 million, and, on that basis, Cleona Lewis argues that the 1853 total for all indebtedness was probably about $375 million.[16] By 1860 the investments in securities alone were thought to have been about $400,000,000.[17]

If the 1850s had matched the 30s, the next decade saw net inflows of unprecedented proportions. Writing at the end of the decade, David Wells, the Special Commissioner of Revenue, reported that foreigners met the outbreak of the War with great suspicion; and that, as a result, about $200,000,000 of American securities were returned in 1861–63.[18] Wells may have been correct, but there is little reflection of the massive repatriation in the net flow figures. The figures for 1861 show capital imports of $103 million, those for 1862 reflect no significant movement, and those for 1863 display a net $13 million inflow.

Whatever the truth of the early years may be, the history of the rest of the decade is clear. Between 1860 and 1869 the net inflow amounted to $761 million, a figure that represents more than $21 per capita. Over that period, the federal government had incurred interest bearing debt of $2.4 billion and state and local indebtedness had increased by some $500 million. "By 1868, according to *Hunt's Merchant's Magazine*, $700,000,000 of United States bonds were held abroad, and they had not netted the American sellers more than 57 1/2 percent. Secretary McCulloch estimated the foreign investments, excluding railway stocks, at $850,000,000. Altogether the amount of American securities held abroad was estimated at $938,000,000."[19] Finally, in 1869, Wells, inventorying all foreign debt except commercial credit, placed the total foreign investment in the United States at $1.465 billion. Cleona Lewis adds some $75 to $80 million for the excluded items and estimates total US indebtedness at "a little above 1.5 billions."[20] Simon, writing some two decades later takes exception to this figure. He notes, "although sizable quantities of government bonds were sold at a discount in European markets, my estimates suggest that Wells' 1869 estimate is clearly extravagant", and he suggests an alternative figure of $1.2 billion – a figure that is close to the $1.216 billion reached by adding the balancing items in the OBE's revisions of the North and Simon series.[21]

Nor did 1869 see the end of the inflow. The net total for the years 1870 to 1873 was $610 million (Bullock, Williams and Tucker estimate the flow for the first eight months of 1873 alone at more than \$100 million), and the years 1874 through 1876 brought an additional \$171 million into the country. Thus, it appears that, over the twenty-seven year span, almost \$1.8 billion was transferred from European savers to American business and government.

Bullock and his co-authors place the beginning of the next episode in 1874 and the end in 1895, while Williamson, with his emphasis on the "long swing", demarks it at 1879 and 1900.[22] A study focused on the net flows alone suggests that their single period may really have been two. The first, spanning the years 1877 through 1881, was marked by four years of capital outflow, and, as a result, a reduction of American net foreign liabilities of \$390 million.[23]

The second "era" stretches from 1882 through 1896. In fourteen of those fifteen years, capital flowed into the country (the exception was 1894), and, in total, the inflows almost equaled the more than \$1.7 billion transferred between 1860 and 1876 – in real terms, the transfer was substantially larger. Both Bullock and Williamson note the preponderance of railway securities in this total, but those years also saw foreign funds flowing into western mining, agriculture, and land development. Bullock and his co-authors argue that between 1890 and 1896 "the net security movement was heavily against the United States, the net annual withdrawal averaging \$60,000,000, or a total of about \$300,000,000."[24] While the net flow estimates do show a decline over the totals of the previous decade, with the exception of 1894, they suggest a continued capital importation of just less than \$90 million a year. If, indeed, \$300 million in portfolio investments were repatriated, those transfers must have been more than offset by increase in short-term capital or new long-term issues.

Like the brief period 1877–1881, the long-term increase of foreign investment was reversed in the nine years 1897–1905 – all years of substantial capital exports. Unfortunately, the period spans the shift in the series from the OBE revisions of North and Simon to the estimates for 1901 to 1918 prepared by Raymond Goldsmith; and, as a result, it is impossible to place an agreed value on the size of that outflow.[25] The net capital series indicate that, by Simon's calculations, the outflow totaled \$827 million between the beginning of 1897 and the end of 1900 and, by Goldsmith's long term estimates, \$712 million for the years 1900 through 1905.[26]

Despite the statistical problems, there can be no doubt that, for the first time, the United States had become a major capital exporter. The best estimates indicate that between 1897 and 1908 American direct investments abroad rose from \$634.5 to \$1,638.5 million (or more than two and a half times), portfolio investments increased from \$50 to \$886.3 million (almost eighteen fold), and, taken together, all foreign holdings rose from

$684.5 to $2,524.8 million (an increase of almost 270 percent).[27] As a result, the nation's net indebtedness declined from a peak of almost $3.3 billion in 1896 to between $2.5 and $2.6 billion in 1900 and, perhaps, to as little as $2.0 billion at the end of 1905.[28]

The last nine years before the outbreak of World War I, however, witnessed a return to the era of heavy American borrowing. In only two of those nine years was the nation a net exporter of capital, and in 1910 the import was a massive $255 million. Overall, despite a more than forty percent increase in American investment abroad, between January 1906 and December 1914, long term capital imports exceeded exports by $493 million.[29] By that latter date the country's net indebtedness once again almost certainly exceeded $2.5 billion.

2

The sources and uses of foreign capital

1. The sources and the industrial disposition of foreign capital (1): the quantitative evidence

Although the data are derived from a number of uncoordinated and often incomplete individual studies, it is possible to glean a general approximation of the industrial distribution of the foreign capital imports at selected dates between 1803 and 1914 and to gain at least some feeling for the relative magnitude of the contribution of Great Britain from the 1860s and that of other European countries from the 1890s onward.

Table 2.1 *Industrial distribution of foreign investments in the United States*

(1)	(2)	(3)	(4)	(5)	(6)	(7)	(8)	(9)
Years	Total Gov.	US Gov.	State & Local Gov.	Rail-roads	Other Private Securities	Direct Inv.	Short Term Inv.	Total Foreign Inv.
				Panel A: Millions of Dollars				
1843	150	0	150	0	53	small	28	231
1853	159	27	132	52	8	5	150	374
1869	1108	1000	108	243	15	25	153	1544
1914	213	nd	nd	3934	1607	1210	450	7414
				Panel B: Percentages				
1843	65	0	65	0	23	0	12	100
1853	43	7	36	14	2	1	40	100
1869	72	64	7	16	1	2	10	100
1914	3	nd	nd	53	22	16	6	100

Source: Cleona Lewis, *America's Stake*, pp. 519–557.
nd = no data.

Table 2.1 is drawn from Cleona Lewis,and it displays her estimates of the distribution of both long- and short-term finance in 1843, 1853, 1869, and 1914. Table 2.2 reports Mira Wilkins' estimates of the distribution of long term investments at six dates between 1803 and 1880, and Table 2.3 Platt's estimates of total foreign indebtedness at a number of dates. It should be noted that Lewis' and Wilkins' estimates for 1853 and for 1869 are based on the same sources.[30] One note: while there may be some question about the size of the total level of foreign investment on the dates in question, there is no reason to believe that the estimates of the sectoral composition and geographic origin of those investments should be badly distorted.

The 1803 total reflects, in part, the French ($4.44 million) and Dutch ($1.85 million) debts incurred during the Revolution and refinanced in the 1790's; but it also reflects the fact that, in 1803, fifty-six percent of all federal debt was held abroad – the highest proportion ever lodged in foreign hands. In addition, it captures the issues of the Second Bank of the United States ($6.2 million) and another $9 million of "Other" bank issues.

Table 2.2. *Industrial distribution of long term foreign investments in the United States*

(1)	(2)	(3)	(4)	(5)	(6)	(7)	(8)
Years	Federal Government	State & Local	1st & 2nd US & Other Banks	Turnpikes & Canals	Railroads	Unidentified & Miscellaneous	Total Long Term Foreign Investment
Panel A: Millions of Dollars							
1803	48.7	0.0	15.2	0.2	0.0	3.4	67.5
1838	0.0	66.5	24.8	2.0	0.0	16.7	110.0
1838°	0.0	3.3	45.3	28.0	16.7	16.7	110.0
1853	27.0	132.5	6.7	2.5	52.1	1.3	222.1
1856	15.0	132.5	6.7	2.5	82.9	1.4	241.0
1869	1000.0	107.5	(a)	5.0	243.0	35.0	1390.5
1880	249.0	97.0	(a)	0.0	899.0	4.0	1249.0
Panel B: Percentages							
1803	72.1	0.0	22.5	0.3	0.0	5.0	100.0
1838	0.0	60.5	22.5	1.8	0.0	15.2	100.0
1838°	0.0	3.0	41.2	25.5	15.2	15.2	100.0
1853	12.2	59.7	3.0	1.1	23.5	0.6	100.0
1856	6.2	55.0	2.8	1.0	34.4	0.6	100.0
1869	71.9	7.7	0.0	0.4	17.5	2.5	100.0
1880	19.9	7.8	0.0	0.0	72.0	0.3	100.0

°Distributes government loans on the basis of their announced purposes.
(a) Included in unidentified and miscellaneous.
Source: Mira Wilkins, *Foreign Investment*, pp. 50, 91, and 147.

International Capital Markets

Table 2.3. *United States of America: total foreign indebtedness (public and private), direct estimates (millions of US dollars)*

Year	Quantity	Year	Quantity
1821	30	1860	400
1822	38	1863	200
1837 (1)	150	1864	271
(2)	200	1865	320
1838 (1)	110	1866 (1)	427
(2)	150–200	(2)	600
1839	200	1867	519
1843 (1)	197	1868 (1)	638
(2)	200	(2)	938
1851	225	1869 (1)	788
1852 (1)	100	(2)	900
(2)	300	(3)	965
1853 (1)	184	(4)	1465
(2)	222	1870	883
1854	225	1871	1047
1855 (1)	230	1872 (1)	1260
(2)	364	(2)	1500
1856 (1)	240	1873	1393
(2)	500	1874	1462
1857 (1)	250	1875 (1)	1000
(2)	300	(2)	1489
(3)	400–500	1876 (1)	1440
		(2)	2250

Source: D. C. M. Platt. *Foreign Finance in Continental Europe and the USA, 1815–1870* (London: George Allen & Unwin, 1984) p. 188.

The 1838 and 1843 enumerations are more interesting. While the federal debt had burgeoned to almost $120 million by the end of the War of 1812, only a quarter was held overseas; and by 1835 the entire debt (including the estimated one-third held in Europe) had been repaid. Those reductions were, however, more than offset by the increase in state and local borrowing; and a substantial fraction, perhaps as much as forty percent, of those funds were raised abroad.[31] Bonds of the state of New York were quoted in London as early as 1817, and other states were gradually added to the list over the course of the next two decades. Even the issues of American cities began to appear in Europe. In 1830, a

Washington DC loan was floated in Amsterdam; and bonds of Philadelphia and Baltimore appeared in London two years later.[32] By 1838 eighteen states had borrowed $170 million; four years later the number of debtor states had risen to twenty and their total borrowings to $197.5 million.[33]

Although it was the states and cities that acted as guarantors, it was the nation's financial and transportation infrastructure that were the ultimate recipients of the bulk of the foreign funds. An industrial breakdown of the 1838 total shows that about thirty-one percent was directed toward the nation's banks, thirty-five percent toward its canals, twenty-five percent toward its railroads, and four percent toward its roads. The figures for 1842 are similar, although the share going to railroads had increased.[34] Thus, if the state and local government loans outstanding in 1838 are reallocated on the basis of their announced purpose (see Table 2.2 entry for 1838), it would appear that something more than $45 million was invested in banking, $28 million in canals and turnpikes, and $17 million in railroads. If the same exercise is repeated with the loans outstanding in 1842, foreign support for railroad investment appears to have been somewhere in the neighborhood of $38 million.[35]

The effects of the financial debacle of the early 1840s are still visible on the distribution of foreign investments in 1853. Although the total net indebtedness changed little between the 30s and 50s, if Lewis's figures are correct, the proportion of short term debt rose from thirteen percent in 1843 to forty percent a decade later. At the same time, the fraction of government debt in total foreign investment fell from sixty-five to forty-five percent, despite the increase in the amount of federal debt held abroad from zero to $27 million. Clearly state and local governments had reduced – partially by default to be sure – their debts from the peak levels of the early 40s. At the same time, the bankruptcy of the Second Bank of the United States reduced the share of banking investments on the nation's international balance sheet.[36] Thus, the proportion of government and bank issues in the total of long-term foreign investment declined from more than four-fifths in 1838 to something less than two-thirds fifteen years later, and the overall decline of those sectors in the aggregate total was probably from more than eighty percent in 1843 to less than forty percent eleven years later.

In addition to the increasing proportion of short-term credit, those reductions in banking and government investments were offset by an increasing commitment to privately financed railroads. Such railroads – roads that had attracted little foreign finance in either 1838 or 1843 – accounted, by 1853, for almost one-quarter of long-term and one-seventh of all foreign investment. Although Platt has argued that, "foreigners were not *directly* interested to any extent in US railway securities until the beginning of the 1850s", Mira Wilkins reports, "in 1848–1853 German, French, Swiss, and then British monies poured into US railroad securities." By 1853 the Secretary of the Treasury noted that seventy-six of the 244 railroads that he had canvassed reported that they had attracted some foreign investors; and he put total foreign investment in American railroad securities at $52.1 million. As much as twenty percent of the common stock of the Illinois Central was held by foreigners; and, in addition, they controlled fifty percent of the total capitalization (stocks and bonds) of the Erie and Kalamazoo, forty-eight percent of the Philadelphia and Reading, forty-three percent of the Western of Massachusetts, thirty-nine percent of the Cleveland, Columbus, and Cincinnati, twenty-seven percent of the Madison and Indianapolis, and fourteen percent of the Atlantic and St Lawrence.[37]

David Wells' 1869 study reflects the massive Civil War borrowing of the Federal government. Those obligations totaled $1.0 billion – seventy-two percent of long term and sixty-four percent of all foreign investment in the US. In addition, it appears that, between 1853 and 1869, the relative contraction of state and local borrowing had continued, perhaps at an accelerated pace (the two sectors' share fell from thirty-six to seven percent of all investment); moreover, the decline was not only relative, but absolute as well.

Short-term investment remained constant in absolute terms but fell sharply when the measure is a relative one. The growth of railroad investment, however, continued to increase at an average rate that exceeded thirty-five percent a year, and, while in the face of the Federal government's voracious borrowing, the proportion of foreign holdings of American railroad securities in all long-term investment declined somewhat, its position among all foreign investment rose slightly. Finally, although the amount involved was small, Wilkins' enumeration includes $10 million of investment in American mining, and that investment represented a precursor of things to come.

The estimates for 1880 are less rich, but they do underscore two trends in the pattern of foreign investment. First, between 1869 and 1880 there had been a dramatic reduction in the role of federal debt, whether the comparison is made in absolute or in relative terms. Second, the vast majority of new investment was directed toward American railroads. Although the rate of increase was somewhat below that of the 1853–1869 period, foreign investment in that sector continued to increase at almost twenty-five percent a year.

Although there is still some dispute about the level of total foreign investment at the outbreak of World War I, Cleona Lewis provides a clear picture of the sectoral distribution of those transfers, and her work makes it possible to garner some insights into the more micro distribution. At the most aggregative level, the fraction of finance channeled to government continued to decline as did the relative role of short term credit. Both trends obviously reflect the maturing of the American capital markets. Although foreign holdings of American rails more than tripled (to $3.9 billion) between 1880 and 1914, at the latter date they constituted a far smaller (fifty-eight as compared to seventy-two percent) proportion of those investors' total long-term American commitments.

In terms of their relative importance, it was the "other securities" and "direct investments" that increased most rapidly. Together, the two categories increased from less than one to almost forty percent of all foreign investment; and, by 1914, they represented some 2.8 billion dollars. Although the exact distribution of those investments is not known, with certain assumptions it is possible to provide a rough estimate of the breakdown of long-term foreign investment (see Table 2.4).[38] Although the conclusion is certainly speculative, it appears that, by the outbreak of the First World War, foreign investment had penetrated almost every aspect of American life.

Who were the foreigners willing to invest their savings in the United States? Up to the end of the nineteenth century, there is a paucity of aggregate quantitative evidence; but there are some spotty quantitative fragments; and there is a substantial body of qualitative information. Cleona Lewis, for example, begins her landmark study, with the observation that "the American colonies were founded and developed by the aid of European capital; largely from Great Britain, but with funds from other countries also participating – particularly from Holland, France and Spain."[39] The debts arising from the Revolutionary War and

Table 2.4. *Estimated industrial distribution of long-term foreign investments in the United States, 1914*

(1)	(2)	(3)	(4)	(5)	(6)	(7)	(8)
Rail-roads	Government	Banks	Breweries & Distilleries	Commercial & Industrial	Agricultural & Land Related	Public Utilities	Oil & Mining
Panel A: Millions of Dollars							
3934	213	32	355	508	972	222	517
Panel B: Percentage							
58.3	3.2	0.5	5.3	7.5	14.4	3.3	7.7

Source: Underlying data are from Cleona Lewis, *America's Stake*, pp. 529–557. For a discussion of the estimation procedure see footnote 38.

the Louisiana Purchase were initially funded by the French and the Dutch, but hardly had the nineteenth century begun before a substantial fraction of those claims had been transferred across the Channel to be absorbed by the British investing public – the same investors who were to make large loans to the Second Bank of the United States within three years of the signing of the Treaty of Ghent.[40] Wilkins estimates that, in 1818, the British held forty-eight percent of the foreign held federal debt and the Dutch forty-three, but a decade later the figures were seventy-four and eleven.[41] Similarly, the "greater part" of the New York State bonds issued to finance the Erie Canal was "bought up by English investors."[42]

British dominance continued into the frenzied 30s; but every major European financial center had private banking houses that dealt in state and local securities; and there is evidence that, after 1838, Continental investors became more heavily involved in American finance.[43] By the 1850s, however, as European capital again began to flow to the United States in large quantities, it was the British who again played the leading role. Jenks, for example, puts that nation's investment in the United States in 1854 at £50 to £60 million ($235 to $292 million), and Hobson concludes that those investments rose from about $300 million in 1852 to about $500 million in 1857. Although Hobson's estimates may to be too large, it would be impossible to argue that the British were not the single most important source of foreign investment.[44]

As to other European contributors, by mid century the Dutch were still important, but they played a much less significant role than they had five decades earlier. The German stake in American railroads had apparently increased, there was a somewhat lesser amount of French investment; some "Swiss monies entered"; and other nationalities were also present.[45] During the postbellum era, both German and Dutch investment continued to increase. In the German case, the increase rested, at least in part, on the close personal ties between emigrant Germans and the banking community at home. In the case of the Netherlands, Dutch bankers organized formal trusts or holding companies to invest in American securities, partiularly railroad securities.[46]

In general, these conclusions are supported by Lewis' research covering the last half of the century. She notes that the Dutch did make substantial investments in railroads in the Mississippi Valley and the West – and were at least twice burned in the process – and that, for a few years at least, the Germans "were the largest buyers" and held the title of "the chief center of European investments in our bonds."[47] On the other hand, she also concludes that "French investments in American rails were negligible, whether in comparison with like investments of other countries or with the aggregate of French capital abroad", although she does note some late nineteenth century French investment in mining and oil.[48]

Herbert Feis argued six decades ago that the securities of American railways had "long enjoyed an active market on the German stock exchanges", that German capital had built branch factories to utilize that nation's chemical and metallurgical patents, and that they had established numerous trading concerns.[49] More recently, Richard Tilly, citing both the close personal connections that existed between German and American bankers and Fei's quantitative study, concluded that, despite the approximate equality of European and overseas investment, "the United States was the largest single recipient of German foreign investment in the late nineteenth century", although "that weight declined after around 1900 – at least for portfolio investment."[50]

Without question, however, the British were the largest foreign investors in the United States. Even as the Germans were being trumpeted as "the largest buyers", the data indicate that British holdings were seven times as large.[51] Although there are still disputes about the exact size of the foreign investments in the US, there are annual quantitative estimates of the British proportion dating back to 1861, and, while certainly subject to some error, they probably provide a reasonable picture of the actual situation (see Table 2.5).[52] At the beginning of the 1860s, Britain may well have accounted for nine dollars of every ten of foreign investment in the United States. Thereafter, however, that nation's position began to erode.

Table 2.5. *Percentage of British investment in all foreign investment in the United States, 1861–1913*

Year	Percent
1861	90.0
1865	88.0
1870	85.5
1875	83.0
1880	80.5
1885	79.5
1890	77.0
1895	74.5
1900	71.0
1905	66.0
1910	61.0
1913	59.0

John H. Dunning, *Studies in International Investment*.

It had fallen to about three in every four by the mid 1890s, and it was probably less than three in five by 1913.

More complete estimates of the sources of foreign investment exist for the years after 1900 (see Table 2.6). Nathaniel Bacon's estimates for 1899 may somewhat overstate Britain's and understate Germany's share, but they do indicate a geographical broadening in the investment base. George Paish's 1908 enumeration is generally considered reliable, and it captures the quite important contributions of the Germans as well as the results of the substantial inflows of capital from the Netherlands and France. Finally, Mira Wilkins' extensions of Cleona Lewis' estimates for 1914 (Table 2.7 column (7)) suggest, in addition, a spread of the capital base across Europe as well as a significant flow from north of the US border.

Table 2.6. *Sources of foreign investment in the United States by country*

	(1)	(2)	(3)
Country/Year	1899	1908	1914
Panel A: Millions of Dollars			
Great Britain	2500	3500	4046
Germany	200	1000	904
Netherlands	240	750	605
France	50	500	390
Other European	110	250	143
Canada	nd	na	263
Other	45	na	400
Total	3145	6000	6751
Panel B: Percentages			
Great Britain	80	58	60
Germany	6	17	13
Netherlands	8	13	9
France	2	8	6
Other European	3	4	2
Canada	nd	na	4
Other	1	na	6
Total	100	100	100

Source: Cleona Lewis, *America's Stake*, pp. 524, 530, and 546.

Table 2.7. *Estimates of long-term foreign investments in the United States by nationality of investor*

(1)	(2)	(3)	(4)	(5)	(6)	(7)
Nationality	1899	1907	1908	1914a	1914b	1914c
Panel A: Millions of Dollars						
British	2500	4000	3500	4000	4250	4250
French	50	300	630	1000	410	480
German	200	1000	1000	1250	950	1100
Dutch	240	600	750	650	635	650
Swiss	75	100	(a)	(b)	(b)	70
Belgian	20	0	(a)	(b)	(b)	30
Other Europeans	15	0	130	(b)	150	180
Canadian	(b)	0	0	(b)	275	225
Japanese	(b)	0	0	(b)	(b)	25
All Others	45	0	0	100	420	30
Total	3145	6000	6010	7000	7090	7090
Panel B: Percentages						
British	79	67	58	57	60	60
French	2	5	10	14	6	7
German	6	17	17	18	13	16
Dutch	8	10	12	9	9	9
Swiss	2	2				1
Belgian	1	0				0
Other Europeans	0	0	2		2	3
Canadian		0	0		4	4
Japanese		0	0			0
All Others	1	0	0	1	6	0
Total	100	100	100	100	100	100

(a) included in "Other Europeans"; (b) included in "All Others"

1899 Nathaniel Bacon, "American International Indebtedness" *Yale Review* **9** (Nov. 1900) pp. 268–279.
1907 Charles F. Speare, "Selling American Banks in Europe" *Annals of the American Academy of Political and Social Sciences*, **30** (1907) pp. 269–293.
1908 US Senate, National Monetary Commission, *Trade Balances in 1908 of the United States* (by George Paish), 61st. Cong., 2nd Sess., 1910, S. Doc. 579, pp. 174–175. Publicly issued securities only. No figures given for any countries outside Europe.
1914a Harvey E. Fisk, *The Inter Ally Debt*, (New York: Bankers Trust Co., 1924), p. 312.
1914b Cleona Lewis, *America's Stake*, p. 546.
1914c Mira Wilkins, *Foreign Investment*, p. 159.
Source: Mira Wilkins, *Foreign Investment*, p. 159.

2. The sources and the industrial disposition of foreign capital (2): the qualitative evidence

(a) 1803–1840

There can be no question that Europeans held a substantial portion of federal debt in the early years of the nineteenth century; there is evidence of investment in land and financial institutions, and they also invested heavily in the Second Bank of the United States. Those latter transfers initially took the form of loans, but they were ultimately converted into permanent investments in the Bank's stock – investments that were estimated to total $3 million in 1820, $4 million by 1828, $8.4 million by 1832, and $20 million by 1838. The latter two figures represent thirty and fifty-seven percent of the Bank's stock then in private hands.[53]

Despite the flows associated with the Second Bank, the majority of capital transfers between 1803 and the early 1830s took the form of short-term commercial credit. Initially, goods, and therefore credit, were channeled through independent non-specialized urban merchants. Those mercantile firms were sometimes of American origin, but often they had been established by British manufacturers to facilitate the distribution of British goods to the very diffused and diverse American market and, on more than one occasion, to dump excess inventories.[54] Although the structure of the system changed after the widespread bankruptcy of American mercantile firms in the mid 20s, short-term capital continued to flow. British mercantile houses, many connected with the cotton trade and operating through branches or agency arrangements, were able, because of their ability to supply capital, to continue to dominate American overseas trade. "In London and Liverpool a group of eight houses, of which Baring Brothers and Brown Brothers were the most active, handled practically all of the exchange and credit relations wth America." These firms not only supplied credit to American importers, but they underwrote much of American exports as well.[55]

In addition, the British short-term capital market "provided banks with funds to carry inventories of gold or securities, it supplied exchange dealers with the sterling bills to reduce fluctuation in the value of the dollar, and it advanced the funds that enabled American railways to continue building while they mobilized longer-term support at home". Overall it appears that much more than a quarter of all American imports were financed in London. In 1836 the three "Ws" – Wiggins & Co., Wilde & Co., and Wilson & Co., – alone had aggregate debts of £7 million, and that total does not include Baring Brothers, the leading American house, or any of the minor firms. Overall, it is estimated that, by 1836, the credit extended to Americans on commercial account totaled £20 million. While there was a drop in 1837 and a major decline in the early 1840s, the £20 million figure appears to capture the flavor of the late 1830s.[56]

While it was state and local government borrowing that dominated the 30s, there were also private placements. In 1830, for example, within the transport sector, the promoters of the Camden and Amboy Railroad sold one-half of the initial capital stock offerings in the United Kingdom, and, in 1838, the C&A became the first American Railroad to be included on the London Stock Exchange's "Official List." Before the decade was over, five other private American railroads, including the Iron Mountain (partly owned by the Rothschilds) had raised at least some of their capital in London.[57] British funds were also channeled into the shares of the Morris Canal and Banking Company and the Delaware and Rariton Canal (a firm that within a few years was more railroad than canal), and the Cairo [Illinois] City and Canal Company was able to borrow $2 to $3 million, most of it in Europe.

The financial sector also received small but significant infusions of capital during the decade of the 30s. Among commercial banks, the Rothschilds invested in shares and bonds of the Louisiana Bank, the Commercial Bank of Albany, the Merchants' Bank of Baltimore, and the Union Bank of Florida. In addition, the Barings invested in the New York Bank of Commerce, British investors purchased the capital issues of at least ten banks located in five states, including a twenty-seven percent share of the Girard Bank of Philadelphia, and Dutch capitalists had invested in five other banks in New York, Louisiana, and Florida. An 1837 Louisiana state report indicated that foreigners had invested in twelve of the states' sixteen banks and that they held fifty-two percent of the state's banking capital. Moreover, although three-quarters of that investment was backed by state guarantees, almost $6 million was not.

It was not only banks but also trust companies that turned to Europe for capital during the 1830s. The North American Trust, the New York Life Insurance and Trust, the American Life Insurance and Trust, the Ohio Life Insurance and Trust, and the New York Farmers Loan and Trust all raised capital abroad. The North American garnered no less than one-half of its $10 million capital from the UK. Farther west, George Smith tapped Scottish investors for more than $1.8 million for the Wisconsin Marine and Fire Insurance Company and his four other land and investment companies.

While there is no evidence of foreign investment in American manufacturing, there were a few transfers of capital into that country's mining (mostly coal mining) enterprises, but they were small and "of little consequence".[58]

(b) 1840–1914: Railroads

Despite Platt's reservations about the earlier period, as the quantitative evidence indicated, from the late 1860s until World War I, railroads received far more attention from foreign investors than any other sector of the American economy. Moreover, if Civil War finance is excluded, that conclusion holds all the way from the late 1840's until the sounds of the "Guns of August". Despite frequent bankruptcies, reorganizations, and skipped dividends, Michael Edelstein has argued that for the period 1872–1894, at least, the United States "was the beneficiary of some combination of enlarged preferences for risky assets and relatively sparse sources of those assets originating elsewhere." Moreover, although certainly risky, those American rails paid substantially higher returns than their UK counterparts in the early years and still somewhat more after 1900, when they appear to have become substantially less risky.[59] Whether the inducement was a desire to hold risky assets, high expected returns, substantial risk adjusted returns, or the dulcet voices of the likes of Jay Cooke, James McHenry, and Henry Villard, the British in particular, and northern Europeans in general, displayed an amazing affinity for the issues of American railroads.

It is estimated that, as early as mid century, Europeans were absorbing between $30 and $40 million in American railroad securities annually.[60] By the early 50s, a British wine grower and merchant, Benjamin Ingham, had become the largest single investor in the New York Central; by 1856 European investors held sixty percent of the Illinois Central's capital stock and an additional $12 million of its bonds; and by the next year the British holdings of the Philadelphia and Reading were so large that its president was selected from the firm's London bankers, the McCalmont Brothers.[61] In 1856 the first American railroad was listed on the Amsterdam exchange; and, by 1860, the number listed in London had risen to seven.[62]

The 50s, however, marked only the beginning of the European investors' love affair with American railroads. By 1864, three-quarters of the Illinois Central's stock was in European hands; the figures for 1873 suggest a somewhat higher figure; and, in the words of the historian Paul Gates, the railroad continued to be "largely owned by English and Continental Investors until the turn of the century."[63] In 1872, when British investors forced Jay Gould's resignation as President of the Erie, foreign holdings of that railroad's stock increased from sixty to almost 100 percent.[64] Between 1870 and 1874 American railroads accounted for almost seventy percent of all foreign and colonial (non Indian) rail and forty-five percent of *all overseas private* securities issued in London, and, in that latter year, it is estimated that foreign holdings of all American railroads totaled $390 million.[65] Foreign holdings of the New York Central's stock rose from five percent in the early 70s to thirty-seven percent in 1895. Over the same period, those investments in the Pennsylvania increased from seven to more than fifty percent; and, between 1879 and 1899, those in the Louisville and Nashville went from 5,000 to 413,764 shares (that is, to seventy-eight percent of the total).[66] William Z. Ripley, railroad expert and banking critic, reported that, in the early 1890s, foreign investors held, in addition to their more than fifty-two percent of the Pennsy's and seventy-five percent of the stock of the Louisville and Nashville, sixty-five percent of the Illinois Central's, fifty-eight percent of the New York, Ontario, and Western's, fifty-two percent of the Philadelphia and Reading's, thirty-three percent of the Great Northern's, and twenty-one percent of both the Baltimore and Ohio's and of the Chicago, Milwaukee, and St Paul's stock.[67]

Among those European investors, the majority lived in the United Kingdom. Robert Fleming, the entrepreneurial force behind three Scottish American Investment Trusts, for example, believed that, "Scottish capital made possible the building of the American rail network many years earlier than would otherwise have been possible", and while he may have somewhat overstated his case, British and Scottish investments were very important.[68] Although they are recognized to have especially favored the Illinois Central in the years after 1851, UK investors also bought "the bulk of the shares as well as the bonds" of the New York and Erie, the Philadelphia and Reading, and the lines running from Marietta (Ohio) to St Louis that were ultimately taken over by the B&O.[69] When, in 1879, a storm of public criticism forced William Vanderbilt to distribute a part of his holdings in the New York Central and Hudson River, it was the British who took some 350,000 shares, and, in 1888, just eighteen of a total of sixty-three British shareholders held a quarter of the stock of the Louisville and Nashville.[70] British investments in US rails are estimated to have risen from $486 million in 1876, to $1.7 billion in 1898, and to $3.0 billion in 1913, and the nominal value of American railroad securities quoted on the London Stock Exchange rose from £82.7 million in 1873, to £1107.5 million in 1903, to £1729.6 million in 1913.[71]

Although some western and southern roads found their way onto the London market, the first postbellum wave of finance – the wave that peaked in 1873 – was primarily associated with the expansion and near completion of the networks in the East and Midwest. In the East, most of the major lines were represented among the twenty railroads that floated their issues on the British market. That group included the Chesapeake & Ohio, the Baltimore and Ohio, the Erie, the Pennsylvania, the Philadelphia and Reading, and the New York Central, but it was not only the majors that turned to "The City" for finance. The London Stock Exchange provided the funding mechanism that permitted a number of very small lines to raise capital as well. The bonds of the Perkiomen railroad – a

Pennsylvania line connecting Perkiomen and Emaus junctions, a distance of 38.5 miles – found their way onto that distant market as did the issues of the Geneva & Ithaca (45 miles) and the Northern Central of Maryland, a line that connected Baltimore and Sunbury, Pennsylvania.

In the Midwest, no fewer than twenty-five railroads drew British finance between 1865 and 1875. As in the East, the major lines were well represented – the list included the Burlington, the Chicago and Alton, the Chicago and Northwestern, the Illinois Central, and the Louisville and Nashville – but it did not end there. Issues of roads like the Indiana and Southern, the West Wisconsin, the Paris and Danville, and the St Louis Tunnel were also present.

In the South, the Alabama and Chattanooga, the East Tennessee, the Virginia and Georgia, and the Galveston, Harrisburg, and San Antonio all tapped the British market. The eight western roads that found a home on the London market included the Central Pacific, the Denver Pacific, the Minneapolis, St Paul and Pacific, the Northern Pacific, and the Union Pacific, as well as the Katy, the Oregon and California, and the Omaha Bridge.

While the East and Midwest continued to draw funds, the geographic focus of the second wave – a wave that peaked in 1880 – shifted south and particularly west. The Alabama and Great Southern drew substantial blocks of finance, but the Alabama, New Orleans and Texas received even more. To the west there were flotations by the AT&SF, the Chicago, Milwaukee, St Paul, and Pacific, the Denver and Rio Grande, the Great Northern, the Northern Pacific, and the Southern Pacific, not to mention those of railroads whose names, while never well known, have long since passed into history – roads like the Central City, Deadwood, and Eastern and the Texas Trunk.

By 1890 the national network was largely in place. From then until 1913, the majority of existing railroads were no longer constructing new lines, but they were in the process of double tracking and otherwise upgrading their facilities. At the same time, although the demand for finance remained high, integration and consolidation had dramatically reduced the number of roads competing for funds. Some small lines including the Colorado Midland, the Cleveland and Canton, the Knoxville and Cumberland Gap, and the Tonopah and Tidewater did enter the market, but it was the "majors" that dominated the list. Between 1905 and 1909 – a period that saw a total call on the London market of $572 million – only twenty-five individual lines were involved.[72]

London subscriptions to American rails totaled $65 million in 1907, $83 million in 1908, are estimated to have been $102 million in 1909, and were $110 million in 1910.[73] As a result, by 1914 British investors owned more than $1 million in the shares of at least sixteen American railroads – railroads that ranged alphabetically from the Alabama Great Southern to the Union Pacific and, in terms of the British commitment, from $58.2 million in the Pennsy to $1.7 million in the Louisville & Nashville. Moreover, the island nation's investments in American railroad bonds were estimated to be two and a half times as large as its holdings of equity.[74]

If the standard is the level of investment in 1914, the Germans appear to have made the second greatest foreign contribution to the American railroad network, although clearly they did not lose in a photo finish. That the *American Railroad Journal* had called them the "largest buyers" of railroad securities in the early 1850s has been noted, and, although their total investment may have reached $42 million by 1856, they could not have remained "the chief center of European investments in our bonds" for more than a few years.

After the Civil War, German investors, like their Dutch counterparts, became interested in the land grant railroads in the West. They funded a $6.5 million loan to the Kansas Pacific in 1869, by January 1870 they had purchased $5.5 million of Central Pacific bonds, and, by March of that year, they had bought $1.7 million of Michigan Central and $2.5 million of Chicago and Southwestern bonds. Between then and the end of the year, they also supported the Kansas & Pacific (again), the St Joseph and Denver City, the Port Royal and Augusta, and the Davenport and St Paul railroads.

Burned by the suspensions that followed the American stock market crash of 1873, German investors appear to have turned away from American railroads, although they did advance some funds to the Denver, South Park, and Pacific in 1876. The reorganizations of the western roads in the early 80s, however, appear to have calmed their fears, and there is evidence of financial aid to the Union Pacific in 1888 and to the San Francisco and Northern Pacific the next year. A decade later, a study of German investments reported holdings of $20 to $25 million in the Northern Pacific and $15 to $17 million in its Southern counterpart. In all, that study reported significant holdings in eighteen American railroads – most in the West or Middle West – that, together, totaled more than $100 million in 1899. The first decade and a half of the twentieth century saw new German advances to the Southern Pacific, the Central Pacific, the Denver and Rio Grande, and the St Louis and San Francisco. Thus, by the outbreak of the World War, the German total was certainly three or more times the end of the century estimate.[75]

The Dutch easily took the bronze medal in the pre-War foreign "race for the rails." Soon after Appomattox the Dutch began to invest in American railroads, particularly those in the Mississippi Valley and the West. Robert Riegel reports investments in the AT&SF, the Cairo and Fulton, the California Pacific, the Central Pacific, the Chicago, Milwaukee and St

Paul, the Chicago and Northwestern, the Denver Pacific, the Denver and Rio Grande, the IC, the Kansas Pacific, the Missouri, Kansas, and Pacific, the Missouri, the Kansas and Texas, the Missouri Pacific, the Oregon and California, the St Paul and Pacific, and the Union Pacific.[76] Despite their early treatment at the hands of James McHenry and, somewhat later, James J. Hill, the Dutch maintained their interest in western rails.[77] In 1888, for example, they participated with the British and Germans in a $4.4 million mortgage loan to the Union Pacific.[78] A 1909 Interstate Commerce Commission report placed Dutch equity holdings (their bonds holdings were not included) in thirteen railroads at $70 million. In that year they joined in a new loan to the Missouri Pacific; the next year they participated with the French in a loan to the St Louis and San Francisco; and in 1912, they, together with the British, absorbed the new debt offerings of the Denver and Rio Grande.[79]

Despite their position as Europe's second largest source of foreign investment, the French, of all the continental financial powers, contributed the least to American railroad development. In part, this position reflected the French government's well documented attempts to direct "the savings of the French people to Russia, Turkey, and other countries where the French had political alliances or economic interests", but in part it also can be traced to the fraudulent sale of Memphis, El Paso and Pacific bonds on the Paris market in 1869. Granted the rare privilege of selling American bonds on the Paris Bourse, the promoters, including General John C. Fremont, bilked French banks and investors out of some $5 million, and, in the process, they managed to close that market to American railroad securities for thirty years.[80]

Thus, with the exception of some direct placements in the 1850s, the French played no measurable role in the development of the American rail network.[81] After the turn of the century, however, French capital again began to filter into the American industry. The Pennsy received $48 million in 1906, the New York, New Haven and Hartford $28 million in 1907, the St Louis & Pacific $17 million in that year and another $10 million in 1910, the Chicago, Milwaukee & St Paul also received a "large loan" in that latter year, and the Central Pacific borrowed $48 million in 1911. By 1914 it appears that the French also had significant equity investments in the Southern Pacific, the Union Pacific, the Central Pacific, and the Chesapeake & Ohio.[82]

(c) 1840–1914: Government Securities

By 1853 the burden of foreign held state and local debt – a burden that had probably amounted to more than $150 million in the early 1840s – had been reduced by repudiation and repayment to about $127 million, and most of the nation's subnational units had resumed payments of principle and interest. The southern states' need to finance the War and post-War reconstruction, however, forced them into the financial markets once again; and, given the political climate, the bulk of those loans were placed abroad. By the early 1870s, the total of the new debts of those states had ballooned to more than $200 million, and eleven states found they could no longer afford to service their obligations.[83] On paper, in addition to passed interest payments, repudiation produced losses to lenders of between $70 and $80 million, and negotiations between borrowers and lenders produced an additional reduction of about $55 million of principal as the states fought to scale down their obligations. Since many of these loans had been heavily discounted at the time of issue, the extent of actual losses suffered by foreign lenders remains unclear.[84] Given the reputation of the American states, the new legal restrictions placed on their fiscal commitments, and the improvements in the domestic capital markets, there is less evidence of further foreign borrowing after the 1870s. Eight states did, however, make some use of the London Stock Exchange. Massachusetts was by far the heaviest user, but the public issues of Alabama, Arkansas, Georgia, Louisiana, New York, Pennsylvania, and Virginia all found their way to London. In 1915, however, *the American Dollar Securities Committee* found evidence of only a single foreign held state loan still outstanding – $37,000 of a New York State loan of 1897.[85]

The federal government also chose to finance a substantial fraction of its wartime activities with borrowed funds. Initially, however, there was a reluctance to look abroad, and, under any condition, public opinion in the UK – in 1863 a £3,000,000 Confederate loan was oversubscribed five times – made it nearly impossible to raise funds in London. In that year, however, the government did sell $10 million on German account, and, with emancipation and the military victories of the last two years of the War, it is estimated that, by 1865, $250 million was held in that country and in Holland; and an additional $70 million had been raised in the rest of Europe. British attitudes, too, appear to have changed, and the six refunding operations effected through the 70s were conducted largely in London, since, by then, British investors were in possession of most of the foreign held US government bonds – holdings that totaled about $1 billion.[86] That debt was gradually reduced, and only once again, in 1895, was the Treasury forced to turn to Europe, and, even then, the evidence suggests that European participation was not really necessary. The American markets had developed sufficiently that the American half of the $62 million issue was oversubscribed six times.[87]

Although the federal, and to a lesser extent the state, governments no longer found it necessary to turn to foreign markets, the same was not true of local government – foreign funds were needed to finance an infrastructure for the nation's rapidly growing cities. A number of smaller cities that had borrowed to underwrite transport developments defaulted in the 70s and 80s, but the major cities maintained their reputations as "good credit risks." Among American cities, St Louis and Boston were the clear front runners; but the list also includes other major urban centers – Chicago, New York, Providence, St Paul, and the nation's capitol – and two relatively minor cities – Duluth, Minn. and Fall River, Mass. Faced by demands for street improvements, water systems, sewers, urban transport, and ultimately electrification, beginning in the 1870s, cities turned to Europe and particularly to London. While the total was small in comparison to the figures for federal or state loans, New York City alone repaid more than $80 million due in Paris and London in the last four months of 1914.[88]

(d) 1840–1914: Land Related Investments

Given the relative abundance of land and other natural resources, and given that a substantial fraction of new transport investment was directed toward bringing that land and those resources into the market, it is hardly surprising that a small, but not insignificant, fraction of foreign investment went to firms organized to exploit those gifts of nature. In the years between the late 1860s and the First World War, there were foreign – almost all European – investments in financial land and development companies, in firms launched to farm or raise cattle in the South and West, in investment trusts that held portfolios of American land and mortgages, in western mines (usually gold or silver but, with increasing frequency, copper), and in oil exploration and production in California, Oklahoma, and Texas.[89]

The history of foreign investment in American lands can be traced back to at least the last decade of the eighteenth century when Robert Morris sold more than a million acres in New York to an investment group headed by Sir William Pulteney and another five million to an association of Dutch investors.[90] Those sales were, however, somewhat of an aberration, and, while there are records of some personal investments, large scale foreign re-entry to the American land market was delayed until after the Civil War. In 1869, for example, the Nevada Freehold Properties Trust raised almost $1.6 million on the London market.

In 1869, John Collinson, a British engineer and promoter, and his friends purchased the Maxwell land grant – "2,000,000 acres of land more or less" – in New Mexico for $1.35 million, and, despite serious questions about the validity of their title, incorporated the Maxwell Land Grant and Railway Company and began to sell bonds in Britain and Holland. By 1870 they had raised more than $2.5 million and were obligated to pay $250,000 in interest each year.[91] At about the same time, William Blackmore, a British promoter, agreed to sell the land covered by the Sangre de Cristo grant – land located in New Mexico and Colorado – to investors in Europe. He incorporated the Colorado Freehold Land and Emigration Company in London to purchase the northern half of the grant, and he organized the Dutch financed United States Land and Freehold Company to develop the southern portion.[92] In addition, between 1872 and 1874 the Californian Land Investment, the Scottish American Investment, the Scottish American Mortgage, the United States Land and Colonization, and the United States Mortgage Company, together, drew almost $6.2 million.

The major foreign boom in American, largely western, lands was, however, delayed until the next decade.[93] Beginning in 1879 with the organization of the Missouri Land Company of Scotland, the Platte Land Company (Colorado), and the Rugby Colony in Tennessee, continuing with firms like the Florida Land and Mortgage Company, Phillips Marshall & Company (Mississippi), and the Capital Freehold Land and Investment Company that, in 1885, received 3 million acres in Texas in return for building the state capitol, foreign funds – particularly British funds – moved into American lands.[94] Lewis reports that at least twenty-nine foreign land companies with aggregate capital of $52 million were registered in the United States between 1879 and 1911, and, in 1909, the *Philadelphia Bulletin* published a list of fifty-four such companies – a list that included only one firm on the Lewis list. Together, the eighty-two companies controlled, at one time or another, between thirty and thirty-five million acres of land.[95]

The western flavor of those investments is captured in the names of the firms that turned to the London market. The list includes the Arizona Trust and Mortgage, Cedar Valley Land, Iowa Land, Missouri Land and Live Stock, Nevada Land and Cattle, Oregon Mortgage, Scottish Mortgage and Land Investment of New Mexico, London and North-West American Mortgage, San Antonio Land, San Jacinto Estate, South Minnesota Land Company, Texas Land and Cattle, Texas Land and Mortgage, Trust and Mortgage of Iowa, and Western Mortgage and Investment.[96]

Land speculation was one important area of foreign investment; direct investment in agricultural activities was a second. By far the greatest number of those foreign farming ventures were in western cattle ranching – an activity that reached a peak in the mid 1880s. As Wilkins notes, "in 1880 there were 800,000 range cattle in Texas and 250,000 in Wyoming; by 1883 there were 5 million in Texas and 1 million in Wyoming. . . . Foreign investors were in large part responsible."[97] Although Lewis identifies only eighteen of those cattle companies (companies that were capitalized at more than $27 million and controlled more than 4.1 million acres), Wilkins lists no fewer than forty, all organized between 1879 and 1889 and with more than half of that number formed in 1882 and 1883. Those forty firms were capitalized at more than £7.8 million and controlled more than twenty-one million acres in ten states and territories.[98] The first experiments were moderately successful, but falling cattle prices, severe weather and outbreaks of disease spelled disaster in the middle years of the decade (capital calls on the London market, for example, averaged less than $400 thousand a year between 1885 and 1887). Some firms survived. For example, one of the oldest ranches, the Prairie Cattle Company, paid dividends of more than twenty percent in 1883 and, while barely struggling through the disastrous 80s, proved to be a very profitable investment in the years before World War I. The firm continued to operate until 1915 when it sold its assets at a substantial profit. During its thirty-five years of life, the Prairie Cattle Company drew on the London market for $4.7 million, but a shareholder who had participated in the initial offering and held on until the end could feel satisfied with his choice of investments. Overall, however, the most successful single cattle ranching enterprise was almost certainly the Matador Land and Cattle Company. That firm posted substantial profits early, and, although losing money during the depression of the mid 80s, survived and proved extremely profitable in the years after 1910. While its profits suffered again during the depression of the 1930s, the Matador became a virtual bonanza in the 1940s, and when, in 1951, it was sold to a group of New York investment bankers, it brought thirty times the value of the initial investment. The Swan Land and Cattle Company, on the other hand, despite more than $9.0 million in British finance, barely struggled on until it was sold to American investors in the 1920s.[99] The picture for the remaining cattle ranching firms is even less rosy. It is estimated that the loss to British investors between 1884 and 1900 was more than $18 million.[100]

While cattle was by far the most important agricultural activity supported by foreign capital, it was not the only one. In 1882, the British North American Land and Timber Company Ltd, together with some firms controlled by Jabez B. Watkins, an American, purchased 1.56 million acres of land in Louisiana. The "syndicate" announced its intention to drain the marshland, innovate a series of newly developed agricultural technologies, and grow rice. The next year, the California Redwood Company Ltd bought timberland and built a number of saw mills in northern California, and the following year, the Scottish Carolina Timber and Land Company Ltd began to cut timber and raise cattle in the eastern United States. Within a decade, the Riverside Orange Company Ltd had begun to irrigate lands and plant orange groves in southern California. By 1894 the Ashley Company Ltd was engaged in growing cotton in Louisiana; in 1911 the Fine Cotton Spinners and Doublers Association purchased 38,000 acres of cotton lands in Mississippi; and, the United States Lumber and Cotton Company, a firm with a pre-World War I balance sheet that reported $3,457,900 in capital stock, raised a total of $2.8 million on the London market in 1909 and 1910 – the firm survived through the 1920s.[101]

Given the level of interest in American lands, it is not surprising that these direct capital transfers were complemented by indirect transfers routed through European mortgage companies and investment trusts. Such indirect foreign investment – investment made primarily by the Scots and English but also supported by the Dutch and Germans – appears to have begun in the late 70s, surged in the 80s, and diminished somewhat between 1890 and 1914. In 1890, the Alliance Trust of Dundee, for example, held almost ninety percent of its portfolio in American mortgages, but that fraction had fallen to less than sixty by the outbreak of the Great War.

Beginning with the organization of the Scottish American Investment Trust and the Scottish American Investment Company in 1873, at least twenty-four Scottish and British intermediaries – intermediaries designed to channel funds into farm mortgages on the other side of the Atlantic – were launched by the end of the 1880s. Although little evidence exists as to the actual size of the activity, it was sufficient to produce political repercussions. "Foreign bashing" became common, and many states passed laws prohibiting aliens from owning land. (See Chapter 3 for more detail.) While Congressman John Davis, a well known "basher", put foreign mort- gage holdings at more than $3 billion in 1899, the true figure, although large, was almost certainly less than $100 million. Of the Scots and British companies organized in this period, at least seven, with total capital of $45 million, were still operating in 1914.

While the Scots and British were the largest investors, the Dutch made a not insignificant contribution – Wilkins, for example, reports thirteen Dutch mortgage banks with loans of $29.3 million in 1913, and Lewis found that, in 1916, no fewer than twelve such banks had American investments totaling $40 million. There is evidence of German participation as early as 1880 – Dutch and German monies were invested in the United States through the Lombard Investment Company, and, in 1890, the Deutsch– Amerikanishe Treuhand-Gesellschaft was launched with a capital of 20 million marks – and of French and Swiss participation two decades later.

Overall, American mortgages appear to have been an attractive altern- ative for European investors. Taking all countries and both institutional and private investors together, Lewis put the total foreign holding of American real estate mortgages in 1914 at "more than $200–250 million." Wilkins' estimate is somewhat more conservative, but she still places the figure at between $200 and $250 million.[102]

While investments in cattle ranching and land development schemes were based on the potential value of the land itself, investments in mines and oil were based on the expectation of profits from assets hidden beneath the surface of that land. While the exact number of American based firms that benefited from infusions of foreign capital is still in doubt, the magnitude of the total investment was substantial. Clark Spence has estimated that, between 1860 and 1914, there were at least 584 mining and milling firms – corporations with a nominal capitalization of £81,185,000 – chartered in Britain in the "inter-mountain West and Southwest."[103] Edward Ashmead identified 659 British firms with a nominal capital of £99,568,738 that were registered between 1880 and 1904 to conduct mining operations in the United States.[104] Wilkins argues that British investment represented more than one-half of all foreign investment in mining; and she estimates that foreign capital financed betwen 1,500 and 2,000 mining and mineral related companies organized between 1875 and 1914.[105]

The investments were, however, not particularly rewarding, at least to the foreign investors. Spence reports that no more than one in ten of the British firms ever paid a dividend, and Lewis reports that, among forty mining companies organized between 1870 and 1895, twenty were gone by 1903, and the remaining twenty had disappeared by 1914.[106] Still, Wilkins reports that, despite the less than satisfactory overall performance, for four decades after 1875, "German, French, Belgian, and Dutch as well as British investors were . . . excited by every announcement of US mineral discoveries, and investors remained dreamers about 'fabulous returns'."[107]

While it was the natural endowments of coal and iron that underwrote American industrialization, it was the lure of silver and gold that truly excited European, and particularly British, investors. Foreign investment had supported California gold mining during the rush of 49; during the 1860s and 70s Europeans invested in gold mines in Montana; and, during the next decade, they followed the miners to new discoveries in Colorado and, a few years later, to Alaska. At least seventeen Anglo-British companies launched between 1895 and 1898 had "Cripple Creek" in their name; the Independence mine in Colorado was sold to the London based Venture Corporation in 1899 for $10 million; and Camp Bird Ltd was organized in 1900 with a nominal capital of £1,000,000.

Similarly, foreign capital moved into silver mining with the discovery of the Comstock Lode. It should surprise no one that Utah's Emma was a silver mine. It has been suggested that foreign ownership played an even greater role in the exploitation of Nevada's silver than it had in Colorado's gold, and a French financed firm even attempted to mine silver in Montana.[108]

This initial outpouring of British finance was not, in most cases, met with the expected reciprocal flow of profits. The list of spectacular failures was led by the notorious Emma, whose Scottish owners were finally forced to sue both its American and British promoters for fraud, and it included Cassels Gold Extracting Company, about which a London financial journal reported that the British investors had fallen victim to "gold extraction with a vengeance".[109] In the words of the editors of *The Economist*, "Looking back over the mining mania of 1871, it has been ascertained that out of more than one hundred ventures then brought forward only ten are now in existence, and but half that number have ever earned dividends".[110] The editors of the same magazine later reported that "there is a pretty general belief that the profits were never honestly made; that, as a matter of fact, the ore bodies which yielded the dividends were planted by human hands and not by nature".[111]

By the mid 1880s, although gold and silver continued to dominate the calls on the London market, the list of mining calls included at least six copper and one quicksilver mine – for example, the Belt Copper Mines raised $414,000; and the Arizona Copper Company, while attracting less than $2 million in the 80s, had, by 1914, drawn a total of $9.2 million from the London market. Moreover, even among the precious metal mines, while names like Old Lout, Sapphire Gold, and Slide and Spur still appeared on the list of calls, those whose contribution to the American economy was somewhat less transitory, Nevada Consolidated, for example, began to appear with greater frequency. It should, however, be noted that the "New" Emma launched in this period ultimately tapped British and Scottish investors for an additional $1.4 million.

Gold and silver may have proved most exciting, but foreign investment was not limited to the precious metals. Although there were some investments in iron ore and coal mining, those commitments were usually linked to investments in iron and steel production. There was, however, a significant level of British, French, German, and Dutch investment in the non ferrous metals – copper, lead, and zinc – as well as in aluminum, phosphate, salt, and borax. The securities of the Montana Copper Company were sold abroad in 1880, and the Scottish owned Arizona Copper Company dates from 1882. In 1895 the Rothschilds purchased a one-quarter interest in the Anaconda Copper Company and, four years later, about one-fourth of all US copper output was foreign controlled. Although the British and French contribution declined substantially from a peak in 1899, they continued to retain a substantial interest, and German investment increased. In 1914, the British still held almost all of the securities of the Ducktown Sulfur, Copper, and Iron Company and of Borax Consolidated Ltd; the French owned 100,000 shares of Utah Copper – nominal value $1 million, market value $6.6 million – and $5.5 million of the securities of the Southern Aluminum Company; and, as late as 1917, the Germans still held forty-nine percent of the stock of the $7 million American Metal Company Ltd.[112]

These later enterprises appear to have fared substantially better than the get rich quick mining schemes floated in the "roaring 70s". Firms like Arizona Copper, Ducktown, Mountain Copper, Camp Bird, De Lamar, and the Natomas Company of California all survived until the outbreak of the Great War, and some lasted much longer. For example, in 1916, Arizona Copper, a firm that had been profitable from the time it was founded in 1882, paid a tax free dividend equal to eighty percent of the initial investments, and, in 1921, the firm was sold to Phelps–Dodge on favorable terms.[113] Even precious metal mines appear to have performed better. The Camp Bird mine, with John Jay Hammond as consulting engineer and Herbert Hoover as chairman of the board, had, by 1911, paid dividends equal to 155 percent of the initial investment; and De Lamar's cumulative dividends were also a rosy 146 percent.[114]

Oil was discovered in Titusville, Pennsylvania in 1859, but foreign investors did not move quickly to exploit that opportunity. Although the English Petroleum and Mining Company was organized in 1865 to buy oil lands in Pennsylvania, it disappeared with hardly a trace, and further foreign investment awaited the market expansion touched off by the innovation of the automobile. Between 1901 and 1914, foreign investors did begin to invest in the American petroleum industry. Again, British investors were the most important, contributing to the exploitation of fields in California, Oklahoma, and Texas.

Recipients included California Oilfields, Pacific Oilfields, the Anglo-California Oil Syndicate, the Kern River Oilfields of California, the Santa Maria Oilfields of California, California Amalgamated Oil, Santa Barbara (California) Oil, and the Consolidated Oil Fields of California. California firms, however, were not the only beneficiaries; there were also flotations by the Kansas, Oklahoma Oil and Refining Company, Oklahoma Oil, Texas Oilfields, and the Tulsa Oil Company.

The British investment firm of Balfour, Williamson, and Company, for example, launched the California Oilfields Ltd with initial capital of more than $1 million in 1901; and, with some aid from the Dutch, that enterprise was followed by Texas Oilfields Ltd, the same year, by Pacific Oilfields in 1907, by the Oklahoma Oil Company and Kern River Oilfields in 1910, the Santa Maria Oilfields (a $5.8 million enterprise) in 1911, and the Kansas, Oklahoma Oil and Refining Company in 1912.[115]

The French and Belgians (with some additional Dutch capital) launched the Société Belgo-Americaine de Pétroles du Wyoming in 1905 to exploit oil discoveries in that state, and the French by themselves organized the Pétroles d'Oklahoma in 1911. By 1914, however, it was the Royal Dutch Shell group that had become the single most important foreign player in the American market. The Shell Transport and Trading Company – incorporated in the United Kingdom in 1897 – had, soon after the turn of the century, begun to buy American oil properties. In 1902 they acquired an interest in the Union Petroleum Company, and in 1913 they bought the California Oilfields Ltd. In 1905 Royal Dutch and Shell merged, and the new organization continued to expand into the American market. For example, in 1910 Royal Dutch acquired the British controlled Dundee Corporation and its Oklahoma properties. Thus, by the outbreak of the War, Royal Dutch had the "greatest direct investment of any single foreign industrial enterprise in the United States." Lewis estimates that the group controlled at least $17.7 million of the total $35 million foreign investment in American petroleum.[116]

(e) 1840–1914: Commerce and Manufacturing

By far the largest foreign investments in American manufacturing were directed toward the nation's brewing industry. Amounting at their peak in 1891 to somewhere in the neighborhood of $90 million, British investment in American brewing alone was greater than the total foreign investmen in cattle ranches, meat packing, granaries, grain elevators, and flour mills. Between 1885 and 1894, of the 187 calls on the London market issued by sixty-five Manufacturing & Commercial firms, ninety-seven were calls of twenty-five breweries. They included nine calls by the Frank Jones and by the Springfield breweries, seven by the Chicago, the Cincinnati, the City of Baltimore United, the Illinois United, and by the New England, and six by the United States Brewing Company. Taken together, the London Exchange alone channeled more than $38.5 million to American breweries.

In the case of almost all of the American breweries that drew capital in London, the British organizers had purchased and reorganized existing American firms. For example, between 1888 and 1891 twenty-four British "syndicates" acquired about eighty American breweries. Although the largest were the St Louis Breweries (capitalization £2.85 million) and the Milwaukee and Chicago Breweries Ltd (capitalization £2.271 million), the movement toward merger was a national one; the twenty-four were spread from coast to coast – in New England, New York, New Jersey, Baltimore, Philadelphia, Washington DC, Cincinnati, Springfield, Ohio, Detroit, Indianapolis, Chicago, St Louis, Denver, and San Francisco. Although investment declined somewhat from its peak in the early 1890s, Lewis put the total in 1899 at $75 million and at $58 million in 1914.[117] In addition to the British investment, at the time of the United States' entry into World War I German investors held about $4.7 million of the securities of seven other American breweries.[118]

Although the British had invested $1.5 million in the Mount Savage Ironworks in 1844, most studies have tended to overlook the role of foreign investment in iron, coal, and steel.[119] George Paish, for example, estimated that, in 1910, British investments in American Iron, Coal, and Steel amounted to a paltry $1.7 million (one tenth of one percent of his total); however, the actual figures were almost certainly much higher.[120] While the totals were modest in comparison with the size of the American industry, there had been significant foreign investment – particularly in the South – at least as early as the British organized Southern States Iron and Coal Company in 1875. In fact, during the 1870s no fewer than eight such firms ranging alphabetically from the Alton Coal, Coke & Iron Company, through the Lehigh & Wilkes Barre Coal Co., to the Southern States Coal, Iron, and Land Co. Ltd received between $24,000 and $8.8 million. By 1914 British, Dutch, German, French, Swiss, and Canadian investors held $122.4 million of the common and $7.5 million of the preferred shares of the United States Steel Company; and those latter figures do not include substantial holdings in both Bethlehem and Otis Steel.[121]

By 1900 almost every major manufacturer of sewing thread in the United States was British owned. Beginning with the manufacturing subsidiaries opened by the Scottish firms of J. & J. Clark in Newark in 1865 and by J. & P. Coats in Pawtucket in 1869, British influence spread steadily. For example, while those two firms continued to play a major role in the American industry, in 1898 the British Linen Thread Company owned five US firms, and the American Thread Company – registered in 1899 with capital of $5.4 million – was completely owned by English Sewing Cotton Limited.[122]

In addition to breweries, iron and steel, and sewing thread, manufacturing tied to the land and to the growing consumer market also benefited from foreign investment. Just as the lure of western lands drew European investment into land and ranching, the potential profits from the products of those lands drew investments into land related manufacturing enterprises. In the 1890s, for example, the British directed funds into milling and meatpacking, but that surge in investment was short-lived.

In 1889, the British purchased Pillsbury mills, the nation's principle flour producer, and launched Pillsbury–Washburn with a capital stock of £1 million and debentures of £635,000.[123] At the time the conglomerate was organized, it included three Pillsbury mills, two Washburn mills, two water power companies, an elevator company, and a number of county grain elevators in Minnesota and North Dakota. Taken together, this newly integrated firm was, at the time it was organized, the largest milling company in the world.[124] About the same time, one British investment group purchased a chain of grain elevators in Minnesota, the Dakotas, and Montana and organized the Chicago and Northwest Granaries Company Ltd, and another acquired the City of Chicago Grain Elevator Line and reorganized its properties as the City of Chicago Grain Elevators Ltd.[125]

Lever Brothers began to manufacture soap in the United States in 1889; they operated three factories in 1900, and, although that number had declined to one by 1914, their investment still totaled $3.75 million. American rayon production was a British preserve after Samuel Courtauld & Company (later Courtauld's Ltd) opened its American subsidiary in 1909, and in addition a number of more traditional British textile firms (and some German ones as well) made direct investments in the United States.

There was also some German, as well as Canadian, French and Belgian direct investment in other manufacturing and commercial enterprises. Friedrich Bayer & Company became a major producer of pharmaceuticals; Kny–Scheerer was the nation's largest maker and purveyor of surgical instruments; Siemens & Halske and Allgemeine Elektriziäts Gesellschaft had major presences in the fledgling electrical industry; and, together, Bosh Magneto Company and Eisemann Magneto Company with an investment of $11.5 million produced half of the magnetos sold in this country.

The Canadian Car and Foundry Company had a New Jersey plant valued, in 1916, at more than $16 million, and the Alabama Traction, Light and Power Company Ltd was organized in Canada when, in 1912, funds could not be obtained locally. The French had, for example, investments in the New York Taxi Cab Company and in the Berlitz language schools, and the Belgians held stock in American chemical companies later included in the formation of Allied Chemical and Dye, Kansas Chemical Manufacturing Company, and the Solvay Process Company. Lewis estimates that in 1914 the level of British investment in American manufacturing and commercial enterprises stood at $36 million, Canadian at $24 million, and French and Belgian at $13 million.[126]

3. American capital called on the London Stock Exchange[127]

Although the actual size of aggregate capital flows to the US is still the subject of some dispute, a significant portion of the flows from the largest supplier, Great Britain, was recorded in rich detail. An examination of the American capital called up on the London market provides clues as to the magnitude as well as more precise estimates of the spatial and industrial distribution of those financial flows.[128]

John Dunning has reworked and combined the estimates of Albert Imlah and Matthew Simon to produce a series on British Investment in the United States between 1861 and 1913.[129] Lance Davis and Robert Huttenback, drawing on reports in *The Investor's Monthly Manual* and *The Stock Exchange Annual Year Book*, have produced a series on "Capital Called Up" in the London market between 1865 and 1913.[130] Table 2.8 displays both the Dunning and the Davis and Huttenback series as well as the results of an attempt to merge the two sets of numbers.

International Capital Markets

Table 2.8 (a).

(1)	(2)	(3)	(4)	(5)	(6)	(7)
Year	Total Foreign Investment in the US	UK Share Foreign Investment in the US	UK Investment in the US (Stock) (2) × (3)	UK Total Foreign Investment (Stock)	Share of UK Investment Going to the US	UK Investment in the US (Stock) (5) × (6)
	(Simon)	(Simon)	(Simon)	(Imlah)	(Imlah)	(Imlah)
	(millions of dollars)	(percent)	(millions of dollars)	(millions of dollars)	(percent)	(millions of dollars)
1865	710	88.0	666	2644	24.0	635
1866	809	87.5	773	2823	25.0	706
1867	963	87.0	868	3051	26.0	793
1868	1039	86.5	973	3247	27.0	877
1869	1217	86.0	1089	3500	28.0	980
1870	1322	85.5	1172	3735	29.0	1083
1871	1428	85.0	1318	4120	30.0	1236
1872	1683	84.5	1499	4652	30.0	1396
1873	1876	84.0	1607	5091	30.0	1527
1874	1963	83.4	1672	5474	30.0	1642
1875	2054	83.0	1701	5751	29.0	1668
1876	2056	82.5	1666	5876	28.0	1645
1877	1996	82.0	1562	5947	27.0	1606
1878	1825	81.5	1414	6033	25.0	1508
1879	1657	81.0	1350	6224	23.0	1432
1880	1688	80.5	1341	6422	22.0	1413
1881	1653	80.0	1373	6776	21.0	1423
1882	1779	80.0	1449	7094	20.0	1419
1883	1843	80.0	1524	7357	20.0	1471
1884	1966	80.0	1586	7748	20.0	1550
1885	2012	79.5	1657	8084	20.0	1617
1886	2171	79.0	1813	8510	20.0	1702
1887	2434	78.5	2032	8984	21.0	1887
1888	2761	78.0	2238	9480	22.0	2086
1889	2999	77.5	2405	9917	23.0	2281
1890	3229	77.0	2550	10449	24.0	2508
1891	3416	76.5	2639	10824	25.0	2706
1892	3502	76.0	2731	11143	25.0	2786
1893	3709	75.5	2779	11429	25.0	2857
1894	3676	75.0	2824	11639	24.0	2793
1895	3880	74.5	2916	11853	23.0	2726
1896	3974	74.0	2938	12160	22.0	2675
1897	3865	73.5	2801	12384	21.0	2601
1898	3768	73.0	2751	12509	20.0	2502
1899	3701	72.0	2665	12738	19.8	2522
1900	3637	71.0	2582	12943	19.6	2537
1901	3614	70.0	2530	13127	19.4	2547
1902	3703	69.0	2555	13307	19.2	2555
1903	3854	68.0	2621	13548	19.0	2574
1904	3975	67.0	2663	13828	18.8	2600
1905	4134	66.0	2729	14268	18.6	2654
1906	4371	65.0	2841	14902	18.4	2742
1907	4550	64.0	2914	15733	18.2	2863
1908	4723	63.0	2975	16569	18.0	2982
1909	5078	62.0	3148	17301	17.8	3080
1910	5427	61.0	3311	18205	17.6	3204
1911	5661	60.0	3397	19268	17.4	3353
1912	5913	59.0	3489	20332	17.0	3456
1913	6166	59.0	3638	21543	17.0	3662

Table 2.8 (b).

Year	(8)	(9)	(10)	(11)	(12)	(13)
	UK Investment in the US (Stock) [(4)+(7)]/2	UK Investment in the US (Flow) [(8) Year 2 – (8) Year 1]	UK Total Foreign Investment (Flow) [(5) Year 2 – (5) Year 1]	US Fraction of All British Overseas Finance	UK Investment in the US (Flow) (10) × (11)	UK Investment in the US (Flow) London Capital Calls
	(Dunning)	(Dunning)	(Imlah)	(Davis, Huttenback)	(Imlah × Davis, Huttenback)	(Davis, Huttenback)
	(Millions of Dollars)	(Millions of Dollars)	(Millions of Dollars)		(Millions of Dollars)	(Millions of Dollars)
1865	650	71	188	0.100	19	25
1866	739	89	179	0.051	9	14
1867	831	92	228	0.063	14	10
1868	925	94	196	0.036	7	9
1869	1035	110	253	0.046	12	12
1870	1128	93	235	0.078	18	25
1871	1277	149	385	0.431	166	262
1872	1447	170	532	0.198	105	117
1873	1567	120	439	0.538	236	365
1874	1657	90	383	0.177	68	81
1875	1684	27	277	0.210	58	53
1876	1656	−29	125	0.700	88	250
1877	1584	−72	71	0.888	63	794
1878	1461	−123	86	0.070	6	14
1879	1391	−70	191	0.056	11	8
1880	1377	−14	198	0.192	38	56
1881	1398	21	354	0.159	56	87
1882	1434	36	318	0.196	62	66
1883	1498	64	263	0.267	70	84
1884	1568	70	391	0.150	59	56
1885	1637	69	336	0.087	29	22
1886	1758	121	426	0.063	27	25
1887	1959	202	474	0.164	78	57
1888	2162	202	496	0.170	84	99
1889	2343	181	437	0.158	69	88
1890	2529	186	532	0.244	130	154
1891	2673	144	375	0.309	116	108
1892	2758	86	319	0.091	29	20
1893	2818	60	286	0.268	77	73
1894	2809	−9	210	0.215	45	28
1895	2821	12	214	0.252	54	102
1896	2807	−14	307	0.095	29	31
1897	2701	−106	224	0.093	21	20
1898	2626	−74	125	0.107	13	40
1899	2594	−33	229	0.069	16	16
1900	2559	−34	205	0.162	33	28
1901	2538	−21	184	0.153	28	36
1902	2555	17	180	0.454	82	302
1903	2598	43	241	0.060	14	9
1904	2631	34	280	0.276	77	131
1905	2691	60	440	0.061	27	47
1906	2791	100	634	0.131	83	61
1907	2889	97	831	0.369	307	264
1908	2979	90	836	0.199	166	183
1909	3114	135	732	0.148	108	140
1910	3528	144	904	0.138	126	133
1911	3375	117	1063	0.140	149	96
1912	3473	98	1064	0.165	176	140
1913	3650	177	1211	0.201	243	211

The London market "Capital Called" series (column 13) reflects the gross export of finance from the UK to the US; it is, therefore, never negative. Dunning's estimates of UK investment in the US (column 9) are net figures and show periods (1876–1880 and 1894–1901) when repatriations exceeded new security purchases. Similarly, the flow estimates based on the Imlah totals and the US proportions reported in Davis and Huttenback (column 12), while showing no negative flows, are also net of repatriations. As one might expect, the estimates based on "Capital Called" are generally much above the Imlah–Davis–Huttenback based estimates of Total Financial Flows (column 12). For example, a large part of the $731 million difference between columns (12) and (13) for 1877, can be explained by a single $500 million US government refunding loan.

A comparison of the Dunning–Imlah and the Davis–Huttenback estimates of the US fraction of UK overseas finance provides some further insight into the relationship between the two series. One caveat, the Dunning–Imlah series has been extrapolated by Dunning from a series of cross section estimates of British financial capital in the US and of total UK financial capital abroad.[131] In any year observations are, therefore, heavily weighted by past investment decisions. The Davis–Huttenback series relate to new calls alone and carry no historical component.

Not surprisingly, the Davis–Huttenback estimates are much more volatile; however, the causes of the significant differences in level between the two series appear to lie elsewhere. While both capture the peaks in the flows in the early 70s and in the 90s, the Imlah series does not capture the minor peak in the early 80s nor the not-so-minor elevations in the first and second quinquennial of the present century. Overall, the Davis–Huttenback series indicate a somewhat lower level of UK overseas investment being directed toward the US. Since the Imlah based series include short- and long-term investments while the Davis–Huttenback series captures only the long-term component, one would expect that the latter would be lower. While the data for short term investment is sparse, Lewis has estimated the 1869 level at $150 million and the 1897 level at $100 million more.[132] Thus, it appears as if an adjustment for change in short term investments can explain at least one half of the observed difference in the level of the two series. It still does not, however, explain the 1880s. Despite the disparity, there is no reason to believe that the Davis–Huttenback capital called series does not provide a reasonable assessment of the spatial and industrial composition of those transfers.

Although not capturing the net financial flows, the "Capital Called" series make an important contribution to any attempt to understand the nature of the relationship between the British and American capital markets. First, the net figures are aggregates and provide no clue as to the industrial or spatial distribution within the US of the international financial flows. The "Capital Called" series, on the other hand, can be disaggregated by industry and, to some extent, by location.[133] Second, since repatriations are not reflected in the data, the "Capital Called" series mirrors the composition of the demand for finance at any point in time. Thus, if in a given year the US Government paid off $100 million in British-held debt while American railroads were, for the first time, able to place $100 million in securities on the London market, the net series would, correctly, show no net flow, but the Capital Called series would, also correctly, indicate that the British had begun to fund American railways.

Obviously, not only British, but also continental investors utilized the London market. As a result, reliance on American capital called in London makes it impossible to cleanly separate British investor sentiments from those of non-British investors, but external evidence indicates that the London market was principally used by British investors. Here we are not dealing with the ultimate ownership, but with the funds that went through the London markets (that is, with "the first foreign parent"). Thus, the "Capital Called" data used here primarily reflect capital flows from Britain to the US; and, as a result, it does not appear to overly distort reality to term the capital calls in London by American firms "British" flows.[134]

A summary of the industrial breakdown of the American flotations and calls appears in Table 2.9.[135] Not surprisingly, given the pattern of American development, railroads were by far the single most important recipient of British savings. It is easy to see why Alfred Chandler has dubbed America's railroads "The Nation's First Big Business".[136] Over the years 1865 through 1913, total railroad flotations exceeded $2.775 billion and averaged almost $57 million a year. In no year did they total less than $3.2 million, and in 1902 they reached nearly one hundred times that amount. They accounted for about one-quarter of the total in the 1860s and 70s, about two-thirds of the total in the next two decades, and more than four-fifths of that figure in the present century.

Railroad construction in the United States proceeded in a series of waves with peaks in 1872, 1879, 1890, 1902, and 1906; the financial data track that pattern closely but lag behind it slightly.[137] The temporal lag strongly suggests that construction – construction undertaken either by the railroad itself or, like the Union Pacific (the Credit Mobilier) and the Central Pacific, through separate construction companies – was initially financed, in the case of land grant railroads, by Government bonds, or by infusions of short term finance.[138] It appears that it was only after construction was completed that the railroads began to search for permanent finance. "Calls" on the London market reached $80 million in 1873, $79 million in 1881, $89 million in 1890, $291 million in 1902, and $210 million in 1907. The timing of the waves was primarily dictated by economic

Table 2.9 (a). *US capital called London Stock Exchange (thousands of dollars) all years 1865–1914*

Industry	Total Calls	Average Calls Per Year	Percent of Total Calls
	1,000s of $s	1,000s of $s	
Transport	2841739	56835	54.4
Government	1603793	32076	30.7
Manufacturing & Commerce	233635	4673	4.5
Agricultural & Extractive	256787	5136	4.9
(Mining)	(103228)	(2054)	(2.0)
(Agricultural)	(30941)	(619)	(0.6)
(Petroleum & Chemical)	(22751)	(455)	(0.4)
(Financial Land & Mort.)	(99868)	(1997)	(1.9)
Finance	79217	1584	1.5
Public Utilities	207417	4148	4.0
Total Calls	5222588	104452	100.0

Table 2.9 (b). *US capital called London Stock Exchange (thousands of dollars)*

Year	MFG., Comm. & Misc.	Finance	Government	Agric. & Extractive	Transport	Public Utils.	Total Cap Call
1865–69	156	3847	3615	1636	49994	8961	68209
1870–74	16207	4869	518972	27233	275338	8369	850988
1875–79	329	331	1009952	3662	93587	11285	1119146
1880–84	4927	21322	0	31084	289908	1269	348510
1885–89	46816	10520	39	34093	190420	9145	291032
1890–94	51578	12791	3931	45205	269022	158	382686
1895–99	34871	3754	65006	13534	89398	2196	208760
1900–04	6517	7549	0	13765	476267	2620	506718
1905–09	19146	3987	0	28140	572260	71891	695424
1910–14	53087	10245	2280	58433	535546	91522	751114
Total	233635	79217	1603793	256787	2841739	207417	5222588

Percentages of Total Calls

Year	MFG., Comm. & Misc.	Finance	Government	Agric. & Extractive	Transport	Public Utils.	Total Cap Call
1865–69	0.2	5.6	5.3	2.4	73.3	13.1	100.0
1870–74	1.9	0.6	61.0	3.2	32.4	1.0	100.0
1875–79	0.0	0.0	90.2	0.3	8.4	1.0	100.0
1880–84	1.4	6.1	0.0	8.9	83.2	0.4	100.0
1885–89	16.1	3.6	0.0	11.7	65.4	3.1	100.0
1890–94	13.5	3.3	1.0	11.8	70.3	0.0	100.0
1895–99	16.7	1.8	31.1	6.5	42.8	1.1	100.0
1900–04	1.3	1.5	0.0	2.7	94.0	0.5	100.0
1905–09	2.8	0.6	0.0	4.0	82.3	10.3	100.0
1910–14	7.1	1.4	0.3	7.8	71.3	12.2	100.0
Total	4.5	1.5	30.7	4.9	54.4	4.0	100.0

Table 2.9 (c). *US capital calls agricultural and extractive industry*
(thousands of dollars)

Years	Total	Mining	Agriculture	Petroleum & Chemical	FLD°
1865–69	1636	1636	0	0	0
1870–74	27233	20259	670	110	6195
1875–79	3662	650	146	0	2866
1880–84	31084	12455	9936	0	8694
1885–89	34093	14549	8115	317	11112
1890–94	45205	3922	5161	82	36041
1895–99	13534	7765	354	73	5342
1900–04	13765	3636	292	6877	2960
1905–09	28140	13632	326	5834	8348
1910–14	58433	24724	5941	9459	18310
Total	256787	103228	30941	22751	99868

Percent of Total Calls

Years	Total	Mining	Agriculture	Petroleum & Chemical	FLD°
1865–69	2.4	2.4	0.0	0.0	0.0
1870–74	3.2	2.4	0.1	0.0	0.7
1875–79	0.3	0.1	0.0	0.0	0.3
1880–84	8.9	3.6	2.9	0.0	2.5
1885–89	11.7	5.0	2.8	0.1	3.8
1890–94	11.8	1.0	1.3	0.0	9.4
1895–99	6.5	3.7	0.2	0.0	2.6
1900–04	2.7	0.7	0.1	1.4	0.6
1905–09	4.0	2.0	0.0	0.8	1.2
1910–14	7.8	3.3	0.8	1.3	2.4

°Financial, Land and Investment
Source: Davis and Huttenback, *Mammon*, "Capital Called" series.

conditions, but the composition of the issues reflects the history of the construction of the American railroad network.

The Transport Sector also contained a few issues by canal and dock and tramway and omnibus companies. At no time could these issues be viewed as large, if the standard of measurement is the funds directed to the railroads, but in the last decade urban transport, particularly the subways of New York and Chicago, drew a small, but not insignificant, share of the total.

It is not surprising that governmental bodies were the second largest recipients of London finance. Over the forty-nine year period, public flotations totaled $1.6 billion; however, unlike railroads, the pattern is not uniform. Calls were made in only nineteen of the forty-nine years, and while they amounted to more than $780 million in 1877 and between $200 and $300 million in 1871, 1873, and 1876, they totaled a mere $39,000 in 1885. Overall, they averaged $32 million a year, but the number and size of calls declined irregularly from 70 and $522.6 million in the first decade to 4 and $2.3 million in the last. While they accounted for more than seven-tenths of the total in the 1860s and 70s, their share had fallen to only six percent in the next two decades, and to a mere one-tenth of *one* percent in the opening years of the twentieth century. That decline, of course, is a reflection of the improved domestic market for *this* type of security.

If there is a surprise in the Capital Called data, it is in the extent of the penetration of finance directed by the London market into the other dimensions of American economic life at a time when the "Frenzied Financiers" of Wall Street were expressing little or no interest in any sector of the economy save railroads, and federal, state and local governments.

Although the figures pale in comparison to the commitments to the transport and government sectors, overall, the British directed almost fifteen percent of their finance to Manufacturing and Commerce, to Agriculture and the Extractive industries, to Finance, and to Public Utilities. Moreover, although the figure for the 1860s and 70s was less than five percent, the total reached almost twenty percent in the 1880s and 90s – the two decades of most rapid structural transformation, and it was still almost that high in the first years of the present century.

Over the five decade period, advances to Manufacturing and Commercial firms totaled almost $231 million – an average of more than $4.5 million a year. The time pattern of those transfers was, however, not smooth. Not surprisingly, there were few transfers in the first years, but there was a peak in the early 70s with calls reaching $9.6 million in 1874. Firms that provided railroad equipment, particularly the United States Rolling Stock Company – a firm organized to provide equipment for the Atlantic and Great Western Railroad and whose directors had chosen General George B. McClelland as president – got a not insubstantial share of those funds.[139] A few miscellaneous firms, like the Anglo-American Leather Cloth Company, received small infusions; however, the most numerous recipients were associated with the infant American iron and steel industry.

The Manufacturing & Commercial sector drew relatively little additional finance between the first surge and the middle 80s (there were, for example, no such calls in 1878, 1879, or 1880), but overall, between 1882 and 1898, the sector received almost twelve percent of all British finance.

The end of the ninth and the beginning of the century's tenth decade saw a renewed British interest in the rapidly expanding manufacturing sector of the American economy. There were $84 million in calls over the three years 1889, 1890, and 1891 – including almost $41 million in 1889 alone. That torrent was in large part a response to the British investor's sudden interest in American breweries. Breweries alone, however, did not account for the entire surge in industrial finance. The other recipients of "London" capital included several milling companies (Pillsbury–Washburn was probably the best known), General Electric, Eastman's, Pullman, and Edison Phonographic.

Given the market possibilities underscored by the obvious British interest, it is not surprising that, for the first time, the New York Stock Exchange began to take a somewhat more serious interest in its department of *Unlisted* Securities – a department not organized until 1885. Although lagging behind its British counterpart by a generation, the Americans did begin to respond to the potential profits offered by the financial demands of the growing manufacturing sector by the 1890s; and, triggered by the explosion of trusts and mergers – to say nothing of the desire of the owners of some industrial firms to take advantage of access to the developing financial markets to diversify their investment portfolios – the Department of Unlisted Securities became the route by which the offerings of a very few American manufacturing companies finally found their way on to the, until then, not so "Big Board".[140]

The American market's increased ability to handle industrial securities combined with the competition provided by new alternatives that had opened for British investors – particularly opportunities north of the 49th parallel – appear to have been sufficient to move American industrial finance away from the London market. There was little American Manufacturing & Commercial activity on the London exchange between 1902 and 1907. There were no such calls in 1902, 1904, and 1905, and, in 1906 they totaled less than $146,000. Beginning the next year, however, the volume of American manufacturing calls began to increase; it reached $24.9 million in 1912 and totaled $50.4 million for the five years 1910 through 1914. Unlike the earlier concentrations – first in railroad equipment and in iron, coal, and steel in the 1870s and then in brewing in the late 1880s and early 90s – there is little evidence of any industrial "bunching" in the pre-War decade. The Indianapolis and the St Louis breweries are represented, as are the Ogilvie Flour Mills, but the list includes an additional almost $7 million of General Electric calls as well as issues of $21.4 million of the British–American Tobacco Company, $8.2 million of Bethlehem Steel's stocks and bonds, and even $50,000 of Quaker Oats securities.

The composition of the early manufacturing and commercial calls, with concentrations in support of iron making, brewing, and milling, suggests something about the natural resource intensity of the nineteenth century American economy, and that conclusion is underscored by the almost five percent of finance channeled to industries that were directly linked with the natural resource base (mining, financial, land, and development, agricultural, and petroleum and chemical firms). Moreover, while the agriculture and extractive sector accounted for only two percent of total calls in the 1860s and 70s, it drew almost eleven percent of British finance between 1882 and 1896, and its share still stood at more than five percent in the last sixteen years of the period. The almost five percent overall figure (two percent to mines, almost two percent to financial land and development companies, six-tenths of a percent to agriculture, and four-tenths of a percent to petroleum and chemicals) translates into a total transfer of $258 million, or an average of about $5.2 million a year. The transfers to the Agricultural & Extractive sector mirror the cyclic patterns found in the Railroad and in the Manufacturing & Commercial groups. There was a peak of $12.5 million in 1872, and a massive transfer of $100.9 million in the years between 1881 and 1891 (calls amounted to almost $48.9 million in the three years 1889 through 1891). Following a slow period in the early 90s, the level of transfers again increased. They rose to $8.5 million in 1897, and, in a final run-up in the years after 1907, the level of Agricultural & Extractive transfers reached $23.9 million in 1910. Unlike firms in the Manufacturing & Commercial sector, however, these Agricultural & Extractive firms seldom found a home on Wall Street before the outbreak of the First World War.[141]

No single story can explain the movements in the sector's totals. That figure is a composite of movements in four quite different industries. Mines were the largest of the four; they attracted a total of $102.7 million (an average of $2.1 million a year). The transfers to firms in the Financial Land & Development sector were, however, almost as large. They drew a total of $101.1 million – an annual average of $2.0 million. Agriculture accounted for an additional $30.9 million ($619 thousand annually), and the chemical–petroleum group $22.8 million, or about $455 thousand a year.

An enumeration of mining calls indicates a transfer of $8.5 million in 1871 and $7.8 million in 1872, five years of substantial flows between 1882 and 1887 (reaching $5.1 million in 1887), another surge in the mid 90s ($5.5 million was called in 1897), and a final crest in the second quinquennium of the present century that culminated in a transfer of almost $12.0 million in 1910. In the transitional decades (the years 1882 to 1898), mining investment represented more than three in every one hundred dollars of British financial transfers.

In the first wave of investment in American mining, the focus was on gold and silver mines in the far West, and firms with mines in the states and territories of Arizona, California, Colorado, Montana, Nevada, Utah, and Wyoming all managed to attract British finance. Between 1865 and 1874, sixty-two American mining companies ranging alphabetically from the Austin Consolidated Silver Mines to the Yreka Creek Gold Mining Company of California issued 95 calls on the London market. The list included $2,435,000 for Utah's Emma Silver Mining, $1,370,418 for Sierra Buttes Gold Mining Limited, $974,000 for South Aurora Mining, and $584,400 for Phoenix Quicksilver Mining. The investments did not, however, generate the profit that had been expected.

Burned, wary, but still hopeful, the British moved somewhat tentatively back into American mining finance in the mid 80s. Although well below the peak level of transfers of the previous decade, the calls reached $3.0 million in 1886 and $5.1 million the next year; over the entire decade, forty-seven mining firms issued eighty-four calls for a total of almost $27.0 million.

During the 1890s, mining calls totaled almost $11.7 million, and the industrial distribution – heavily biased toward gold and silver but including nine calls from five copper mines and a smattering of other metals – looks much like the pattern of the previous decade. While Mountain Copper did raise over $4 million, the major difference was the evidence of the Alaskan gold rush found in the offerings of firms like Felix Klondyke and Golden Klondyke River.

While there were no American mining calls in 1913, the years between 1905 and 1912 saw more financial transfers ($33.9 million) than even the heady early 70s ($20.2 million between 1870 and 1874). The mix had, however, shifted. Of the eighty-six calls made by a total of twenty-seven firms, forty-six were made by copper mining companies. If the five calls by the Ducktown Sulfur, Copper, and Iron Company (a total of $309,000) are included, those demands summed to more than $18.8 million, or about three-fifths of the mining total for the years in question.

The British–American Financial Land and Development connection was established early, and overall accounted for a total transfer of $101 million, or about $2 a million year. While those figures represent less than two percent of all finance, the sector drew more than five percent of the total in the years between 1882 and 1898. The time pattern of the sector's financial flows followed the pattern observed in ranching, and generally the pattern of mining finance. There was a peak in the early 70s, but the 1880s were *the* decade of British investment in the American West. From the beginning of 1881 through the end of 1891, financial land and development calls totaled $50.3 million, and over $21.1 million was transferred in 1890 alone.

Western mines and financial land and development companies came early to the attention of the British investor; however, the lure of potential agricultural profits were muted in the 60s and 70s and did not become important until the next decade. Although firms like the Anglo-American Oyster Company did receive small infusions in the 70s, the only important transfer was the result of an 1874 call for $250,000 by the South Carolina Rice Plantation and Trust. Over the entire period, however, despite the fact that Agricultural calls were zero in twenty-five of the forty-nine years, financial transfers to those enterprises totaled $30.9 million, or about $619,000 a year. While accounting for far less than one percent of all transfers in the years 1865 through 1881 and 1899 through 1914, they amounted to more than two percent in the seventeen years 1882–1898. Thus, the $30.9 million figure turns, in large measure, on the industry's growth in the 1880s. A flotation of the Anglo-American Cattle Company in 1879 marks the beginning of the British investors' flirtation with western cattle ranching. It was the early 1880s, however, before it was possible to speak of a significant shift in British finance toward that industry. Total calls exceeded $1.9 million in 1882, $4.7 million in 1883, and $2.2 million the following year. As a result of the poor performance of the British owned cattle ranches, agricultural calls after 1890 were fewer in number and value. The few surviving cattle companies aside, thereafter finance went to lumber companies (for example, the Arkansas Timber and Cotton, Columbia River Lumber, and the United States Lumber and Cotton) and firms developing agricultural properties in California and Florida (The Riverside Orange Company, Ltd, for example).

The chemical and petroleum group of the Agricultural and Extractive sector received a total of $22.7 million, or about $455,000 a year. Those transfers were, however, almost all concentrated in the twentieth century. Although there was a single call for $110,000 for a rock asphalt firm in 1871 and calls totaling almost $400,000 in 1886, 1887, and 1891 to firms like Colorado Nitrate, Natural Portland Cement, and Old Swan Borax, there were no other transfers in the nineteenth century. Between 1900 and 1914, however, the industry attracted more than one percent of all finance. There were peaks in 1904 ($5.8 million) and again in 1910. Those twentieth century transfers were dominated by oil companies, particularly those located in California, Oklahoma and Texas. Outside of petroleum, there were issues of the Virginia–Carolina Chemical, and the American Cyanamide Company.

Given the pattern of urban growth in the United States, American Public Utilities received less British financial support than one might have expected. Overall, firms producing gas and electricity, telephone and telegraph and urban public transport services, and purified water for public consumption received $207.4 million, or about $4.1 million a year. That figure amounts to about four percent of all finance, but eighty percent of the sector's receipts were concentrated in the years 1898–1914 when public utilities accounted for more than eight percent of the total.

There was an early surge of telegraph finance in the first quinquennium that culminated in transfers of almost $9.0 million in the four years 1865 through 1868. A second wave, divided in the ratio of about one dollar to three between gas and telegraph companies, peaked at $8.8 million in 1875. The former industry underwrote a flow that crested at $8.7 million in 1889, but that year was an exception. Finally, however, the year 1907 and those from 1909 onward witnessed the highest volume of Public Utility calls observed at any time between 1865 and 1913. The figures for the years 1909 through 1913 were $11.4, $11.9, $5.6, $17.7, and $42.7 million respectively. The largest issues were made by telephone companies (particularly AT&T and New York Telephone) and by firms providing electricity to American cities. On the whole, however, while there were public utility shares traded on the New York, as well as on the London exchanges, they did not represent a significant fraction on either.

Of all of the six sectors, Finance benefited the least from the British financial network. The one and a half percent of London calls that were directed toward the Financial sector were received by a handful of commercial banks, a few insurance companies, and an assortment of trust companies, but it was the last named industry that received the bulk of the sector's finance. Calls by Finance firms aggregated $79.2 million, or about $1.6 million a year. The movements were cyclical, mirroring closely the patterns displayed by the other sectors, although the peaks in the 70s and in the early twentieth century are less pronounced while those in the 1880s and 90s are more so. In 1873 Financial calls reached $4.9 million. There were, however, no calls in five of the six years between 1874 and 1880, but 1882 saw more than $10.0 million channeled into the sector, and the flow averaged almost $3.2 million a year for the decade. Subsequently, there is evidence that British demand had shifted and legal restrictions had raised the costs of such investments. At the subsequent peak (in 1890) the total reached only $7.6 million, and the 1911 peak was a mere $2.3 million.

Of the three industries that constitute the Financial sector, neither the commercial banks nor the insurance companies were important.[142] Over the entire period, only nine commercial banks drew funds from the London market; there were no calls in thirty-nine of the forty-nine years and none in the present century. Of the nine, five (the British and California, the Anglo-Californian, the London Bank of Oregon, the London Bank of Utah, and the London and San Francisco Bank) were located in the West. There were even fewer (four) calls by insurance companies, and they, like the 1881 call for $243,500 by Scottish–American Accident Insurance, were relatively small. On the other hand, the finance that went to trusts that specialized in American investments was not trivial. Altogether, the trusts received $73 million (almost $1.5 million a year).

3

The economic, social, and political response to foreign investment

1. The American response to foreign investment

As Mira Wilkins suggests, American reaction to European investment, although on occasion angry and strident, was most often muted, and, surprisingly often, positive.[143] In fact, the most common response was not "Pommey go home", but a simple demand that foreign investors not be given special favorable treatment. Over most of the nineteenth century, there was a general recognition among Americans that foreign investment made a substantial contribution to domestic growth. In the words of the financial editor of the *New York Evening Mail*:

"Without the accumulated and unemployed pound sterling of the Englishman, the francs of the Frenchman, the Belgians, and the Swiss, the gilder of the Dutchman and the marks of the German, the material progress that has been the lot of these United States ever since the close of the Civil War could not continue."[144]

The marriage between foreign investor and the American borrower was not, however, always all sweetness and light. Xenophobia among rural and working class Americans was not new – those groups had long displayed a dislike and distrust of foreigners, and at times those beliefs were reflected in their attitudes toward foreign investment as well. Although, by the last quarter of the century, the term "Manifest Destiny" had long been passé, the growing strength of the domestic economy had convinced many Americans that it was time for the United States to take its rightful place in the international hierarchy, and it caused them to wonder why the US did not take control of both its finance and commerce and "proclaim herself mistress of the seas".[145] The intellectual ground was fertile, and, over the last quarter of the century, western farmers and workers found support for their anti-foreign investment bias in other regions and even among business and industrial groups.[146] The most active opponents of foreign investment, however, shared three characteristics – they were western, they were farmers and workers, and they were most vocal

50

during the years of agricultural depression from the mid 1880s to the mid 1890s.

Although there were some complaints about foreign ownership of American railroads, those alleged grievances differed little from the complaints by shippers about the "watered capitalization" and monopolistic behavior of all railroads – American or foreign owned. By far the most vigorous, and the most effective, assaults on foreign – and particularly British – investment, came from farm groups. Those attacks were directed at foreign investment in land and in farm mortgages, and they centered on the question of alien ownership of American land.

Although pioneering farmers had begun to complain about the behavior of the managers of foreign owned ranches in the 1870s, it was the next decade before the complaints were translated into public policy. By the middle of that decade, almost all of the arable land in the public domain had been settled, and frontier farmers found themselves pushing against the fenced range – range that had frequently been fenced illegally – of the British owned cattle ranches.[147] At the same time, farmers in parts of the Old Northwest Territory and in the trans-Mississippi West found themselves faced by a severe drought – a drought that was to last for almost a decade.

Faced with land they could not farm and mortgages they could not pay, the agricultural community, ignoring the geographic and climatic causes of their problems, turned on the "villain" closest at hand – the foreign investor. "A passionate, hitherto unmatched fury mounted against foreign investment in the United States" – a fury that was so intense that, as late as 1892, "a New York law firm doubted its client (a foreign investor) could obtain fair treatment in the Illinois courts, because, 'of the prejudices of the West against English capital'."[148]

Politicians react to voter discontent, and the more focused the discontent, the faster the reaction. Although a bill prohibiting alien ownership of land in the Territories failed to become law in 1883, by 1884 the platforms of both major political parties called for some control on alien land holdings. Given the wide-spread public support and the intensity of the lobbying activity, it is not surprising that, in March 1887, a bill forbidding "any absentee alien, or resident alien who had not declared the intention of becoming a citizen, to gain possession in the future of real property in the territories, except property acquired by inheritance or through the collection of debts previously contracted" and, in addition, requiring that, "at least four-fifths of the stock of any corporation thereafter acquiring real estate in the territories had to be held by citizens", was passed by both Houses of Congress and signed into law.[149]

What the federal government did for the territories, the states did for themselves. Beginning with Indiana, similar laws were passed by the majority of the Western States, and, by 1900, thirty of the forty-five states had passed laws that in some way restricted alien ownership of land. The Nebraska, Missouri, Oklahoma, Texas, Iowa, and Washington laws were the most stringent, but anti-foreign feelings were so intense that voters in both California and Kansas demanded that their state's constitution be amended to remove long standing guarantees of property rights.[150]

As draconian as the legislative response was, and, despite intense agrarian political pressure to expand the "reforms" to include the repudiation of, or at least a moratorium on, foreign held debt, "in every instance the operations of mortgage companies – their right to enforce contracts by foreclosure sales and their right of ownership of real estate, usually for a short term of years – were safeguarded".[151] Despite the bitter attacks upon foreign money-lenders, in the capital deficit West, even the most Anglophobic politician was ultimately forced to recognize that foreign finance was still necessary if the region was to develop.

Although the reaction was nation-wide, the original complaints that had triggered the reaction were largely localized both in time and space, and they were generally not representative of American attitudes in other times and in other places. Even in the West, the center of the most vocal opposition to foreign investment, the citizens of the mining regions resisted legal restrictions on such transfers, and they remained strong proponents of continued infusions of overseas capital. It may only have been the memory of the westerners' "success" in unloading the Emma and the Cassels Gold Extracting Company on gullible foreigners that induced the editor of the *New Mexico Interpreter* to complain, "The mining industry in the Territories has been largely fostered by foreigners, and [because of the new federal legislation] hundreds of mines which would have been sold this year will now go without purchasers perhaps for years."[152] Whether the editor had the Emma in mind or not, there was a widespread belief in the mining regions "that foreign investors in mines in the territories had 'facilitated the development of the country, enabled farmers to find a market, and all other industries to prosper' ".[153] Although Colorado passed a law prohibiting alien ownership of property, mineral lands were excluded (the law, itself, was soon repealed), and in Montana, Idaho, and Utah, among the strongest arguments for statehood was the claim that the new political regime would make it possible to abolish the ownership restrictions imposed by the federal law of 1887. Although Idaho ultimately passed an alien ownership bill, the Act, like the ones passed by the Arizona and Colorado legislatures, exempted mining land. Politicians and businessmen in the mining territories protested the passage of the federal law of 1887 arguing "that it would do them great harm by stopping the flow of capital to them, and within a short time the governors of Wyoming, Idaho, Dakota, and Utah asserted that this gloomy prophecy had been realized".

Again, the repeal of the Colorado law was based on the recognition that the legislation of 1887 had "deprived the state of any part of the dazzling influx of British capital".[154]

Although the populists, the grangers, and the Knights of Labor railed against British money lenders and foreign ownership of land, their complaints about other forms of overseas investment, although at times no less strident – they argued, for example, that British capital and American industry constituted an "unholy alliance" designed to put "shackles" on the American people and that the reinvestment of the Englishmen's profits from their American investments would mean, in ten years, "that masses of our people would become interest paying toilers for the aristocracy of the old world" – were, in large measure, identical to their attacks on all "Big Business".[155] Thus, their attacks on the Pillsbury–Washburn flour milling conglomerate – a restructuring that made the firm the world's largest milling enterprise – and on the sale of Chicago's Union Stockyards to British investors were focused almost solely on the potential for monopoly.[156]

Nor were the majority of Americans, even competitors, particularly concerned about the potential market power of foreign investment in the manufacturing sector. In the Pillsbury–Washburn case, for example, the editors of the *Northwestern Miller*, the regional trade journal, wrote:

"We do not believe that our mills become any less American from the introduction of foreign capital any more than our railways are less American because they are built by capital which is largely foreign. Money is cosmopolitan. It talks in all languages. The very number of the holders of the stock is sufficient guard against the denationalization of trade. Moreover, we look to see a large increase in capacity . . . The result will be an enormous increase in our milling business, an improvement in our export trade."[157]

The more common public response recognized the nation's need for foreign capital, although that recognition was often coupled with a demand that the owners of that capital be granted no special treatment. Mira Wilkins' survey of government policy suggests that some state governments took actions to help attract or retain particular businesses or investments from abroad, but she concludes that such behavior was neither common nor particularly important. Moreover, she concludes that the federal government had offered no special inducements designed to attract foreign investments and that even the government's 1875–1879 and the 1895–1896 appeals to foreign lenders to aid this country's public finances, did not involve any offer of special privileges to those investors.[158]

Both state and federal governments did pass anti-trust laws and regulatory legislation, but those laws applied evenly to foreign and domestic business. Most states regulated both banks and insurance companies, and foreign institutions did not escape. Similarly, in the tobacco and thread cases, the government merely "sought to compel investors to conform to American rules, that is, to compete rather than cooperate".[159] At the private level, the editors of *Banker's Magazine* wrote, "So long as the number of persons wishing to borrow on American lands is large, and so long as their desire to borrow is eager and urgent, there is nothing to prevent the flow into that business of a good deal of British capital, but, of course", the article continued, "there should be equality of tax treatment."[160]

It should be noted that, their feelings of justice and equal treatment aside, Americans kept their options open. In 1889, the New York correspondent for the *Economist* commenting on the surge of British investment in American brewing noted that "should Americans go to war with Britain, Americans could always take over British properties".[161] Similarly, many New Mexicans – the governor, both political parties, and the territory's business community – applauded the British owned Rio Grande Dam and Irrigation Company when it set out to build a dam on the Rio Grande at Elephant Butte. However, when after nine years of struggling with local, State, Federal, and Mexican regulations the company lost its capital and the Federal government had taken over the project without providing compensation, the same New Mexicans applauded again.[162]

How then is it possible to account for the Jekyll and Hyde American response to foreign investment? Xenophobia and national destiny aside, there were probably two important underlying factors that shaped the public response: the state of the economic environment and the nature of the investment.

There had been foreign investment in the United States since the country was founded; but, by the 1870s, the experience with financiers like Jay Gould had convinced many British investors that the "wars between the railroad kings were ruining the property of British bond and shareholders." The *Economist* wrote, "there is absolutely no security, even in the state of New York, that the most solid properties may not fall into the hands of a Fisk, Gould, and Vanderbilt gang, and be applied to Opera House orgies and purposes".[163] These investors began to seek alternatives that were not American controlled – and the free standing company became the institution of choice.

What was optimal for the British would not, however, have been the choice of the Americans. As Clements suggests, "British investment in national or state debt, even in railroads, aroused no [American] interest because they were impersonal, subject more to general influences than to individual preferences. British investment in the Trans-Mississippi West between 1870 and 1890 consisted much more of enterprises that made western development bend to British purposes and interest".[164] Carl Solberg has made a similar point, although in a different geographic context –

"British capital was much more visible in Argentina than in Canada – and, thus, more open to nationalistic attack".[165] That characterization – bending to British purpose and interest (the British assumed that American law, a legal system based on British common law, would protect them from "nationalistic" attack) – was, however, precisely the goal the British were trying to achieve. They discovered, much to their chagrin, that laws can be changed and that, although the westerners may have thought that foreign capital was desirable, outside control, particularly alien control, was not.

Moreover, the timing of the British shift in the geographic focus of their investment portfolio could hardly have been worse. Not surprisingly, given the time (the 1880s) and the level of development of the American capital market, the British looked to the West. Although the shift in industrial focus also took place in the eastern component of their portfolio, that region was already relatively well developed. The geographical shift to the West, however, occurred contemporaneously with the development of the states in that region, and, as a result, English investment, although quantitatively not large, was of much greater relative importance. Even its relative importance might not have been enough to trigger the "nationalistic attack" had the frontier not "dried up" both geographically and climatically and had the land in question not been part of the public domain.

In the ensuing political battle, the words *public domain* carried great political significance, but they had an economic significance as well. A ranch on unfenced, and legally unfenceable, public lands required little capital to operate. Nineteenth century cattle ranching was labor, not capital, intensive. The frontier rancher, who needed hardly more than a sod hut, a horse, a rope, a branding iron, and a few head of cattle suffered no measurable loss when British capital was withdrawn. In those parts of the public domain that were endowed with mineral deposits, however, the case was quite different. Unlike ranching, mining was capital intensive, and, without capital, the mineral lands could not be developed. To those would-be mining entrepreneurs, foreign capital was necessary, and the British investor was a hero not a villain.

Over most of the nineteenth and early twentieth centuries, however, Americans viewed foreign capital as a blessing not a disease. Even in the agricultural West, foreign mortage money was given grudging respect. Moreover, with the lifting of the drought and as British investment in the region declined both relatively and absolutely – relatively as the domestic sector grew and absolutely as dismal returns caused the British to reposition their portfolios – the public's Anglophobic mood began to dissipate. After the turn of the century, while xenophobia was not dead, there is little evidence that it affected the economic environment.

2. The foreign response to American investment

In the nineteenth and early twentieth centuries, British investors were involved in a long lasting, passionate, and stormy romance with the American economy. There were certainly moments of bliss and periods of contentment, but, as in many such long term affairs, there were dark years as well, and the years of the early 1840s were among the darkest. In the private sector, the panic of 1837 coupled with the business fall-out that occurred during the ensuing depression had hit British investors in American banks, shipping lines, and mercantile houses with a series of major losses and bankruptcies – the list of bankrupt firms included, for example, that pillar of the American financial community, the Second Bank of the United States. The worst, however, was yet to come. States had borrowed heavily to underwrite investments in banks, canals, and railroads, and in the course of 1841 and 1842 nine states stopped payment of interest on their debt. Two (Michigan and Mississippi) repudiated them outright; Florida "pleaded minority; she was only a territory, a ward of the federal government, when her debt was incurred"; but the legislatures of Indiana, Illinois, Louisiana, Arkansas, Pennsylvania, and Maryland merely shrugged their collective shoulders and announced that they were unable to pay.[166]

The Europeans reacted with horror and outrage. In the press, the editors of the *Times* denounced all Americans and "prophesied that the American name would not recover for half a century [from] the slur which had been cast upon it by the temporary or complete failure of some states to pay their debts". American agents seeking new infusions of British capital were faced not only by the anger of the editors of the *London Times* – "that there is a certain class of securities to which no abundance of money, however great, can give value; and in this class their own securities stand preeminent" – but also by a refusal of British bankers to even discuss new loans. As Paris Rothschild told Duff Green, "You may tell your government that you have seen the man who is at the head of the finances of Europe, and that he has told you that they can not borrow a dollar, not a dollar."[167] Finally, in perhaps the most devastating of all rejections, "at least one American of irreproachable antecedents was barred admission to a London club specifically because he belonged to a republic which did not fulfill its engagements".[168]

In the short run, the *Times'* prophecy appeared to be correct. In 1842 the United States government found it impossible to float a loan in any European money market despite the fact that, "the federal government had a long and honorable record of paying its debts".[169] Memories are, however, short, and as European interest rates declined, they tended to become even shorter – fifty years became eight, and, perhaps, less. With British three percent consoles trading above par, the siren call of six, seven, and eight percent returns could be heard emanating from the other side of the Atlantic, and the British investor, although still wary, appeared prepared to listen. In 1848, despite the fact that Arkansas, Florida, Michigan, and Mississippi had still shown no sign of making any amends for their fiscal indiscretions, United States six percent stock – an issue that was aggressively pushed by both Baring Brothers *and the Rothschilds* – was selling at higher prices in the London market than French threes. By the next year, not only had the US stock prices risen to 106, but Massachusetts five percents (a sterling issue) were trading at 100, New York 5s and Ohio 6s at 93 to 95, Virginia 6s at 91 to 93, and even Pennsylvania 5s at 80 (a decade earlier they had found few buyers at 3 1/2).[170]

British and continental investors, seduced by the higher rates of interest offered by American investments, gradually again began to make their funds available on the western side of the Atlantic. This time, however, they moved to provide themselves with some additional protection. They purchased the advice of, and they channeled their investments through, responsible American financial houses; they tried to add supplementary guarantees to the issues of state governments, and, in the case of privately owned railroads, they – particularly the French and German investors – sent agents to the United states to critically examine "all the projected public works" and to study "their condition and prospects, until they were enabled to form a correct opinion of their merits and the value of the securities on which they were based".[171]

The new policies were helpful, but they hardly provided a magic elixir. On the one hand, by 1856, foreign portfolio investment in the United States was probably in excess of $200 million, and, of that total, state issues probably amounted to something more than $90 million.[172] On the other hand, the investors' confidence could hardly have been bolstered by the "scandalous disclosures of the frauds and forgeries perpetrated by Robert Schuyler, the president of the New York and New Haven Railroad" or by the level of financial distress that still marked many American railroads in the wake of the financial panic of 1857. Perhaps the editors of *The Times*, London, captured the situation neatly when they argued that "as long as British capitalists thought they could gain an extra one or two percent interest upon their investments that they would never manifest 'any want of credulity so long as even credulity could hold on' ".[173]

Certainly that argument appear to have captured the spirit of those capitalists' response to the post Civil War market for state bonds. With political control vested in fiscally irresponsible radical reconstruction governments and with their war ravaged economies badly in need of capital to rebuild, states across the South turned to the European capital markets. They had barely managed to float their bonds when the Panic of 1873 and the subsequent "hard times that prevailed in all sections of the country" combined to make it difficult for those states to meet their fiscal obligations. At the same time, the political counter-revolution led to the election of government officials who felt little or no responsibility for the debts "fraudulently" contracted by their "carpet bag and scalawag" predecessors. During the late 70s and early 80s eight states – Alabama, Arkansas, Florida, Louisiana, North Carolina, South Carolina, Tennessee, and Virginia – defaulted.[174]

Again it was the European investors who, despite their precautionary measures, were caught holding the bag, and, even if the level of their rhetoric was somewhat less harsh than it had been in the 40s, resentment was, almost certainly, longer lived. The individual states' responses differed, but in every instance the end was similar – some combination of repudiation, downward revaluation, and forced refinancing at lower interest rates. Alabama, for example, repudiated $7.7 million of its $25.5 million debt and revalued the residual down from $17.8 to $12.6 million; Arkansas repudiated some $12 to $13 million of its $18 million debt on the grounds that it was fraudulent, unjust, and illegal; South Carolina after determining that $11.8 of its $29.2 million debt was legal, offered bondholders $4.5 million; and Tennessee offered new three percent bonds worth fifty cents on the dollar to the holders of the $28.8 million seven percent debt.[175]

Needless to say, these offers did not leave the European debt holders totally pleased. While, by 1890, all nine states had made some arrangement about their debt, in aggregate, these "arrangements" represented a repudiation of between $70 and $80 million (only Tennessee and Virginia resumed payment without some outright repudiation) and a downward revaluation of at least an additional $55 million.[176] As late as the 1930s, the question of the appropriate political reaction to the intransigence of the American states in regard to the question of their debt was still being debated in Parliament, the Corporation of British Bondholders put the amount still in default at $60 million, and Monaco tried unsuccessfully to sue the state of Mississippi over its defaulted debt.[177]

Nor were the relations between America and Europe much better in the private sector. Most foreign investment was in railroads, and, given the history of the financial high jinks perpetrated by the Goulds and Vanderbilts, there would almost certainly have been problems, even if the economy had not been subject to periodic downturns.[178] The depression of the 1870s forced the Erie, the Northern Pacific, the Kansas Pacific, and many smaller roads into bankruptcy. During the next decade an even larger number of roads succumbed, and in the 90s no less than thirty percent of all of the nation's outstanding railroad securities were subject to some receivership proceeding. In that decade, the list of bankrupt railroads included the B&O, the Norfolk & Western, the "Santa Fe", the "Frisco", the Union Pacific, the Northern Pacific, the Central of Georgia, and most of the predecessors of the Southern. From 1884 to 1900, 60,000 miles of line were involved, just less than one third of the nation's total mainline mileage. Nor did the new century bring respite, between 1907 and 1914, the Père Marquette, the Chicago & Eastern Illinois, the Rock Island, the Missouri Pacific, the Missouri, Kansas & Texas, and the "Frisco" – again – were added to the list. In the words of one transportation historian, "the financial record of these years was not one to inspire confidence in the judgment of many of the railroad leaders or their banker associates", and he might have added "or of the British and continental investors who provided the financial support."[179]

As Dorothy Adler has noted, the average Englishman was not called "John Bull" for nothing, and "in the nineteenth century the bulldog quality of perseverance was applied no less to his financial operations than to other aspects of his life".[180] Given the fiscal peccadilloes that marked American railroad finance decades, some overseas investors responded by shifting their portfolios to other industries and other regions, but the vast majority did not. Instead the British innovated a number of new financial institutions designed to protect investors, and, if an investor were careful and if he were willing to pay the cost, it was possible to escape the worst consequences of railroad entrepreneurship run amok.

The first, and by far the most successful of these new arrangements, was the establishment of close and continuing relationships between individual American railroads and one of a set of very reputable British financial houses.[181] The "relationship" worked for the American railroad in much the same way that a "listing" on the New York Stock Exchange provided an imprimatur to reassure the American investor about the quality of his investment (see Chapter 4). The "house" – would at first have been a merchant banking house (both the Barings and the Rothschilds, for example, had connections with the Louisville & Nashville, and while the AT&SF primarily used the American firm, Kidder Peabody, the Barings stood as indirect "guarantor"), but later it might have been a stockbroking firm, (for example, Vivien, Gray, and Company served as an intermediary for the Norfolk and Western) or even an individual (the Scotsman Robert Fleming acted for a number of roads). This "house" provided advice, short-term finance, and usually held a substantial enough block of the road's equities to guarantee that management would listen carefully to its advice.[182] Moreover, if the road did find itself in trouble, the "house" often had sufficient influence to make it highly probable that its shareholders were protected in any proposed reorganization.[183] Of course, such services were not offered free, and the investor, after having paid his admission fee, might always awaken one morning to discover that the road had switched "houses".

The second institution was the "Protective Committee", a device first implemented in the case of American railroads during the Illinois Central's financial problems of the 1850s.[184] The Committee would usually send an investigatory team to the United States, and on the basis of that report the Committee attempted to negotiate some concessions in return for the promise of additional funds. Initially perceived as a short-term solution, after 1879, when the British began to realize the problems were chronic, the Committees tended to take on a permanent or semi-permanent character. The institution's weakness, of course, lay in its inability to adduce some political leverage to support its demands – the railroads involved had often not floated their shares "through a merchant house or established stockbroker" but had, instead, used the services of "jobbers or arbitrageurs", and thus they were beholden to no financial house. Unless the road's management was amenable or the Committee was able to restructure the railroad's board in its image, its power was limited. In the most successful of such interventions – the Ontario, the Rio Grande, the Atlanta Great Southern, and the Wabash – the railroad agreed to appoint one or more members of the committee to their board.[185]

Representation of the Board was a third alternative, and, by itself, it was probably the least effective. Not only did the road's current board have to agree, but, even if appointed, it was difficult for any Englishman to attend more than an occasional meeting and almost impossible for him to provide continuing guidance. Moreover, if an American was chosen as a surrogate, it was necessary for someone in England to formulate a managerial strategy, transmit that strategy to the shareholders' representative, and monitor its implementation – all from a distance of several thousand miles.

Finally, on occasion, the foreign investors actually foreclosed on the mortgages, assumed ownership, and developed the property. Foreclosure and development was used by the British in the case of the Alabama Great Southern, and it was used more frequently by German and Dutch investors in their attempts to extricate themselves from the financial difficulties generated by their early forays into western roads – the Brunswick and Albany (a Georgia railroad) provides an example of a successful foreclosure. The process was, however, costly, and it was never clear that the foreign investors had either the expertise or the interest needed to develop and operate a railroad.

These four institutions, although frequently employed with more than a modicum of success, were essentially defensive – that is, they were designed to minimize the adverse impact of decisions made by American entrepreneurs for their – the Americans, that is – benefit. At times, however, the British investors adopted a more aggressive stance. Competition and rate wars, although good for the shippers, were not good for a railroad's profits, and, on occasion, the British investors provided the driving force behind any attempts to impose a collusive solution when "cut-throat" competition had gotten "out of hand". J. P. Morgan is usually credited with arranging the so-called *"Corsair"* or "West Shore" deal to halt the violent competition that had broken out between the New York Central and the Pennsylvania, but, although Morgan was certainly the "broker", the standard accounts leave out the crucial role played by the British owners of the New York, Ontario, and Western. Again, when the aggressive pricing tactics of the Chicago, Milwaukee, and St Paul began to threaten the profitability of the Chicago and Northwestern and several other roads that linked Chicago to the wheat lands to the west, British investors operating through the aegis of the firm of Junias Spencer Morgan – in fact, "matters were entrusted directly to Morgan" – took control of the railroad, halted its expansionist policies, and organized the Western Traffic Association in an attempt to control railroad rates in the region.

4

Two securities markets: London and New York

1. The London and New York Stock Exchanges in the late nineteenth century

In light of the significant financial flows from London, it is natural to examine the state of the domestic American capital market. Although that market was gradually maturing, the process was slow, and certain sectors were unable to attract sufficient finance from domestic sources. To provide some evidence of the level of development of the American market and of the industrial and geographic distribution of the industries that the domestic market did not serve, American securities listings on the London Stock Exchange can be compared with those listed on the premier domestic securities market – the New York Stock Exchange. Table 4.1 reports the number of American firms whose stocks were traded on the New York Stock Exchange and the number that were traded on the London exchange in 1870, 1880, 1890, 1900, and 1910.[186] It also provides a very broad industrial classification of those issues.

Among the American stocks listed in London in 1870, there were six railroads, two mining companies (the Colorado Terrible Load and the Eberhardt & Aurora), and one telegraph company. The twenty-seven stocks listed in New York included twelve rails, and among the fifteen other issues of twelve firms were two coal and one quicksilver mine (the American and the Pennsylvania Coal Companies and Quicksilver Mining), four express companies (Adams, American, Wells–Fargo, and US), Western Union, the Boston Water Power Company, and the Pacific Mail steamship line.[187] Only a single stock issue, the $100 shares of the New York Central Railroad, was traded on both exchanges.

The increase in American stock listings on both exchanges from 1870 to 1880 suggests rapid American economic expansion – an expansion that involved major shifts both in the geographic and in the industrial structure of the economy – and it is obvious that the financial demands engendered by that expansion were placing a severe strain on the nation's adolescent capital market. The total number of firms whose shares listed on the New York exchange nearly quadrupled while the number of American issues on

Table 4.1. *Number of US stock issues traded on the London and New York Stock Exchanges*

	Total Stocks	RR Stocks	Misc. Stocks
1870			
LSE	9	6	3
NYSE	27	12	15
1880			
LSE	47	19	28
NYSE	103	73	30
1890			
LSE	108	37	71
NYSE	118	90	28
1900			
LSE	135	51	84
NYSE	273	143	130
1910			
LSE	133	42	91
NYSE	306	146	160

the London exchange more than quintupled. The forty-seven stocks listed on the London exchange included nineteen railroads, still a large fraction of the US stock listings, but it was the non-railroad issues that had increased most rapidly. In 1870, only three non-railroad firms were listed in London; the 1880 listings included two telegraph companies, two banks (the Anglo-Californian and the London and San Francisco), four investment trusts, one wagon and railway carriage company (United States Rolling Stock), and eight mines.

Although the 1880 listings on the New York exchange indicate some institutional response to the increased demand for finance in the non-railroad sectors, nearly three-fourths of the companies listed were railroads. The number of non-railroad listings doubled between 1870 and 1880, but New York's appetite for railroad shares was even more voracious – the number of listings increased from twelve to seventy-three. While the New York rail total had been twice that of London, it was now nearly four times as large. Clearly, although much of the expansion of the New York exchange can be traced to an increasing focus on railroad securities (their share of a much increased total increased from forty to seventy percent), the number of non-railroad shares also increased. In 1880 the list included telephone and telegraph companies, mines, express companies, and a water and power company. In 1870 those New York non-rail listings had outnumbered their London counterparts by five to one. A decade later, although the New York list had risen from fifteen to thirty, there were no fewer than twenty-eight such listings on the British exchange.

In 1890, the total number of American shares listed in New York was still slightly greater than the number listed in London; however, if the focus of attention is turned to the non-railroad sector, the London market was servicing over two and a half times the number of enterprises that were supported by the New York exchange. While railroads still accounted for one-third of the American issues traded on the London market, the listings included seventy-one American firms drawn from at least nine different industries. There were two gas and waterworks, two iron, coal, and steel firms, four telephone and telegraph companies, seven land and building enterprises, seventeen land, mortgage, and financial firms, four trusts, one wagon and railroad carriage company, three mines, and eleven breweries. In addition there were nine other enterprises including Borax Ltd, the Chicago and Northwestern Granaries, Eastman's, J&P Coats, and the Pillsbury–Washburn Flour Mills. Over the previous two decades, the number of American equity issues traded on the New York Stock Exchange more than quadrupled; over the same period the number traded on the London Stock Exchange increased twelve fold. The financial demands required to support the rapid pace of economic growth were clearly straining the newer nation's domestic financial network.

The degree of that strain is reflected in a comparison of the ratio of non-railroad American equity issues to all issues listed on the two exchanges (see Table 4.2). In 1870, the ratio tilted toward non-rail issues on the New York exchange (.56) but toward rails (.33) on the London market. A decade later the results were very different. As the demand for finance

Table 4.2. *Percentage breakdown of US stock issues traded on London and New York Exchanges*

Year	London		New York	
	Railroad	Non-Rail	Railroad	Non-Rail
1870	.67	.33	.44	.56
1880	.40	.60	.71	.29
1890	.34	.66	.76	.24
1900	.38	.62	.52	.48
1910	.32	.68	.48	.52

for new industries – industries often located in the South and West – grew, the British exchange reacted quickly, the New York Stock Exchange much more slowly. The proportion of non-rails on the London market had increased by half, while the fraction in New York had declined to one-half its former level. Nor was the trend reversed over the next decade. The British figure continued to increase (to two-thirds of the total), but the American proportion continued to decline (to one in four).

In fact, despite the overall expansion of the New York exchange, the number of non-railroad issues traded declined slightly between 1880 and 1890. The twenty-eight issues that were listed included those of five of the firms that had been included two decades previously (Adams Express, the United States Express, Pacific Mail, Quicksilver Mining, and Western Union) and an additional seven issues by five companies that *The Times* referred to as "unlisted but traded". Those "unlisted" securities included three issues of the American Cotton Oil Company, three of the Sugar Refineries' Trust, and one of the Distillers and Cattle Feeders Trust. One new express company (the Atlanta) had been added; the Colorado Coal, Iron, and Steel, the Colorado and Hocking Coal, and the Tennessee Coal and Iron companies had joined the list of iron, coal, and steel firms; the shares of four gas companies including the Chicago, the Consolidated, and the Laclede were listed as were nine miscellaneous firms – the latter included Edison General Electric, the National Lead Trust, the National Linseed Oil Company, and the Pullman Palace Car Company.

Of the thirty-seven American railroad stocks listed in London in 1890, twenty-two were also traded in New York, but there were no issues of "non-railroad" firms traded on both exchanges. Even if railroads are included in the enumeration, such jointly traded issues were rare (see Table 4.3). There had been almost no overlap in 1870, and, while the fraction of jointly traded issues increased through the turn of the century, it never exceeded two in nine. A similar lack of overlap is found in a study of bond issues traded on the two exchanges. In 1900, for example, only twenty percent of the total issues were traded on both markets. Though the data provide some evidence of increasing market integration, it remains clear that the London market supplied capital to firms still incapable of attracting finance on the New York exchange.

By 1900, however, New York had begun to respond to the "non-railroad" demands of American enterprise. Over the last decade of the nineteenth century, total American issues on the London exchange increased by about twenty-five percent, but the share of "non-rail" enterprises actually declined slightly. On the other side of the ocean, the number of listings on the New York Stock Exchange rose by more than 130 percent, and the proportion of "non-rail" issues almost doubled. The New York trend away from rails continued – albeit more slowly – over the first decade of the

Table 4.3. *Percentage of total American*
stock issues traded on both the New York
and London Exchanges

Year	Percentage
1870	.056
1880	.107
1890	.204
1900	.221
1910	.182

present century, and, in that latter year, for the first time since 1870, rails made up less than one half of the total stock listings. The American market was maturing rapidly.

The 1900 "non-rail" enumeration for London of companies with substantial American investments had an eclectic flair. The list included ten breweries, nineteen land, mortgage, and investment companies, two telephone and telegraph companies, seven investment trusts, an equal number of mines, two banks, and ten firms listed under "other companies" – the latter included American Thread, Cassell & Co., Fraser & Chalmers, Kodak, Redfern, Spratt's Patent, in addition to the previously listed Borax Ltd, J. & P. Coats, Eastman's, and the Pillsbury–Washburn Flour Mills.[188]

The extent to which the New York Stock Exchange had emerged as a conduit for capital to the previously neglected sectors of the American economy is captured in an enumeration of the listings that begin with the word "American". The list includes American Beet Sugar, American Car and Foundry, American Coal, American Cotton Oil, American District Telegraph, American Express, American Ice, American Linseed, American Malting, American Smelting and Refining, American Spirits Manufacturing, American Steel Hoop, American Telegraph and Cable, American Tin Plate, American Tobacco, and, finally, American Woolen.

By 1910 the NYSE was certainly teenaged, if not yet adult. While London listed one hundred and thirty-three American stock issues (forty-two "non-rails"), three hundred and six were traded on Wall Street, and, of that number, one hundred and sixty were from sectors other than rails. American commercial and industrial firms, breweries, iron, coal, and steel firms, investment trusts, and land, mortgage, and financial firms were still listed in London, but such firms also appeared on the New York exchange. Despite the obvious movement toward maturity, however, the same firms were seldom listed on both exchanges. What joint listings there were,

were dominated by rails, the only "non-rail" equity issues listed on both exchanges were of the United States Steel Company, AT&T, Anaconda Copper, and Amalgamated Copper.

One recent addition to the New York listings might have provided a glimpse into the future for those investors with foresight. The 1910 list included a British firm – the Underground Electric Railways of London. On the Big Board, it joined the shares of the Canadian Pacific Railroad, the Cuban–American Sugar Company, and the Northern Railways of Mexico. In that year the Board also listed bond issues of the governments of Argentina, Japan, and Panama. Wall Street had begun to dip its toes into the waters of international finance.

Moreover, as far as domestic finance was concerned, the New York list began to resemble the lists we know today. The one hundred and sixty "non-rail" listings ranged alphabetically from Allis Chalmers to Western

Table 4.4. *Number of US bond issues traded on the London and New York Stock Exchanges*

	Total Bonds	RR Bonds	US Fed. Bonds	US State Bonds	US City Bonds	Misc. Bonds
1880						
LSE	128	97	4	11	7	9
NYSE	267	190	15	64	0	0
1900						
LSE	216	171	2	1	4	38
NYSE	590	505	11	10	0	64

Percentages

	RR Bonds	US Fed. Bonds	US State Bonds	US City Bonds	Misc. Bonds
1880					
LSE	.758	.031	.086	.055	.070
NYSE	.712	.056	.240	0	0
1900					
LSE	.792	.009	.005	.018	.176
NYSE	.856	.019	.017	0	.108

Note: The 1880 totals were derived by sampling *The New York Times* financial data for the entire month of December. The 1900 totals come from a complete bond listing also found in the *Times*.

Union. It included some old friends – although Adams Express and Quicksilver Mining had disappeared, both the Pacific Mail and Western Union remained from the 1870 close. From the 1890 roster, American Cotton Oil was now formally listed, and Colorado and Hocking Coal and Iron, Consolidated Gas, Distiller's and Cattle Feeder's Trust (now Distiller's Securities), General Electric, Laclede Gas, National Lead, North American, Chicago Gas (now People's Gas), and the Pullman Palace Car Company (now simply the Pullman Company) remained. In addition, since 1890 the exchange had expanded to include the offerings of a set of firms that are still household names today – Allis Chalmers, American Tobacco, Bethlehem Steel, International Harvester, National Biscuit, Republic Steel, Sears Roebuck, United States Rubber, and United States Steel. The New York Stock Exchange was becoming a truly economy wide capital market.

Although the data on bond listings is probably less reliable, they too confirm the pre-War trends apparent in the equity market. While both the London and the New York exchanges responded to the demands for finance originating in the rail and government sectors, the London exchange responded more quickly than its New York counterpart to the demands of the other sectors of the economy (see Table 4.4). As with the equity issues, it appears that it was the turn of the century before New York began to list substantial numbers of those offerings.

2. The American domestic capital market and the demand for foreign capital

Given the size and the composition of the flows from savers in Britain to capital using firms in the United States, the question remains – why did those American firms look abroad for financial support when domestic help was so much closer at hand? The answer to that question is not simple – it has at least three different but not entirely unrelated components. First, while the American savings rate was high, the available savings were not great enough to have underwritten the short-term surges in investment demand that marked this nation's development. Second, British savers were probably more sophisticated than their American counterparts. That is, while there may have been clusters of American savers who were willing to risk their accumulations in enterprises far removed from their everyday experience, most were not. Third, the institutional structure of the New York exchange was different to that of its London counterpart. That is to say, the New York market was constrained by an institutional structure and a set of operating rules that, although designed to reassure investors, made it somewhat difficult to adjust to rapidly changing demand considerations.

Although there may be some question of the direction of causality in the second and third, the evidence for the first component is relatively straightforward. The surges of foreign finance were temporally correlated with the Civil War and with periods of most rapid American growth and structural transformation: 1814–1819, 1832–1839, 1869–1875, and 1882–1896. Although there is a substantial literature on the question of the relationship between American investment demand and the foreign supply of capital, the most convincing analysis can be found in Edelstein's study of *Overseas Investment in the Age of High Imperialism*. Edelstein shows that, over the four overlapping quinquennial between 1834 and 1858 and the five between 1869 and 1898, there was a strong positive relationship between the ratio of American Gross Domestic Capital Formation to Gross National Product and the ratio of Net Foreign Investment to Gross National Product. Thus, he concludes that it was the American demand for capital rather than the foreign supply of capital that was the engine that powered the movement of finance from Europe to the US. He also finds, however, that, in the last two overlapping decades (1894–1903 and 1899–1908), there is evidence that the positive relationship no longer held. "Crudely, US real domestic capital formation rates rose more rapidly than the US real domestic saving, owing to explosive investment demand and/or slower moving savings desires, and the gap was filled by net foreign borrowing. Once the slower moving savings desires reached their long-run target, net foreign borrowing disappeared."[189]

Most scholars agree that both the second and third components contributed to the problem, but, to some extent, they disagree about the relative weights to be assigned to each, and the evidence is indirect and somewhat ambiguous.

As early as the mid 1930s, M. M. Postan had become intrigued by questions about the evolution and integration of both national and international markets, and his concerns have led to a steady flow of work that focuses on questions of institutional innovation and capital market evolution.[190] More recently, Robert Zevin and Larry Neal have independently examined the question of the degree of integration of international capital markets. Zevin concludes that the international markets were well integrated by *at least* the end of the last century and probably before.[191] In a similar vein, Neal argues that, while international markets were reasonably well integrated in the eighteenth century, the international market disintegrated in the early nineteenth century and was only gradually reintegrated over the course of that century.[192]

Postan concluded that pre-modern capital transfers were usually not founded on market exchanges between unrelated savers and investors, but on direct transactions based on personal relations. Before a modern capital market could develop, it was necessary to educate savers, to prove to them that investment in depersonalized "symbolic capital" (capital that was mobile and divisible – that is, liquid paper claims on assets rather than the assets themselves) was as safe as direct ownership of the physical asset itself. In the case of Britain, Postan argued that this educational process began with the sleeping partnerships of the sixteenth century, but it was not completed until savers had, first, come to recognize the profitability of investments in government bonds issued during the Napoleonic Wars and, then, had discovered the ultimate safety of investments in railroad securities during the "height of unsafety" – the early 1840s.[193] He then went on to draw parallels in the histories of Russia, Germany, and France.

In the case of the United States, it has been argued that, because of the greater geographical distances between savers in the East and investors in the South and West and because of the marked disparity between the new expanding industries that required finance and the older traditional activities that were the source of savings, the problem was even more complex. The educational process in the United States was, however, similar, to that experienced on the other side of the water – similar at least, as far as the North and West were concerned, but in the US, the process was delayed by at least half a century. Thus, eastern and mid western savers' experience with the 5–20s during the Civil War provided the same lessons as the British Napoleonic War debt, and during the 1870s, 80s, and 90s, their experience with US railroad bonds duplicated the lessons of the Hudson years in Britain.[194] In the South, however, investment in Confederate bonds did not have the same effect on the southern saver's education. Despite the southern experience, to the north, the educational process had proceeded far enough by the early twentieth century to lead Frank A. Vanderlip, a prominent New York banker, to argue that "the whole great Mississippi Valley gives promise that in some day distant perhaps it will be another New England for investments. There is developing a bond market there which is of constant astonishment to eastern dealers".[195]

That day was, however, in the twentieth century. Earlier, the situation was markedly different. Naomi Lamoreaux, in a study of New England commercial banking, has shown just how personalized capital remained despite the existence of an apparently depersonalizing institutional structure.[196] From her examination of the records of a number of nineteenth century New England banks, she concludes that it was not market forces but kinship connections that structured the loans made by those institutions.

Drawing on a different body of evidence and making a distinct, but parallel, argument, Kenneth Snowden has demonstrated that as late as

1890, after the effects of risk have been netted out, there still remained significant inter-regional differences in mortgage interest charges. "Mortgage rates were substantially higher for borrowers in the South and West and represented a tangible financial burden. Effective rates of interest on both home and farm mortgages were two to three percent higher in many of the western regions than identical loans would have been in the Northeast. Borrowers in these regions do not, however, appear to have been the victims of eastern monopoly power. Instead, I conclude that home as well as farm borrowers paid high rates in the West and South because of the direct costs of moving funds between regions and uneven diffusion of financial innovation."[197]

Yet a third avenue of support for the immobility argument can be found in an examination of the monopoly profits earned by those few American financial capitalists who were able to exploit their personal ability to mobilize capital. The list includes, but is not limited to, Jay Cooke, John D. Rockefeller, and, of course, J. P. Morgan – who, as late as 1912, was able to control more than two billion dollars of the savings of Americans who were willing to put their funds into enterprises that he backed, although they were still unwilling to trust the formal depersonalized financial markets.[198] Moreover, recent work by Bradford DeLong indicates that, given the existing structure of the financial markets, relative earnings prove that those savers were far from foolish.[199]

It seems, therefore, safe to conclude that, until the end of the nineteenth century, at the very least, the London capital market served a far more sophisticated group of savers than its New York competitor.[200] Obviously the two markets did not exist in isolation, but it appears that a substantial fraction of the American securities traded in London were not even imperfect substitutes for many of the stocks and bonds traded in New York. That is to say, while the British contribution to American capital formation was never large, the financial flows were not trivial, and, more importantly, they were often targeted at economic activities that lay outside the scope of the still embryonic American financial market. Moreover, they were particularly important during the last two decades of the nineteenth century when the American economy was undergoing a very rapid structural transformation.

While a part of the relatively slow development of the New York market may merely reflect the preferences of the savers with which the market dealt, a part at least, can be traced to the institutional differences between the New York and London exchanges. The New York Stock Exchange was organized by a collective to engage in the creation and maintenance of a securities market and it was owned by that collective. While the London Stock Exchange was organized for ostensibly the same purposes, it was not owned solely by traders:

[When the LSE] decided to build its own exchange in 1801 it did so by issuing shares which could be purchased by anyone. Consequently, there was a divorce between those who used the building for the conduct of their business – the members – and those who controlled the building and saw it as a business – the owners. In 1878, for example, there were 2,009 members of the London Stock Exchange but only 508 shareholders, a number of whom were non-members.[201]

The New York Stock Exchange building, constructed in 1868, was fully financed by its membership. Thus, the wedge between owners and members that marked the London market was absent in New York – there, the sets of owners and of members were identical.

The London market's pronounced cleavage between owners and members was clearly reflected in the exchange's governing structure. Two committees – the Committee of Trustees and Managers and the Committee for General Purposes – were jointly vested with ultimate control over exchange matters. As their names suggest, however, the committees represented different interests: the Trustees and Managers Committee represented exchange owners, and the General Purposes Committee represented members. Inevitably, their interests collided.[202] The identity between owners and managers of the NYSE meant that there would be no in-fighting between the two groups. One committee, the Governing Committee, was final arbiter on all issues affecting the exchange, although it delegated much of its authority to subcommittees. As a collectively owned firm, the NYSE adopted policies typical of collectives in general, and those policies were quite different from the policies of the shareholder-owned London exchange.[203]

On the one hand, the evidence suggests that the rewards associated with organizing as an efficient cartel were high relative to the costs. On the other hand, the cartel carefully screened potential issues and implemented rules that, while providing a valuable service to some, made trading on the NYSE more expensive than on other competing exchanges. Firms willing and able to sustain these costs were, in effect, buying a signal – a signal that assuaged the doubts of skeptical investors – and thus those firms were able to attract a fairly wide range of relatively unsophisticated investors and, thus, build a national market for their securities. Of course, some investors felt no need to rely on NYSE certification to gauge the attractiveness of uncertain investment opportunities, and some firms were unable or unwilling to bear the additional costs.

The more sophisticated investors refused to bear the high NYSE transaction costs and took their business to rival exchanges. It seems reasonable to assume that this group was small relative to the number of unsophisticated investors – by 1910 the NYSE handled the lion's share of transactions in domestic securities (see Table 4.5). Because the numbers of sophisticated investors were small, the rival domestic exchanges were unable to

Table 4.5. *US securities markets, sales in 1910*

Market	Stocks Number	Stocks Proportion	Bonds Par Value	Bonds Proportion
New York Stock Exchange	164,150,061	68.5%	$635.0m	90.6%
Consolidated Stock Exchange	32,238,773	13.4%	—	—
New York Curb Market	18,671,438	7.8%	$10.8m	1.5%
New York: Total	215,060,272	89.7%	$645.8m	92.1%
Boston Stock Exchange	15,503,336	6.5%	$32.7m	4.7%
Philadelphia Stock Exchange	8,341,599	3.5%	$14.6m	2.1%
Chicago Stock Exchange	894,362	0.4%	$7.4m	1.1%
Total	239,799,569	100.1%	$700.5m	100.0%

Sources: Reprinted from Michie, p. 170. NYSE: New York Stock Exchange, Special Committee on Commissions, Memorandum, 1924; Consolidated: Consolidated Stock Exchange, Annual Report, year ending 31 May 1910; Curb: Jones & Baker, *Profits and Dividends on America's Second Largest Stock Market* (New York, 1919); Boston: J. G. Martin, *Stock Fluctuations* (Boston, 1911); Philadelphia: A. W. Barnes (ed.), *History of the Philadelphia Stock Exchange, Banks and Banking Interests* (Philadelphia, 1911); Chicago: F. M. Huston and A. Russell, *Financing an Empire – History of Banking in Illinois* (Chicago, 1926), Vol. 1.

mobilize sufficient capital to meet the demands of all the myriad of firms whose growth reflected the transformation of the industrial profile of the United States. Thus, British entrepreneurs were given an opportunity to purchase American enterprises, reorganize them as "free standing companies" and, through the aegis of the London exchange, raise capital from the relatively more sophisticated British investors. At the same time, some American firms began to utilize the services of the London market themselves. From the point of view of the Governors of the New York market, however, given the relative numbers of the two groups, the decision to forego the business of sophisticated investors in an attempt to attract the business of larger blocks of relatively unsophisticated investors appears to have been a sound one.

The minimum commission rule provides perhaps the clearest example of the exchange's desire to impose a single pattern of behavior on its membership – a pattern of behavior that would guarantee efficient cartel operation. NYSE members were permitted to charge no less than one-eighth percent on every transaction they handled for non-members. The minimum NYSE rate was high, and members of rival domestic exchanges, in an attempt to divert business to themselves, frequently undercut the exchange's minimum commission, but, because of their relatively small size, they failed to provide effective competition. Traders on two rival New York exchanges – the Consolidated and the Curb Market – and those on the Philadelphia Stock Exchange typically charged half the NYSE commission rate, but when, in 1875, twenty NYSE brokers petitioned the

Governors to charge one-sixteenth percent commission on large volume trades for non-members, their request was flatly refused. The importance attached to the minimum commission rule was most clearly stated by the Governing Committee in 1894; "The Commission Law is the fundamental principle of the Exchange, and on its strict adherence hangs the financial welfare and the life of the Institution itself."[204] While such language may seem overly melodramatic, it is nevertheless apparent that NYSE rule-makers sought to eliminate any commission competition between its members – differences in commission rates would not be tolerated.

The Governing Committee also attempted to secure higher individual profits for members by strictly limiting membership. In the wake of its 1869 merger with what had been called the "Open Board", the committee placed a 1,060 cap on membership. Between then and 1914 that cap was increased just once (to 1,100). As business on the exchange grew – 1879 stock sales were $73 million as compared with a pre-World War I high of $262 million in 1906, and bond sales had grown from $571 million in 1879 to a $1,314 million pre-War peak in 1909 – the price of seats rose. Michie notes, "Reflecting the fact that membership was restricted, and did not meet demand, was the fact that the cost of purchasing a place rose [from] between $14,000 and $26,000 in 1880 to between $65,000 and $94,000 in 1910, or approximately fourfold".[205] Restricting membership, a tool employed by many collectives, kept numbers manageable, and, as seats became increasingly expensive, it guaranteed that only the relatively wealthy could join the fold.[206]

Because it was organized as a traders' cartel, the NYSE was able to pursue a collective strategy designed not only to maximize short run profits but also to foster rapid growth in the volume of transactions. In the mid to late nineteenth century, the typical American saver was relatively unsophisticated and, therefore, plagued by high levels of uncertainty about domestic investment opportunities.[207] The informational asymmetry faced by potential investors was great, and, in an effort to attract large national markets for its listed securities, the NYSE devised a set of procedures and trading rules that were designed to reduce the level of uncertainty. In such an environment, potentially viable firms faced what is still a standard problem in their attempts to attract capital:

"Higher quality parties are usually adversely affected by the presence of lower quality parties; either the higher quality parties are pooled with the lower quality parties, to their detriment, or they must invest in signals beyond the point that they would if there were no informational asymmetry to distinguish themselves from their low-quality peers.[208]

Market screening undertaken by the NYSE allowed certain firms to invest in costly signals to separate their securities from those of competing ventures.[209] An NYSE listing itself became a signal to American investors of the "quality" of an investment opportunity.

The most obvious of the NYSE's screening policies was its stringent vetting procedure – a procedure that required potential listings to meet high minimum standards in terms of, "size of capital, number of shareholders, and proven track record." [210] The Exchange made a deliberate effort to attract large, widely held and, price wise, relatively stable issues. The rules also imposed additional costs on securities whose prices dipped below par value, and they made it virtually impossible to trade a security that did not generate the required high level of trade volume in sufficiently large trade blocks. Moreover, an addendum to the commission rules mandated that commissions would be based not on the market price of the security but on a minimum $100 par value. Thus, the rule dictated that members demand at least 12.5 cents on every share traded on behalf of non-members, even if the share price was well below $100. The importance of par values as a signal to relatively unsophisticated investors is emphasized in one study of capital market development:

"A prerequisite for anonymous public markets was the development of mechanisms to enable outside investors better to estimate the value of businesses; this has been a very slow and arduous process, which even today appears far from complete. A rudimentary step, when most available accounting data was entirely unreliable, was the use of par value as a benchmark."[211]

Similarly, the Exchange imposed a minimum size requirement for a single transaction. Although in the 1890s the rules were relaxed to permit members to deal in "odd lots", until then members had been prohibited from dealing in quantities less than the "normal" lot of one hundred stocks or bonds.[212] In short, a firm that passed the admittance tests and continued to demonstrate that the market for its issues was active and stable had purchased an expensive signal about the probable quality of those issues.

The "par value rule" discriminated not only against $100 securities trading at less than that amount, but also against "low denomination" securities issued at values well below $100. Low denomination securities were most often offered by companies with small capital bases, and there were many such firms in the industrial, in the land, mortgage, and financial, and in the mining industries. Even if investors were willing to trade in normal lots, and it is likely that the small investor preferred odd lots, the par value rule made purchases or sales very expensive. It is, therefore, not surprising that most of these securities were listed on exchanges with more liberal trading rules.

Institutional rules are, however, not set in stone, and changing conditions led to changes in institutional structure. The NYSE did not, for example, turn away business because of an irrational prejudice against certain types of securities – they were, in fact, interested in any security that passed their "signal" test and, equally importantly, could attract investors from all regions and all walks of life. As long as a security was of interest to only a small or to a geographically concentrated group of investors, there were few benefits to be gained from a listing on the "Big Board"; and neither the issuing firms nor the investors themselves were willing to pay the price of admission. By the mid 1880s, however, the continued viability of certain industrial, land–mortgage–finance, and mining shares on rival exchanges led the Governing Committee to conclude that those issues were beginning to attract a broad range of investors. As a result, in order to permit its members to share in those potential profits while not diluting the Exchange "quality" signal, the Board of Governors created the "unlisted department" – a department designed to permit members to trade in certain securities without granting those issues an official quotation.

Despite this institutional innovation, by the turn of the century the majority of those issues had still not managed to attract a truly national clientele, and, since the trade rules (i.e. commission and trade block regulations) were not weakened, the attractiveness of the new market was obviously limited. Although the unlisted department struggled along until 1910, few of its issues generated any significant trading volume. In 1895, for example, of the surprisingly large number of industrial stocks (435) covered by the department, the securities of just three firms – American Sugar Refining, National Lead, and US Leather – generated ninety-four percent of the department's $13.6 million sales total.[213] When, in 1910, the unlisted department was dissolved, securities from these three firms were added to the quoted listings.

In part, at least, as a result of the Exchange's trading rules, many firms were not listed on the NYSE, and they turned to other American (the Boston, the Philadelphia, or perhaps the Consolidated), or foreign (that is, London) exchanges. Because potential American investors in these enterprises often tended to be geographically concentrated, some mining and land, mortgage, and financial firms were adequately served by other – more local – American exchanges. The San Francisco and the Boston Exchanges and the Curb Market in New York listed a wide array of mine shares throughout the years 1880–1914. Before the turn of the century, land companies and investment trusts were also often listed on the Boston Exchange.[214] Other firms – those whose capital requirements could not be met by domestic savers – turned to the more broadly based British market. It was not that mining and land ventures could not find homes for their securities in the United States; many could and did, but that home was not the New York Stock Exchange.

In general, as long as rival exchanges steered clear of transactions in NYSE issues, peaceful coexistence was possible. For example, the Curb Market appears to have served as a proving grounds for securities unable to measure up to the rigorous standards required for an NYSE listing. NYSE brokers, moreover, recognized that there were small pockets of investors willing to channel savings into securities that did not pass the Exchange's screening procedures:

"The Curb existed in uneasy harmony with the New York Stock Exchange, never officially recognized but extensively utilized by its membership to fill orders for clients throughout the country . . . An estimated 85 percent of the Curb's total business was on behalf of members of the NYSE, with whom constant contact was maintained through the use of messenger boys, signaling from upper office windows, and conveniently sited telephones at ground-floor window level." [215]

Interestingly, this quote not only underscores the tacitly accepted division in function between the two exchanges, but it also suggests that Curb listings enjoyed something more than local or regional interest.

The continued existence and viability of regional exchanges indicates that there was also a fragmentation between investors in different regions of the country. If there were gains to be had from consolidation of trade activity in national issues, at some point in the period one would have expected the smaller American exchanges to handle only regional listings as national issues gradually gravitated to New York. Through at least 1910, however, the Boston Stock Exchange, for example, listed land, mortgage and financial firms and mining concerns located throughout the country. At least one market observer, Charles Head, a member of both the New York and Boston Exchanges, noted the regional fragmentation between investors:

"We do a pretty large business in Boston which does not come to this city [New York] at all – where the customers are Boston men, and the business is done there. We do large business in these Boston stocks – in all the copper stocks." [216]

The persistence of trade activity unique to a single exchange – the Boston (and to a lesser extent the Philadelphia) – suggests that the exchange served a group of relatively sophisticated investors who did not rely solely on the New York Stock Exchange's "certification" to reduce their uncertainty. Arthur Johnson and Barry Supple argue that Boston investors' early experience in the China trade made them particularly suited to investment in the American West. In their words, those investors were "a close-knit group, accustomed to managing far-flung enterprises, they appeared on the domestic scene at a time when the West offered great opportunities to capital and entrepreneurial talent." [217] In sum, it is quite apparent that not all American savers were equal in their abilities to evaluate uncertain investment opportunities, and, even at the turn of the century, the majority, even of those willing to hold paper securities at all, still demanded "official certification".

The combination of rapid increases in the demand for capital, relatively unsophisticated investors, and restrictive trade rules meant that firms in certain sectors of the American economy, particularly corporations located in the South and West, went unserviced by the New York market; they were, however, often able to attract capital on the London market.[218] Certainly by the end of the period the New York market had begun to display evidence of approaching maturity – that is, its traders and specialists had begun to serve a wider array of enterprises; however, it lagged its London counterpart by at least two decades. Domestic land, finance, and investment companies, as well as mining, agricultural, and other land based firms, were forced to retain their London connections until well into the present century.

In the final analysis, except perhaps in the short run, it was not lack of American savings that led American firms to the London capital market. While there may still remain questions of the level of American savings in the antebellum decades, there is little doubt that the gross savings rate averaged almost twenty-five (and the net rate more than eighteen) percent from about 1870 to at least 1908, and these rates were far higher than those observed in Britain.[219] Instead, it was a combination of the organizational structure of the New York exchange and the perceptions of the majority of American savers – savers who were unwilling to risk their accumulations in enterprises far removed from their usual experience. As those savers became more sophisticated, the potential economies of scope from a more broadly based exchange increased, and ultimately it paid those who governed the New York exchange to increase their listings – at least somewhat.

Despite the very high rate of domestic savings, the New York exchange failed to mobilize sufficient savings to provide finance for the entire range of investment opportunities then available in the United States. That problem became particularly acute in the decades following the Civil War as the rapid transformation of the American economy generated a substantial demand for finance in sectors of the economy that were well outside the normal experience of American savers. At the same time, European, and particularly British, savers possessed sufficient resources and demonstrated a willingness to fill at least a part of the gap, but they appear to have been more comfortable dealing with their local brokers and a known market than with strangers and strange institutions located thousands of miles away.

5

American investments abroad

1. Introduction

For more than a century after Virginia became the tenth state to ratify the decisions of the Constitutional Convention, the United States was the world's largest international debtor, but, while World War I triggered what appears on the surface to have been a revolutionary regime change, there was evidence at least two decades earlier that the flows through the international financial network had already begun to reverse. Although they do not offer conclusive proof, the net capital flow figures tend to confirm that conclusion. Between 1790 and the end of 1896, the net capital import totaled $3.4 billion; however, over the last eighteen years of the pre-War period and despite massive foreign investments in the United States, the net capital *outflow* totaled about $1.4 billion. Similarly, although the figures are certainly subject to error, it appears that the ratio of long-term US investment abroad to long-term foreign investment in the US rose from .22 in 1899, to .42 in 1908, and to .50 in 1914.[220]

2. The early years: 1797–1896

For the earlier period, Bullock and his co-authors concluded, "American investments abroad were insignificant until the late nineties", and, in a similar vein, a decade later, Cleona Lewis wrote, "Until the closing decade of the nineteenth century, the outward flow of capital . . . was of negligible proportions."[221] Moreover, both the fragmentary quantitative as well as the qualitative evidence that remain appear to substantiate the conclusion reached by those scholars. While there were American trading companies in Canada since the early eighteenth century, in China since 1783, in Argentina since 1801, in Mexico and Brazil since the 1820s, and in Japan since the 1850s, there is little evidence of extensive American investment.[222] Similarly, although two Americans established a paper mill in Quebec in 1804, Samuel Colt opened the first foreign branch of an American manufacturing firm in Britain in 1852, and three Baltimoreans were apparently "extensively engaged in building locomotives, cars, casting of cannon, and making a variety of machinery for government" near

St Petersburg in 1857, there is little evidence of successful American investment in manufacturing abroad until well into the 1860s. In the UK during that decade, the Pullman Company established a plant, R. Hoe and Company began to build printing presses, and the Singer Sewing Machine Company invested more than a quarter of a million dollars in a facility.[223]

Even in the case of railroads, the recipient of the bulk of this nation's foreign investment, American forays abroad were quite limited before the last decades of the nineteenth century. In the early 1850s American investors contributed to the construction of the Great Western Railroad in Canada, but that investment – an investment made in the hope of providing a link between the New York Central and the Michigan Central – turned sour when the railroad's management adopted a 5'6" gauge.[224] More success marked the $8 million invested in the Panama Railroad (chartered 1849, opened 1855), but success did not lead to a flurry of further investment. Such decisions awaited the 1870s when the American railroad network was extended into Canada and construction of the Boston financed Sonora railroad in Mexico began, but even then American investment did not become a permanent part of the economic environment.[225]

There is, in fact, little evidence of substantial and continued American investment abroad before the late 1890s, but, the industrial profile of the investment pattern in those early years set the pattern that was to continue as American foreign investment surged in the years between the late 1890s and 1914. In fact, the surge continued until the Depression of the 1930s (see Tables 5.1 and 5.2). Aside from the capital needed to underwrite the export of the products of American technology or of the country's natural resources – and the specialized knowledge inherent in domestic production often led, in the long run, to American investment in foreign production – the bulk of American foreign investment was in activities that can best be viewed as extensions of the American domestic market (see Table 5.3).[226]

In 1897, American financial commitments in Mexico and Canada represented just less than sixty percent of all American long-term foreign investment, and Cuba, the West Indies, and Central and South America accounted for an additional fifteen percent. Although, by 1914, the relative role of Mexico had declined by a small amount and the proportion directed toward South America had increased somewhat, overall, the patterns had changed little. In fact, as late as 1935 the western hemisphere still accounted for almost sixty-five percent of all American long-term commitments – by that date only Asia and Oceania had increased their relative shares significantly.

The major exceptions to the "home market" scenario were American firms that had found a European market for their products. On the one

Table 5.1. *American investments abroad by geographical area (millions of dollars)*

Region	1897	1908	1914
1. Direct Investments			
Europe	131.0	369.3	573.3
Canada	159.7	405.4	618.4
Cuba & other West Indies	49.0	195.5	281.3
Mexico	200.2	416.4	587.1
Central America	21.2	37.9	89.6
South America	37.9	104.3	323.1
Africa	1.0	5.0	13.0
Asia	23.0	74.7	119.5
Oceana	1.5	10.0	17.0
International Banking	10.0	20.0	30.0
Total Direct	634.5	1638.5	2652.3
2. Portfolio Investments			
Europe	20.0	119.9	118.5
Canada	30.0	291.9	248.8
Cuba & other West Indies	0.0	30.0	55.0
Mexico	0.0	255.6	266.4
Central America	0.0	3.1	3.6
South America	0.0	25.4	42.6
Africa	0.0	0.0	0.2
Asia	0.0	160.5	126.4
Oceana	0.0	0.0	0.0
International Banking	0.0	0.0	0.0
Total Portfolio	50.0	886.3	861.5
3. Direct and Portfolio Investments			
Europe	151.0	489.2	691.8
Canada	189.7	697.2	867.2
Cuba & other West Indies	49.0	225.5	336.3
Mexico	200.2	672.0	853.5
Central America	21.2	41.0	93.2
South America	37.9	129.7	365.7
Africa	1.0	5.0	13.2
Asia	23.0	235.2	245.9
Oceana	1.5	10.0	17.0
International Banking	10.0	20.0	30.0
Total Direct & Portfolio	684.5	2524.8	3513.8

Source: Cleona Lewis, *America's Stake*, p. 606.

International Capital Markets

Table 5.2. *American investments abroad by geographical area (percents)*

Region	1897	1908	1914
1. Direct Investments			
Europe	20.6	22.5	21.6
Canada	25.2	24.7	23.3
Cuba & other West Indies	7.7	11.9	10.6
Mexico	31.6	25.4	22.1
Central America	3.3	2.3	3.4
South America	6.0	6.4	12.2
Africa	0.2	0.3	0.5
Asia	3.6	4.6	4.5
Oceana	0.2	0.6	0.6
International Banking	1.6	1.2	1.1
Total Direct	100.0	100.0	100.0
2. Portfolio Investments			
Europe	40.00	13.5	13.8
Canada	60.0	32.9	28.9
Cuba & other West Indies	0.0	3.4	6.4
Mexico	0.0	28.8	30.9
Central America	0.0	0.3	0.4
South America	0.0	2.9	4.9
Africa	0.0	0.0	0.0
Asia	0.0	18.1	14.7
Oceana	0.0	0.0	0.0
International Banking	0.0	0.0	0.0
Total Portfolio	100.0	100.0	100.0
3. Direct and Portfolio Investments			
Europe	22.1	19.4	19.7
Canada	27.7	27.6	24.7
Cuba & other West Indies	7.2	8.9	9.6
Mexico	29.2	26.6	24.3
Central America	3.1	1.6	2.7
South America	5.5	5.1	10.4
Africa	0.1	0.2	0.4
Asia	3.4	9.3	7.0
Oceana	0.2	0.4	0.5
International Banking	1.5	0.8	0.9
Total Direct & Portfolio	100.0	100.0	100.0

Source: Cleona Lewis, *America's Stake*, pp. 578–604.

Table 5.3 (a). *America's direct foreign investments, 1897–1914 by geographic region and class of investment (millions of dollars)*

	1897	1908	1914	1897	1908	1914
		Total			Sales	
Europe	131.0	369.3	573.3	80.0	125.0	215.0
Canada	159.7	405.4	618.4	10.0	15.0	27.0
Cuba & other West Indies	49.0	195.5	281.3	5.0	8.0	12.0
Mexico	200.2	416.4	587.1	1.5	2.0	4.0
Central America	21.2	37.9	89.6	0.0	0.5	0.5
South America	37.9	104.3	323.1	13.0	26.0	40.0
Africa	1.0	5.0	13.0	1.0	3.0	9.0
Asia	23.0	74.7	119.5	20.0	48.0	55.0
Oceana	1.5	10.0	17.0	1.0	4.0	7.0
International Banking	10.0	20.0	30.0	0.0	0.0	0.0
Total	634.5	1638.5	2652.3	131.5	231.5	369.5

(Percents)

	1897	1908	1914	1897	1908	1914
		Total			Sales	
Europe	20.6	22.5	21.6	12.6	7.6	8.1
Canada	25.2	24.7	23.3	1.6	0.9	1.0
Cuba & other West Indies	7.7	11.9	10.6	0.8	0.5	0.5
Mexico	31.6	25.4	22.1	0.2	0.1	0.2
Central America	3.3	2.3	3.4	0.0	0.0	0.0
South America	6.0	6.4	12.2	2.0	1.6	1.5
Africa	0.2	0.3	0.5	0.2	0.2	0.3
Asia	3.6	4.6	4.5	3.2	2.9	2.1
Oceana	0.2	0.6	0.6	0.2	0.2	0.3
International Banking	1.6	1.2	1.1	0.0	0.0	0.0
Total	100.0	100.0	100.0	20.7	14.1	13.9

Source: Cleona Lewis, *America's Stake*, Appendix D, pp. 575–606.

Table 5.3 (b). *America's direct foreign investments, 1897–1914 by geographic region and class of investment (millions of dollars)*

1897	1908	1914	1897	1908	1914	1897	1908	1914
Mines			Oil			Agriculture		
0.0	3.0	5.0	0.0	3.5	8.0	0.0	0.0	0.0
55.0	136.0	159.0	6.0	15.0	25.0	18.0	25.0	101.0
3.0	6.0	15.2	1.0	2.0	3.0	24.0	92.3	144.3
68.0	234.0	302.0	1.5	50.0	85.0	12.0	40.0	37.0
2.0	9.6	11.2	0.0	0.0	0.0	3.5	18.2	36.5
6.0	53.0	220.8	2.0	5.0	22.0	9.0	11.0	25.0
0.0	2.0	4.0	0.0	0.0	0.0	0.0	0.0	0.0
0.0	1.0	2.5	0.0	0.0	0.0	0.0	0.0	12.0
0.0	0.0	0.0	0.0	0.0	0.0	0.0	0.0	0.0
134.0	444.6	719.7	10.5	75.5	143.0	76.5	186.5	355.8

(Percents)

1897	1908	1914	1897	1908	1914	1897	1908	1914
Mines			Oil			Agriculture		
0.0	0.2	0.2	0.0	0.2	0.3	0.0	0.0	0.0
8.7	8.3	6.0	0.9	0.9	0.9	2.8	1.5	3.8
0.5	0.4	0.6	0.2	0.1	0.1	3.8	5.6	5.4
10.7	14.3	11.4	0.2	3.1	3.2	1.9	2.4	1.4
0.3	0.6	0.4	0.0	0.0	0.0	0.6	1.1	1.4
0.9	3.2	8.3	0.3	0.3	0.8	1.4	0.7	0.9
0.0	0.1	0.2	0.0	0.0	0.0	0.0	0.0	0.0
0.0	0.1	0.1	0.0	0.0	0.0	0.0	0.0	0.5
0.0	0.0	0.0	0.0	0.0	0.0	0.0	0.0	0.0
21.1	27.1	27.1	1.7	4.6	5.4	12.1	11.4	13.4

Source: Cleona Lewis, *America's Stake*, Appendix D, pp. 575–606.

Table 5.3 (c). *America's direct foreign investments, 1897–1914 by geographic region and class of investment (millions of dollars)*

1897	1908	1914	1897	1908	1914	1897	1908	1914
Manufacturing			Railroads			Public Utilities		
35.0	100.0	200.0	0.0	0.0	0.0	10.0	12.8	10.8
55.0	155.0	221.0	12.7	51.4	68.9	2.0	5.0	8.0
3.0	18.0	20.0	2.0	43.2	23.8	0.0	24.0	58.0
0.0	10.0	10.0	110.6	56.8	110.4	5.6	21.6	33.2
0.0	0.0	0.0	15.7	9.0	37.9	0.0	0.6	3.5
0.0	2.0	7.0	2.4	1.0	3.6	4.5	5.3	3.7
0.0	0.0	0.0	0.0	0.0	0.0	0.0	0.0	0.0
0.0	5.0	10.0	0.0	0.0	10.5	0.0	15.7	16.0
0.5	6.0	10.0	0.0	0.0	0.0	0.0	0.0	0.0
93.5	296.0	478.0	143.4	161.4	255.1	22.1	85.0	133.2

(Percents)

1897	1908	1914	1897	1908	1914	1897	1908	1914
Manufacturing			Railroads			Public Utilities		
5.5	6.1	7.5	0.0	0.0	0.0	1.6	0.8	0.4
8.7	9.5	8.3	2.0	3.1	2.6	0.3	0.3	0.3
0.5	1.1	0.8	0.3	2.6	0.9	0.0	1.5	2.2
0.0	0.6	0.4	17.4	3.5	4.2	0.9	1.3	1.3
0.0	0.0	0.0	2.5	0.5	1.4	0.0	0.0	0.1
0.0	0.1	0.3	0.4	0.1	0.1	0.7	0.3	0.1
0.0	0.0	0.0	0.0	0.0	0.0	0.0	0.0	0.0
0.0	0.3	0.4	0.0	0.0	0.4	0.0	1.0	0.6
0.1	0.4	0.4	0.0	0.0	0.0	0.0	0.0	0.0
0.0	0.0	0.0	0.0	0.0	0.0	0.0	0.0	0.0
14.7	18.1	18.0	22.6	9.9	9.6	3.5	5.2	5.0

Source: Cleona Lewis, *America's Stake*, Appendix D, pp. 575–606.

Table 5.3 (d). *America's direct foreign investments,
1897–1914 by geographic region and class of
investment
(millions of dollars)*

1897	1908	1914
	Miscellaneous	
6.0	125.0	134.5
1.0	3.0	8.5
1.0	2.0	5.0
1.0	2.0	5.5
0.0	−0.0	−0.0
1.0	1.0	1.0
0.0	0.0	0.0
3.0	5.0	13.5
0.0	0.0	0.0
10.0	20.0	30.0
23.0	158.0	198.0

	(Percents)	
1897	1908	1914
	Miscellaneous	
0.9	7.6	5.1
0.2	0.2	0.3
0.2	0.1	0.2
0.2	0.1	0.2
0.0	−0.0	−0.0
0.2	0.1	0.0
0.0	0.0	0.0
0.5	0.3	0.5
0.0	0.0	0.0
1.6	1.2	1.1
3.6	9.6	7.5

Source: Cleona Lewis, *America's Stake*, Appendix D, pp. 575–606.

hand, there were firms like Singer, Westinghouse, and Edison General Electric that exploited their patents on new technical developments, and on the other there was Standard Oil, a firm that, when faced with Russian competition, moved quickly into international distribution and ultimately into production as well.[227]

The Singer Sewing Machine Company, for example, had built its first foreign manufacturing plant in Glasgow in 1868; it opened a very modern facility with a capacity equal to that of its largest American plant near that city in 1881; and two years later it also had plants operating in Canada and Australia.[228] Westinghouse was producing air brakes for railroad cars in Paris in 1879 and in the United Kingdom two years later.[229]

Similarly, in the years before 1896 nearly all of the modern electrical giants received infusions, either direct or portfolio, of American capital. By 1880, one of Edison's companies had invested in Deutsche Edison Gesellschaft; the Edison Swan Electric Company Ltd was organized in Britain in 1883; and within a decade General Electric itself had invested $1 million in the Canadian General Electric Company Ltd and paid $1.2 million for Thomson–Houston International, a subsidiary, that soon began manufacturing in France. Within a few years Thomson–Houston had developed an extensive sales network in South America, built an arc-light station in Hammerfest, Norway – a station that for years remained the most northerly electric installation in the world – and sold its products in Egypt, Russia, and Spain.[230]

As early as 1882, the Bell Telephone and Telegraph Company established the Bell Telephone Manufacturing Company in Antwerp. With the organization of AT&T, the Belgian firm was taken over by the Western Electric Company, and, between 1910 and 1915, it established manufacturing enterprises in France, Britain, Italy, Spain, and Norway and acquired part ownership of competitors in Austria and Hungary.[231]

Faced by potentially stiff competition from the Russian petroleum industry, Standard Oil began to invest in foreign distribution facilities in 1879, and the company's distribution network soon spanned most of the world.[232] In that year the Standard also opened a refinery in Galicia (Austria–Hungary) in which they invested the munificent sum of $32,300. Although that enterprise was not a success, within a decade the firm's subsidiaries were operating refineries in Cuba and Mexico, and, during the next decade, the list was expanded to include Canada, France (two), and Germany. Investment in foreign production, however, was delayed until the organization of the Romana–Americana Societate Anonima Pentra Industria, Comertul si Exportal Petrolium, in 1905.[233]

The US was a part of the international economy, and it is not surprising that American investment underwrote a small part of the international communications network. Thus, in 1854 Cyrus Field had raised $1.5 million in New York to help fund the New York, Newfoundland, and London Electric Telegraph. In 1866, the International Telegraph Company drew on American finance to fund a cable connecting Florida and Havana; and, a little more than a decade later, the same entrepreneur, James A. Scrymser, organized both the Mexican Cable Company and then, with the help of J. P. Morgan, the Central and South American Telegraph Company. The two firms together provided a telegraphic link that by 1882 had connected Brownsville, Texas to Mexico City, El Salvador, Nicaragua, Panama, Colombia, Ecuador, and Peru. Finally, in 1884 the American financed Commercial Cable Company completed two submarine cables to Europe.[234]

It was, however, the extension of the American market into Canada and Mexico that drew the majority of American foreign investment in the years before 1897. In the case of Mexico, the largest single recipient of American long term investments, it was the extension of the American railroad network and the expansion of the western mining frontier that drew almost ninety percent of the total. As in the case of European investment in the United States, the railroads alone accounted for over half the total. Between 1877 and 1897 Mexico's railroad network grew from 417 to 7,311 miles, and, while there were infusions of British, French, Dutch, and German capital, much of the growth was American financed. The western American railroad entrepreneurs, Huntington, Gould, Sage, and Harriman, were all involved in the promotion and construction of one or more of a long list of Mexican lines that included the Mexican Central, the Mexican National, and the Southern Pacific of Mexico.[235]

Railroads accounted for fifty-five percent of American investment, but mining ventures contributed another thirty-four. While there had been American mines in Mexico as early as the 1820s, it wasn't until Diaz imposed "order and stability" and the legislature had passed the laws of 1884 and 1892 that guaranteed property rights that capital began to flow in substantial proportions. In the early years it was gold and silver alone that attracted American interest, but gradually the focus shifted slightly toward industrial minerals, and, by 1897, precious metals accounted for less than three-quarters of the American financed activity.

In 1886 there were estimated to have been forty American companies mining gold and silver south of the border. By far the most profitable was the Botopilas Silver Mining Company (chartered in New York in 1880) – a firm that, in 1887, merged with five other American producers to form the Botopilas Mining Company with an initial capitalization in excess of $9 million. In 1890, the Cia Metallurgica Mexicana was chartered in New Jersey; its organizer, Robert S. Towne, sold $4 million of stock, built a smelter in San Luis Potosi – the first of its kind in Mexico – and acquired silver and lead mines in the region.[236]

In that same year the Guggenheims received a federal concession to build three smelters, and the next year they received a supplementary agreement from the state of Nuevo Leòn. On the basis of those concessions, they organized the Compaña de la Gran Fundiciòn Nacional Mexican (the Great National Smelting Company), built a smelter in Monterrey and leased mines, "the Cedia for iron, the Reforma for lead, . . . [and] the Encantado and the Pereña." In addition, they also purchased the Tepezala copper mines. The Monterrey furnace, built to serve northern and eastern Mexico, was "blown in" in 1892, and from the "very outset this plant operated at a net profit of $60,000 a month." The experiment was so successful that, the next year, the family opened a second smelter in Aguascalientes to serve the south-central parts of the country.[237]

While American investment in Mexico was concentrated in transport and mining, the pattern of investment in Canada was much more varied. In 1897, for example, the twenty-nine percent of total American long-term investment that was directed towards mining was almost as large as the proportion of mines in the Mexican total; however, in Canada manufacturing drew an equal proportion. Moreover, even if railroad securities constituted all of American portfolio investment in Canada – and they certainly did not – that sector drew less than one-fourth of the total, and it was probably substantially less. In addition, sales agencies, oil production and distribution, and agriculture all received substantially larger fractions of the total capital flow than their Mexican counterparts. In many ways American investors appear to have viewed Canada much as they viewed states like Michigan or California – a potential market and a source of raw materials.

In terms of mines, for example, in 1877, when Boston capitalists were increasing their investment in Michigan copper, they also put $300 thousand into the Orford Nickel and Copper Company – a firm organized to mine ore in Quebec and process it in New Jersey. By 1880 Americans also had interests in antimony and manganese mines in New Brunswick (the Queen's Manganese Company and the Hibbard Antimony Company) and in gold and copper mines in Quebec. The Colonial Gold Mining Company with capital of $2.5 million was operating in the Beuce section, and Eustis Copper – Canada's oldest active mine – had been controlled by Americans since its discovery in 1865. Between 1882 and 1885 at least five firms (each with nominal capital of between $1 and $2 million) were organized by New York and St Paul investors to mine for gold, iron ore, and mica on the prairies. In 1886, Samuel Ritchie, an Ohio carriage builder and railroad entrepreneur, having paid $35,000 for 10,000 acres in Ontario, incorporated both the Canada Copper Comany ($2 million) and the Anglo

American Iron Company ($5 million) and arranged with the owners of Orford Nickel to process the ores. All told, it is estimated that American investors contributed one-half of all Canadian mining capital during the 1880s. Note, however, that these were direct investments, not funds routed through the New York Stock Exchange.[238]

While the American Screw Company may have been the first American manufacturing firm to build a plant in Canada, between 1875 and 1879, Lewis reports that twenty-three American firms located branches in that country. Over the next quinquennial, she counted an additional thirty-two firms, although Wilkins reports that she can confirm the existence of only forty-seven American subsidiaries operating between 1876 and 1887. Both agree, however, that metal working firms tended to predominate, although there were also concentrations in textile and woodworking In addition, Wilkins concludes that no fewer than four American drug manu-facturers, including Parke, Davis & Co., began manufacturing in Canada between 1879 and 1887.[239]

Similarly, American insurance firms including the "Big Three" – New York Life, Equitable, and Mutual – early began selling policies in Canada, and those sales meant, at first, investment in real estate, and then, when Canadian regulations began to bind, the investment of their reserves in a wide range of enterprises.[240] In addition, although, with the exception of some early Canadian Pacific Railroad offerings, total Canadian security sales in the US were not large, American portfolio investors did begin to add some Canadian securities to their holdings. Three million dollars in Quebec bonds were sold in the US in 1879, and, over the next decade, American investors appear to have purchased small blocks of the bond issues of the cities of Winnipeg (purchased by a St Paul Group) and Brandon and of the Queen Victoria Niagara Falls Park. They also pur-chased $1 million in the stock of the Northwest Land Company, and they appear to have owned about a fifth of the Great Western Railroad. More-over, midwestern investors were the source of the majority of the original funds employed by the Manitoba and Southwestern Railroad, although they sold their holdings to the Canadian Pacific in 1884.[241]

At least two decades before the Platt Amendment turned Cuba into a *de facto* American colony, businessmen had, on a very small scale, begun to draw Cuba and the rest of the Caribbean region into the American domestic market.[242] While Mexico contributed minerals and Canada minerals, lumber, and wheat, the Caribbean supplied sugar and fruit to the American market. Still, the levels of investment were not large; in 1897, for example, Cuba, the West Indies, and Central America accounted for little more than ten percent of total American long-term investment abroad. Moreover, if railroads are excluded (particularly the $15.7 million invested in the Panama and in the Guatemala Central railroads) almost ninety percent of the Caribbean total was invested in Cuba, and sixty-five percent was in Cuban agriculture.

American merchants had long financed Cuban sugar growers, but, in the wake of the Ten Years War, defaults left those merchants in control of a number of operating plantations. In 1883, the Boston based E. Atkins & Company somewhat unconsciously made the first major American investment in the sugar industry when, in recompense for a defaulted loan, it took over Soledad, one of the Sarria family's agricultural estates. At the time, the estate consisted of a 4,500 acre plantation, and "ten years later they had enlarged this property to 12,000 acres; nearly 5,000 in cane, with the rest used chiefly as cattle land", and they had built twenty-three miles of private railway. Changes in markets caused the management of the more progressive of these American plantations to expand into milling as well as production, and, although "such mills represented large capital expenditures . . . they were tremendously efficient and greatly reduced the unit costs of production." In time these new grower–refiners became the center of the Cuban sugar production and distribution network – they financed the small growers, contracted for their output, processed the product, and used their own railways to ship the refined sugar to the seacoast.[243]

In the case of bananas, the initial investments can be traced at least as far back as 1870 when Captain Lorenzo Dow Baker discovered that a secondary cargo of bananas could be almost as profitable as his primary cargo of fish. Formalizing the trade, he began to regularly ship fruit from Jamaica to Andrew Preston, the agent for Seaverns and Company, a small Boston produce company. So successful was the experiment that, in 1885, he was able to persuade Preston and nine partners to organize the Boston Fruit Company (the predecessor of United Fruit). Baker himself left fishing and purchased plantations in Jamaica and Santo Domingo.[244]

The years before the mid 90s also set the boundary conditions for the political–economic model of future American political involvement in the Caribbean. As early as 1853, marines were landed in Nicaragua to prevent "any depredations of the property of the Accessory Transit Company", and two years later the company underwrote a revolution that overthrew the nation's government. Forty years later marines were again landed, this time to make certain that the Maritime Canal Company's concession was not canceled, and, in 1895, marines landed to protect American merchants and banana planters in Panama.[245] It is particularly revealing that, in all three instances, the sums involved were relatively trivial. Total investment in the Accessory Transit Company did not exceed $4 million, and only a tiny fraction was ever threatened. Construction of the Maritime Canal across Nicaragua was never begun, and total American agricultural investment in *all* of Colombia was only $3 million in 1897.

3. Towards maturity: 1897–1914

Between 1897 and 1910 American long-term foreign investment surged. Direct investments increased more than four fold, portfolio investment more than seventeen times, and the total from less than $700 million to more than $3.5 billion (see Table 5.1). Despite the quantitative increase, the geographic pattern of investment was little altered. A slight decline in the fraction of long-term investment in Mexico was almost exactly offset by an increase in the share flowing to South America, and a similar fall in Europe's proportion was about equally matched by an increase in Asia's share (see Table 5.2).[246] The industrial composition of investment, however, did change markedly. The fraction of total capital that was invested in railways fell by more than half, while the proportion directed toward manufacturing and mining – particularly the mining of industrial minerals – increased (see Table 5.3b, c).

Outside of the "extensions of the home market", American direct investments continued to reflect the areas of American technological leadership and the nation's still dominant position in petroleum production. Between 1897 and 1914, direct investments in the American sales network increased almost three times, those in manufacturing more than five times, and those in oil production and distribution more than thirteen times. If Canada and Mexico are excluded, Europe drew about sixty percent of the foreign investment in sales, eighty percent of the investment in manufacturing, and a quarter of the investment in oil production.[247]

By 1911, Standard Oil had twenty-two foreign subsidiaries that represented a combined investment of at least $150 million; and the firm controlled, in all, at least sixty-seven foreign enterprises. Most of those sixty-seven were marketing companies, but there were also transport and refining firms as well as two firms engaged in oil production – Romano–Americana with capital of $2.4 million and Imperial Oil (of Canada) with assets of $4 million.[248] Moreover, Standard's domination of the overseas market for American oil was at least partially undercut by the entry of the Pure Oil Company in the 1890s and the Texas Company (Texaco) in 1905. By the end of the 90s, Pure was annually selling more than a million barrels of kerosene in Germany and the Low Countries, and it also had sales organizations in Great Britain, Scandinavia, and Switzerland. Between 1905 and 1911, Pure withdrew from those European markets, but Texaco organized a subsidiary, the Continental Petroleum Company with a terminal in Antwerp, to handle its exports to Europe. By 1913 Texaco also had agencies in Latin America, Australia, Africa, and in several Asian countries.[249]

Aside from oil, while firms like Singer continued to expand their foreign marketing and manufacturing activities, new entrants from the rapidly expanding domestic manufacturing sector began to make their presence felt. For example, The Pittsburgh Wire Company had begun to employ its own foreign sales force in 1893, and that investment proved so profitable that it was soon copied by its competitors. Thus, in 1901, the United States Steel Company turned its attention to the foreign market, and, by 1913, its foreign subsidiary, the United States Steel Products Company, had 268 sales agencies in sixty foreign countries. By 1900 the Deering Harvester Company had begun to manufacture abroad, and, by 1911, its successor, International Harvester, had plants in Canada, Sweden, France, Germany, and Russia that together accounted for more than forty percent of the company's total sales. Similarly, by 1901 the American Tobacco Company was operating four manufacturing plants in Australia as well as single plants in Canada, Japan, Germany, and the United Kingdom. US Rubber began manufacturing in Canada in 1907, and B. F. Goodrich established a French plant three years later.[250]

Construction firms, drawing on American expertise in electric products and the financial strength of a nation's newly emerging investment houses, increased this country's foreign public utility investments six fold between 1897 and 1914. For example, in 1903 the construction firm of J. G. White and Company, the banking house of Speyer and Company, and the Westinghouse Electric and Manufacturing Company jointly contracted to build a street railway and lighting plants in Manila, and, by 1905, a series of American consortia that included either Westinghouse, Western Electric, or General Electric had contracted for work in the Netherlands, Mexico, the UK, Ireland, and South America.[251]

Finally, American portfolio investment in foreign enterprises increased from $50 to $862 million, and Europe and Asia accounted for one-fourth of that increase. In the words of Bullock and his co-authors, "in the year 1900 . . . there was a marked influx in English, Swedish, and German loans. From July to November they amounted to sixty million dollars, in the eleven months after March 1900, to no less than 118 million."[252] During the year 1900, the British received $40 million, the Germans $23 million, the Swedes $10 million, and the Russian Vlakikavkas and Southern Railroad an additional $25 million. The total for 1901 was $125 million, of which the British received $97 million. In 1902 foreign government borrowing totaled $29 million – the UK share was $24 million. So rapid was the increase that, in 1902, the Secretary of State, John Hay, was moved to say:

"The 'debtor nation' has become the chief creditor nation. The financial center of the world, which required thousands of years to journey from the Euphrates to the Thames and Seine, seems passing to the Hudson between daybreak and dark."[253]

Nor had the surge ended. In the six months between the spring and fall of 1904, $535 million of Japanese loans flooded the American and European markets, and when in 1907 twenty percent of those bonds were refunded, half were found to have been carried by American financial houses.[254] In all, between 1901 and 1905 the influx of foreign bonds reached $460 million (including $192 million of Japanese loans), and between 1906 and 1914 the American investors absorbed an additional $442 million. Of the $902 million total, $596 million represented European and Asian loans – including $17 million for the London underground.[255] Despite the attraction of European securities, it was the Western Hemisphere that drew most of the attention of American investors in the years between 1897 and 1914. While the proportion of long-term investment flowing to both Canada and Mexico had declined somewhat, and although the former had edged out the latter for first place on the list of the American investors' most favored countries, the two were still by far the largest recipients of American capital.

In the case of Mexico, the nationalization of the Mexican Central and the Mexican Nation railways reduced the level of direct American investment in railroads, but that decline was more than offset by the increase in portfolio holdings of the securities of the two roads.[256] Moreover, the capital invested in the extension of the Southern Pacific of Mexico into Mexico City meant that, despite partial nationalization, by 1914 direct investment was as high as it had been in 1897.[257] Overall, despite the fact that the railroads' share of the US total had declined from fifty-five to about forty-five percent, American investment in Mexican railroads had increased from $111 to *at least* $387 million.

Conversely, the fraction of investment flowing to mining gradually increased; however, the distribution between precious and industrial metals changed dramatically. Gold and silver had accounted for almost three-quarters of the total in 1897, but, in spite of the fact that Mexico had passed the US and had become the world's leading silver producer, in 1914 precious metals represented less than half (46 percent) of the mining total.[258]

In 1902 the US State Department estimated that there were 294 American financed mining ventures in Mexico, in 1908 the Mexican government announced that American investors controlled 840 of the 1000 foreign owned mines, and two years later those same officials argued that Americans controlled fifty percent of all mines in Mexico and that those mines represented seventy percent of all mineral output. In that latter year, the American Consul General, Alfred L. M. Gottshalk, placed American investment in Mexican mining and smelting at $125 million.[259] Although the long-run implications proved negligible, some questions remain about the value of these investments in the years immediately after the Revolution of 1911. Lewis, in her study of the records of 110 of the American owned mining companies, found that only fourteen continued to operate between 1914 and the end of 1919 and "the idle capital involved amounted to 180 million dollars, out of the 1914 total of 302 million invested in Mexico by these companies."[260]

Before the Revolution, however, there is little question that American investors took a very rosy view of the potential profitability of Mexican mines. For example, the American Smelting and Refining Company (ASARCO) had originally been organized in 1899 to merge sixteen corporations and one partnership engaged in smelting ores and the treatment of lead bullion, copper bullion, and copper matte.[261] Although originally organized to "monopolize" the American domestic market, two years after its charter, in an early example of a leveraged buy-out, ASARCO was merged with and taken over by the Guggenheims. The brothers already owned two Mexican smelters, and, with the takeover, their attentions were directed south, since, with some sixty-four mining properties scattered over Mexico, ASARCO was now the largest single foreign investor in that country.[262]

Again, when in 1898 "Bill" Greene, a western cattleman, discovered traces of copper at Cananea Mountain, he was able to obtain sufficient funding from entrepreneurs on Wall Street to organize the Greene Consolidated Copper Company, and the company invested $12 million on the development of the properties. His associated ventures were failures and Greene lost control of his companies, but, in 1906, the copper mines were taken over by the owners of the Amalgamated Copper Company – the parent company of Anaconda – and the reorganized firm was capitalized at $50 million.[263]

Even before Greene had made his discovery, the Guggenheims were mining some copper near Nacozari. Their efforts proved unprofitable, and in 1895 they were delighted to sell out to a Phelps-Dodge subsidiary, the Copper Queen Consolidated Mining Company. That firm, in turn, incorporated the newly acquired property in West Virginia as the Moctezuma Copper Company, and, between 1895 and 1914, Moctezuma paid its parent dividends totaling $9.7 million. The copper rush continued. In 1900 Americans organized the San Luis Mining Company ($3 million) and the Indiana Sonoma Copper and Mining Company ($3.7 million); in 1901 it was the Transvaal Copper Company ($5.3 million), the Cieneguita Copper Company ($7.6 million), and the Jimulco Mining Company ($1 million); and the next year saw the organization of the Bufa Mining, Milling, and Smelting Company ($1 million) and the Choix Consolidated Mining Company ($3 million).[264]

Mexican lands produced not only gold, silver, and copper, but oil as well. While oil had been discovered in 1876, there was no commercial development until, in 1900, Edward Doheny bought 280,000 acres of potentially productive oil land for $325 thousand and organized the Mexican Petroleum Company of California. The company brought in its first well in

1904; however, the real bonanza for Doheny and the "Golden Lane" awaited the success of Juan Cassiano No. 7 – a well that yielded eighty million barrels between 1910 and 1919. By 1911, Mexico had become the world's third largest producer of petroleum, and half of its production was controlled by American owned companies. In 1914 the holdings of Doheny's operating companies (subsidiaries of his Mexican Petroleum Company Ltd – a Delaware corporation) were valued at $57.9 million.[265]

Agriculture, too, continued to draw about two percent of American finance. Early in the century, Flores, Hale & Company bought and leased "thousands of square miles" of land in Lower California. By 1902 the Chicago based Sonora Land and Cattle Company was reported to have 1.3 million acres, and four other companies each held between seventy-five and five hundred thousand acres. Within a few years, they were joined by another nine companies each owning between ninety thousand and a million acres. In 1910 the American Chicle Company owned three million acres, and at least seven American agricultural enterprises and cattle companies each held between 800 thousand and two million acres.

Beginning in the late 1890s, the sector received an additional fillip as American investment in Mexican rubber boomed. Although of negligible long-term importance, it is estimated that by 1902 American investments exceeded $17 million, and by 1912 those investors controlled sixty-eight percent of Mexico's rubber business. By 1910, the Intercontinental Rubber Company, for example, had purchased between two and three million acres of scrubland covered with guayule, a shrub that they hoped would yield a rubber substitute.[266]

In the case of Canada, the four and a half fold increase in American investment was fueled by an increase of $220 million in portfolio investment, but American direct investment in agriculture rose more than five times, in manufacturing four times, and in mining almost three times. Investment in the agricultural sector went largely into timberlands (in 1909 it was estimated that ninety percent of the available timber in British Columbia was controlled by Americans or American companies), but there was some investment in western farms, and there were large speculative holdings of land in British Columbia and the prairie provinces.[267]

In the manufacturing sector, the first decade of the twentieth century saw more large American corporations – firms like General Electric and Westinghouse, lured in part by the developing market and in part by a desire to operate behind the Canadian tariff wall – move part of their production north of the border. American millers and other food processors opened plants, International Harvester began to manufacture farm machinery, Ford and Buick cars, and US Rubber and Goodyear rubber products.[268]

Americans, however, also continued to establish and finance Canadian firms. In 1902 the American General Consul at Montreal included in a list of American financed enterprises $6 million investments in both the Canadian Steel and Coal Company and in the Federal Sugar Refining Company, a $2 million investment in The Northern Cereal Company, $1 million investments in the American Abell Engine Thrasher Company, in the Locomotive Machine Company, and in an unnamed cold storage company, and one-half million dollar investments in the Canadian Coral Marble Company and in the Northern Aluminum Company.[269]

Despite these miscellaneous industrial investments and the northward migration of a number of large American corporations, the largest American investments in Canadian manufacturing were reserved for the pulp and paper industry. Lewis estimates that in 1897 there was $20 million of American direct investment in the pulp and paper industry; in 1899 the International Paper Company (capital $45 million) announced that it owned about 1.6 million acres of Canadian timberland; and, in 1905 the company began to turn those logs into paper in the Dominion. The major surge of investment, however, came after 1911 when a change in the American tariff schedule permitted Canadian newsprint to enter the US duty free. In 1912 a subsidiary of the *Chicago Tribune*, the Ontario Paper Company, began to construct a mill to supply the paper with newsprint; other US firms immediately followed; and, by 1914, investments in pulp and paper mills represented more than a third of the $221 million American investment in manufacturing.[270]

In mining, the twentieth century saw the Canadian Copper Company and the Anglo American Iron Company merge to form the International Nickel Company, a firm that, when capitalized at $24 million, instantly became the world's largest producer of nickel. The American Consul-General's 1902 list included a $1 million investment in the Clover Leaf Mining Company; in 1910, Johns Manville began to mine asbestos in Quebec; and Field's 1913 enumeration of American investments in Canada included $60 million in British Columbian mining. In terms of precious metals, among the early lode ore mines was the American-owned Le Roi in British Columbia, a mine described in 1896 by a contemporary expert as "one of the best in the world".[271]

Less is known about the composition of Canadian portfolio investment but it appears that it represented about $33.5 million of the 1901–1905 total, and, of that figure, $31.9 million were the issues of railways and other Canadian controlled private companies. In 1913, American holdings of the stock of the Canadian Pacific Railway totaled $29 million, and between 1906 and 1914 Americans appear to have publicly purchased $153 million of the bonds of Canadian municipal and provincial governments, railways, and other private corporations that were not American controlled. To this figure should be added the totals for private placements – a figure that Viner puts, for the years 1905–1913 at $73 million ($35 million of municipal and $38 million of other issues).[272]

Altogether, Field placed American investments in Canada at $279 million in 1909, $417 million in 1911, and $637 million in 1913. The 1913 total was broken down into $135 million invested in 450 Canadian branches of American firms, $124 million of government, municipal, and corporate bonds, $71 million of British Columbia mills and timber lands, $68 million of investments by American life insurance companies, $62 million in British Columbia mines, $60 million in speculative land holdings in that province and $41 million in similar investments in the prairie provinces, $20 million in city and town property, and the remainder in a series of miscellaneous activities that included $3.5 million in theatrical enterprises and $1 million in fox farms on Prince Edward Island.[273]

Given the anti-imperialist rhetoric of the Mexican Revolution and, half a century later, the focus of Canadian nationalistic rhetoric on the subject of American investment, it is surprising that there is little evidence of similar feelings in the years before 1911.[274] In the case of Canada, there appear to be at least three possible explanations for the seemingly mild response: one economic, one political, and one demographic – and the three are not mutually exclusive.

In 1871, Canada was a relatively poor country, and, over the next three decades, the rate of growth of per capita income was lower than the comparable figure for its large southern neighbor. Between 1871 and 1900, real Canadian GNP per capita increased at an average annual rate of 1.6 percent. In contrast, in the US, GNP per capita grew at an annual compound rate of 2.1 percent.[275] Neither the British nor the American investor appear to have been impressed by the Canadian performance; over those years the annual British per capita transfers averaged only $4.44, and the transfers to the agriculture and extractive sector – the focus of most of the American complaint – was only $0.26.[276] Although the evidence on the views of the American investor is less conclusive, it tends to support the same conclusion. In 1897, total American direct and portfolio investment in Canada was only $159.7 million, or about $31 per capita.[277] In fact, although the ratios were soon to change, in 1900, total American investment was less than one-sixth of British.[278]

Politics, however, must also have played a role. When, immediately after the Civil War, the US Congress made it clear that reciprocity was dead, the Canadians were forced to abandon any hope of a "continental" policy, and Sir John A. MacDonald turned instead to his now famous national policy – "a program of railroad building, industrialization, tariff protection, and western settlement inaugurated in the years after 1879".[279] Having imposed tariffs in the hope of convincing British and American firms to open branches in Canada, it would seem that it would have been the height of folly to complain when the policy proved successful. In addition, the "national" policy contained some inconsistent elements: the high tariff policy made it profitable to invest in Canadian manufacturing, but it also reduced the profitability of western agriculture and slowed the rate of western settlement.[280]

Finally demographics may have played a role. The center of anti-foreign sentiments had been in the American West, but because of the Canadian government's policy of encouraging immigration, by the mid 1890s, the trickle of American farmers that had begun moving north as the arable land in the American public domain was filled up had became a steady stream. In 1881, despite the fact that Manitoba had sixty-two thousand residents and British Columbia almost another fifty thousand, the total population residing west of Ontario totaled only 168 thousand. Two decades later, the total population in the western region had risen almost three times, to 646 thousand.

While the results may be biased by the heavy migration in the first decade of the present century, the Census of 1911 reported that US born residents constituted over forty percent of all foreign born and that two-thirds of all foreign born in Canada resided in the prairies, in the Territories, or in British Columbia.[281] If Americans were at least as likely to live in the West as in the East – the actual migration patterns indicate that they were substantially more likely – those figures suggest that there were almost 240,000 American born residents of the four provinces and two territories. In 1911, the total population of the six was 1.7 million.[282]

After the turn of the century, capital flows into Canada surged, and while it was British capital until the outbreak of the War, it was American capital from then until the mid 1930s. In 1935, American direct and portfolio investment stood at $3.7 billion, or about $350 per capita.[283] The US may have been a political threat to Canada in the nineteenth century (the Canadians certainly thought that it was), but that has certainly not been true for the past 100 years.[284] It is interesting to note that, as the political threat disappeared, some Canadians came to believe that the economic threat had increased. Despite some bickering, however, recent events suggest that the majority do not, and a continental rather than a national policy has, 125 years after the first failed attempt at institutional innovation, finally begun to emerge.

In the case of Mexico, from 1877 until the revolution, as the economy gradually shifted from stagnation to growth, the government also adopted a southern version of Canada's national policy.[285] First, that policy called for political stability and peace. Second, it was a major tenant of Porfiriato policy that investment from abroad, and particularly from the US, be encouraged. Third, given stability and investment (much of it in railroads), the policy was designed to encourage the integration of the economy both internally and internationally.[286] In the words of one critic of the policy, "The state did not merely submit to foreign pressures on the debt; it threw open the doors to foreign investment in an attempt to marshall sufficient capital and technical expertise to generate economic growth for the benefit of domestic and foreign monopolies."[287]

Although the political, structural, and distributional results of the policy have long been debated, there can be no doubt that "southern national" was, at least in part, an economic success. By 1910, precious metals made up less than one-half of the nation's exports – they had accounted for almost eighty percent in 1877 – and, in the decade 1900–1910, per capita GNP grew by 2.2, manufacturing production by 3.6, and mining and petroleum production by 7.2 percent a year.[288]

Much of that growth can be traced to the importation of foreign capital. By the end of the period, the inflow of capital left:

(1) The largest extractive industries, the electric power and other public utilities, the railroads, and the international banks almost entirely under foreign control;
(2) a substantial share (perhaps half) of manufacturing in foreign hands; and
(3) some fraction of agriculture – cattle ranches in the north, cotton, rubber, sugarcane, and coffee plantations – owned by foreign investors.[289]

Given the nature of government policy, its "success", and the degree of political control exercised by Díaz, it is hardly surprising that there were few voices raised against the foreign imperialist investors.[290] It should be noted, however, that when the encouragement of foreign capital becomes the central tenant of governmental policy, it is likely that it will become the focus of attack for groups attempting to replace that government. Moreover, to the extent that the American experience with Mexican tropical agricultural was typical of American investment in land related activities in general, it appears that Mexican entrepreneurs were as willing to take advantage of risk seeking gringos as Western mine owners had been willing to "extract gold" from British investors' a quarter of a century before.[291]

Given the market opportunities presented by the Spanish American War and the political environment created by the Platt Amendment, it is not surprising that the fraction of American investment directed toward Cuba and, to a lesser extent, the West Indies rose from just more than seven in 1897 to something less than ten percent in 1914. By that latter date, long-term American investment in the region totaled more than $335 million. Despite the fact that agriculture's share of total investment declined from just less than half to forty-three percent, $120 million of the new funds were directed toward that sector. In addition, however, there were substantial commitments to public utilities ($58 million), and additions to the portfolios of American investors ($55 million).

About three-quarters of the agricultural investment was in sugar, and of that amount more than eighty percent was invested in Cuba. By 1898, E. Atkins & Company was already probably the largest sugar proprietor on the island, but the American invasion had hardly begun. R. B. Hawley, for example, began to invest in the Cuban sugar industry just before the turn of the century, and he soon owned some 73,000 acres and the island's largest sugar mill – a mill with the capacity to process ten percent of the sugar crop of the entire island. Later he added the island's only remaining sugar refinery to his holdings and purchased the Unidad Sugar Company. In 1906, his holdings were consolidated in the reorganized Cuban–American Sugar Company – a firm with assets that initially exceeded $14 million and that had, by 1914, grown to more than twice that amount. In that latter year, the Cuban–American Rionda family controlled some 250,000 acres; as early as 1900 the United Fruit Company (organized in 1899) had spent more than $1 million building a sugar mill; and even H. O. Havemeyer of the American Sugar Refining Company (that is, the Sugar Trust) was a minority investor in four Cuban companies. It is estimated that by 1905 there were some twenty-one American-owned mills processing about a fifth of the island's crop – a proportion that had doubled by 1909.[292]

Once the island became independent, investment in Cuban utilities, particularly in electrification, also began to lure American investors. The Havana Electric Railway, Light and Power Company, a firm that produced both electricity and transport, was, for example, nearly bankrupt when, in 1907, it was taken over by an American, Frank Steinhart. To finance the buy-out, Steinhart drew on the resources of the Catholic Diocese of New York and on Speyer & Company, the New York bankers. Although ultimately the target of anti-imperialist attack, the firm was revitalized by its new management, and the value of the firm's shares had, by the mid 1920s, risen from the 1907 low of eleven to 240.[293]

Except for the American bankers' twenty percent holding of the National Bank of the Republic of Haiti (value $400 thousand) and Kuhn Loeb's $13.5 million refunding of the $20 million Santo Domingo debt ($4.6 million still outstanding in 1914), most of the reported portfolio investment in the Caribbean was in Cuban securities. About $35 million were in government and about $11.4 million in private issues.[294]

In 1911, the American Consul General, J. L. Rogers, argued that American investment in Cuba totaled about $205 million. Of that sum, he estimated that $50 million was invested in sugar, $15 million in other lands, $10 million in other agriculture, $25 million in railway equity and an equal amount in mines, mercantile activity and manufacturing, $5 million in both shipping and banking, $20 million in mortgages and credit, $20 million in public utilities, and $30 million in the island nation's public debt.[295]

While the proportion of American long-term investment directed toward Central America declined slightly between 1897 and 1914, the fraction flowing to South America almost doubled. Taken together, the Latin American commitment increased from just less than $60 million to almost $460 million. More than half of that total was directed toward mining, but railroads and agriculture together represented another $100 million, and portfolio investment, an item that had been absent in 1897, added an additional $46 million to the total.[296]

Although there is evidence of assorted American mining investment in Costa Rica, Honduras, Nicaragua, Salvador, Bolivia, Brazil, Colombia, and Ecuador, by 1914 the largest financial commitments were to copper mines in Chile and, to a lesser extent, in Peru. In the case of the latter country, lack of transport and the technical difficulties associated with production at altitudes up to 14,000 feet delayed development until, in 1902, American finance (J. P. Morgan) combined with American technological know-how (the Hearst-Haggin group) to organize the Cerro de Pasco Mining Company.[297] Although the entrepreneurs initially believed that an investment of $5 million would be sufficient to underwrite production, technical and labor problems proved difficult to solve, and the American financial commitment rose to $12 million by 1907 and to $25 million by 1912. By that latter date, the firm had finally begun to produce some copper, but the demand for additional capital investment continued to absorb operating profits for another five years.[298]

American investment in Chilean copper dates from 1904, when William Braden, supported by investors associated with ASARCO, incorporated the Braden Copper Company in Maine, sold $625,000 in preferred shares, received permission to do business in Chile, and began to exploit the low grade ores in the Andean region southeast of Santiago. The need for additional developmental funds induced Braden to seek help from the Guggenheims, and the Guggenheim Exploration Company invested $500,000 in the Braden company's bonds. Even that infusion proved inadequate and, in 1909, the Braden Copper Mines Company, a holding company, was organized to take over the assets of the Braden Copper Company. The new firm issued $4 million in convertible bonds, enough, after retiring existing bonds and preferred stock, to provide $2.5 million in working capital. The holding company was initially capitalized at $10 million, but that figure was increased to $14 million in 1911, and, with the new funds invested in plant and equipment, output was increased from three million pounds of copper in 1908 to sixteen million in 1913.[299] The company ultimately proved so successful, that when, in 1915, ninety-five percent of the firm was sold to Kennecott Copper, the sales price was $57 million.[300]

Braden's initial success convinced the Guggenheims of the profit potential of the porphyr ores, and in 1911 they joined with A. C. Burrage of Amalgamated Copper to buy a number of "exhausted" mines in Chuqicamata in northern Chile for $100,000. The next year, they organized the Chile Exploration Company (Chilex) to develop the properties. The initial investment was $1 million, and exploratory work revealed the existence of 154 million tons of 2.23 percent copper ore. Despite the favorable report, the Guggenheims found it necessary to invest an additional $11 million in developing the facilities needed to reach even the most easily accessible ore (about 300,000 tons). "Huge mechanical shovels carved Chuquicamata into the largest open pit mine in the world, while the brothers' engineer, E. A. Cappelen-Smith, developed a new concentration process utilizing sulfuric acid and electrolytic precipitation to treat the mine's ore." Recognizing the need for additional finance, they organized the Chile Copper Company with a capital of $110 million to acquire the physical properties of the Chile Exploration Company. Ultimately, however, even that sum proved insufficient and another "100 million dollars was poured into the desert before Chile Copper was a success".[301]

In addition to copper, Americans invested smaller amounts in other South American minerals. They invested in gold mines in Ecuador and Colombia; and, by 1914, Alcoa had purchased bauxite rich land in British Guiana, although they had not yet begun to exploit it. Between 1909 and 1912, W. R. Grace & Company and the du Ponts together acquired perhaps $12 million worth of Chilean nitrate *oficinas*, but those investments represented no more than three percent of total foreign investment in that activity. In 1913, US Steel paid about $300,000 and invested an additional $3 million in manganese properties in Brazil.[302]

While it was sugar that dominated American agricultural investment in Cuba and the West Indies, it was tropical fruit in general, and bananas in particular, that drew the bulk of such investment to Central and South America. While sugar production in Colombia and Peru absorbed about $8 million of American capital in 1914, tropical fruit accounted for all of the $36.5 million invested in Central and $8 of the $25 million invested in South American agriculture.

Much of that investment was channeled through the United Fruit Company, a firm chartered in New Jersey in 1899 to combine the agricultural and ocean transport holdings of the Boston Fruit Company and Minor Cooper Keith's land, banana plantations, and railroads in Costa Rica and Colombia (Keith owned land both on the mainland and in Panama). Although capitalized at $20 million, the initial subscription was a disappointing $2.7 million, but, within a year, more than $11 million had been raised. Even the initial funding was, however, sufficient to permit the company to open and operate sales agencies in Boston, New York, Philadelphia, Baltimore, and New Orleans and plantations in Cuba, Jamaica, Santo Domingo, Costa Rica, Colombia, and Nicaragua, to underwrite the export of fifteen million stems of bananas to the United States, and to expand the company's activities into Guatemala. At the time it was initially chartered, United Fruit had title to 212,394 acres of land (61,263 in production), eleven steamships, and 112 miles of railroad.

Within a very few years, although the Cuban lands were converted to sugar and those in Santo Domingo were completely abandoned, the firm expanded into Honduras and increased its holdings in Nicaragua, Jamaica, and Colombia. Between 1900 and 1910, United Fruit accounted for well over three-quarters of the total number of banana stems imported into the combined North American and European markets.

Success breeds competition. The old Atlantic Fruit and Steamship Company, an original competitor, was forced out, but it was soon reorganized with more secure financial backing as the Atlantic Fruit Company, a Delaware corporation. More importantly, in 1911 Samuel Zemmuray organized the Cuyamel Fruit Company to grow bananas in Honduras, and that firm soon became United's chief competitor. Despite these intrusions, United Fruit maintained its near monopoly position until the outbreak of World War I, and by 1913 owned or leased more than 850,000 acres, of which 221,837 were under cultivation.[303]

While South American railroads had absorbed large quantities of British investment, it was Central America that attracted the American investor with an interest in rail transport. Of that region's 1897 total of $37.9 million, almost eighty percent was invested in Guatemala. American contractors had built both the Central and the Western Railways, but much of the Guatemala investment was in Minor Keith's New Jersey incorporated Guatemala Railroad – a railroad that connected Puerto Barrios on the Atlantic with Guatemala City. In 1912 the Northern took over the Western, and the enlarged firm was reorganized as the International Railways of Central America. Of the remaining $7.3 million invested in Central American railroads, $1.5 million represented two American banks' (Brown & Co. and J. & W. Seligman) fifty percent share of the Pacific Railway of Nicaragua and the remaining $5.8 million American investment in the Salvadorian system.[304]

In terms of portfolio investment, the United States appears to have absorbed something more than $64 million of Central and South American issues, and, of that total, some $46 million were still outstanding in 1914. While funds were directed to the governments of nine countries, the major recipients were Argentina (forty percent), Brazil (thirty-two percent), and Bolivia (twelve percent); the total included loans for railroads in Bolivia and to the Brazilian state of Sao Paulo to support a coffee valorization scheme. In the case of Argentina, the $25 million advanced had not been repaid by 1914, and, at that time, it represented more than one-half of American investment in the region's portfolio issues.[305]

Despite the fact that, by 1914, the relative share of American investments in Cuba, the West Indies, and in Central America had increased only marginally over 1897 (from ten to twelve percent of the overseas total), the level of American political interference in the region's political affairs had increased almost exponentially. Even if this country's overt and covert support for the Panamanian "revolution" is ignored – that support was almost certainly not engendered by a desire to protect American investments in the region but by far more global military and economic concerns – there appears to have been a near exponential increase in direct intervention.[306]

The Treaty of Paris that ended the Spanish–American War permitted the direct annexation of Puerto Rico, and, indirectly, it produced the Platt amendment to the Cuban constitution. That amendment, among its other provisions, prohibited Cuba from concluding any treaty with a foreign power, "which will impair or tend to impair the independence of Cuba", and from incurring any foreign debt where interest and payments to the sinking fund could not be met with "the ordinary revenues of the Island of Cuba". It also granted the United States military bases in Cuba, required that the Cubans invest in sanitation to protect the people and *commerce* of Cuba, and permitted the US to intervene militarily for the "protection of life, property, and individual liberty, and for discharging the obligations with respect to Cuba imposed by the treaty of Paris, now to be assumed and undertaken by the government of Cuba".[307] Not only did the American government successfully object to attempts by the Cuban government to borrow funds, but American troops intervened directly in 1906, 1912, and 1917.[308] Interestingly enough, however, it was not the American investor who was the chief beneficiary of this country's involvement in Cuban affairs. Although American investment had increased, in 1914 European capital was still predominant.[309]

An executive agreement concluded in 1904 and modified and ratified as a treaty in 1907 gave the United States the right to collect the customs of Santo Domingo and to distribute fifty-five percent of the funds collected to foreign creditors until such time as that nation's foreign debts had been repaid. Although attempts to annex Santo Domingo had been made during Grant's presidency, direct political interference was delayed until 1902. At that time, an American firm, the Santo Domingo Improvement Company, appealed for intervention to protect an $11 million claim. The following year, the two countries signed an executive protocol that required the Santo Domingan government to pay the US $4.5 million to cover the claim. In 1904, however, Santo Domingo was unable to pay; Kuhn Loeb and Company agreed to advance $20 million to cover the foreign debts; and the Santo Domingan customs houses were taken over to guarantee that payments would be made. A new loan, under similar conditions, was negotiated in 1914. Thus, American control of Santo Domingan customs continued for half a century after the initial agreement had been signed. Control of the island's custom was, however not the extent of American involvement. In 1912, the American government forced the resignation of the Santo Domingan president; it supervised elections there in 1913 and in 1914; and, two years later, the country was invaded by American marines.[310]

The basis of American political penetration of Haiti can be traced at least as far back as 1910 when New York bankers purchased one-fifth of the shares of the National Bank of Haiti – a purchase that was much facilitated by pressure applied by the American Secretary of State.[311] Direct military intervention, however, did not occur until half a decade later, but at that time the resulting treaty reduced the island republic to the status of an American protectorate – a status that continued for almost two decades and of which there is still some evidence today.

Nicaragua had seen marines land to protect American investments in the 1890s, but those incursions were merely the opening guns of a much larger campaign. In 1909 and 1910, the US provided direct and indirect support for a revolution against the governments of both José Zelaya and his successor José Madriz. The next year, despite the support of the American Secretary of State and, perhaps, because of the protests of the Nicaraguan population, negotiations for a $15 million loan failed only because the US Senate thrice refused to ratify the Knox–Castrillo agreement – an agreement that would have given the United States control of Nicaragua's customs. The bankers, Brown Brothers and J. & W. Seligman, however, gained some measure of revenge by negotiating a smaller loan secured by a lien on customs – the customs to be collected by an American chosen by the banks and approved by the State Department. Other loans with similar conditions followed and, perhaps not surprisingly, the marines landed in 1912, and, with only a brief interruption, they remained until 1933.[312]

Clearly the political and military interference in the lives of the residents of Cuba, Santo Domingo, Haiti, and Nicaragua laid the foundation for some seven decades of anti-American feelings, but it is difficult to rationalize the level of intervention with the size of the American's investment stake in those countries. In 1914 the total amount of American investment in all of Cuba, the West Indies, and Central America (excluding Mexico) did not exceed $430 million. Granted Cuba was somewhat important; the island accounted for almost eighty-five percent of that total figure ($129 million in agriculture, $58 million in utilities, $20 million in manufacturing, and $13 million in railroads). Investment in the other countries that witnessed direct American intervention was, however, trifling. The total for Nicaragua (mostly in mining, railroads, and fruit) probably did not exceed $2.5 million; the figure for Panama (outside the Canal Zone) was probably not more than $4 million; for Haiti it could hardly have been more than $11 million; and the Santo Domingan total may have reached $16 million – a grand total of less than $33 million, a third of the amount invested in Canadian agriculture and about equal to the level of investment in that industry in Mexico.

While direct military intervention is guaranteed to raise hackles, the level of rhetoric raised against "Yankee" *economic* imperialism is much more difficult to explain. Not only was the level of American investment in Latin America not large, but the evidence suggests the level of profits was hardly exploitative. Very early Leland Jenks concluded that American involvement in Cuba was more beneficial to the Cubans than to the Americans, and more recently Vasquez and Meyer have come to a similar conclusion about Mexico. Again, William Schell in his study of American investment in tropical Mexico also concludes, "Here the prevailing flow of wealth was from north to south."[313]

Finally, Stanley Lebergott in his more general study of US imperialism reached much the same conclusion.

"In summary, American imperialism after the Spanish American War worked systematic effects on interest groups in Latin America. (a) It increased the income of workers and peasants because it expanded the demand for labor . . . (b) Workers' real wages often increased more than their money wages . . . (c) Imperialist investment increased the value of land held by landlords . . . (d) American imperialism injured the vested interests of the existing native business group by destroying monopoly profits . . ."

In his last conclusion, Lebergott may have discovered the root of the anti-American rhetoric. In his words, "The heart of the anti-imperialist struggle, then, may prove to be a squabble between two capitalist groups, one native and the other foreign, fighting over the spoils of progress."[314]

6

Summary and conclusions

It is difficult to summarize more than one hundred years of international transfers but three issues stand out. The first deals with the reliability and comparability of the data, the second with the role of foreign capital in American development, and the third with the relationship between capital exports, "dollar diplomacy", and the origins of the belief in "Yankee economic imperialism".

The data in this chapter are drawn from two quite different sources: the net flow estimates are derived from an analysis of the nation's balance of payments; the estimates of the stocks of foreign investment in the United States and of American investment abroad are the product of enumerations – censuses, if you like – of the nation's debit and credit balances. In theory, of course, the two are closely related, but, like many empirical exercises, the two are more closely linked in theory than the data often suggests.[315] This problm is one that concerned both North and Simon, and it still cannot be completely resolved.

Table 6.1 displays the estimated stocks and the sum of the net flows for a number of years in the nineteenth and early twentieth centuries.[316] Although at first glance there appears to be a substantial discrepancy in the 1843 figures, closer examination reveals that the residual, while still substantial, is not as large as it first appears. Clearly, the estimate of a negative $75 million of American investment abroad is absurd; however, it should be kept in mind that the summed net flow figures do not capture the state debts that went permanently into default or that were substantially written down between 1839 and 1843.[317] In addition, Lewis acknowledges that her $28 million estimate of short term indebtedness – a figure assumed to be equal to one-third of the 1836 total – is low. Thus, if the net flow figure is reduced by $24 million to account for the defaults and the short-term component of the stock figure is increased by $28 million – to two-thirds of the 1836 total – the resulting residual (–$23 million) represents a believable statistical discrepancy.

Despite North's concern, it is not difficult to rationalize the two sets of 1853 estimates.[318] The Lewis estimate of the stock is $377 and the flows sum to $378 million leaving a small negative residual of $1 million – a figure that appears to be well within normal bounds, particularly given the fact that the

Table 6.1. *Rationalization of summed capital flows with stocks of foreign investment in US and US investment abroad*
(millions of dollars)

	(1)	(2)	(3)	(4)	(5)
	Stock 1 Foreign in US (measured)	Summed Flows	Stock 2a US in Foreign (estimated)	Stock 2b US in Foreign (measured)	Residual
1843a[1]	225	300	−75	(small)	−75
1843b[2]	253	276	−23	(small)	−23
1853a[3]	377	378	−1	(small)	−1
1853b[4]	381	378	+3	(small)	3
1869a[5]	1546	1235	+311	75	+236
1869b[6]	1116	1235	−119	75	−194
1869c[7]	1246	1235	+11	75	−64
1897a[8]	3395	3388	8	685	−677
1899a[9]	3400	3109	+291	+500	−309
1914a[10]	7540	3109	+4431	3514	+917
1914b[11]	6623	3109	+3514	3514	0

1. Lewis, *America's Stake*, pp. 519–521.
2. 1843a adjusted for $24 million defaulted state bonds and with short-term capital assumed equal to $56 million.
3. Lewis, *America's Stake*, pp. 521–522. Secretary of the Treasury's estimate for foreign long term investment plus an 1857 estimate of short-term investment ($222 million + $155 million).
4. Stock 1 adjusted for $4 million defaulted Florida loan.
5. Lewis, *America's Stake*, pp. 522–523. Commissioner Wills' estimates of foreign long- and short-term investment in US adjusted for an additional $80 million in short-term investment. U.S. investment abroad from Lewis, p. 442.
6. Stock 1 adjusted for sale of US bonds at a 43 percent discount.
7. Stock 1 adjusted for sale of US bonds at a 30 percent discount.
8. Lewis, *America's Stake*, p. 442.
9. Lewis, *America's Stake*, p. 529. Lewis' adjustment of Bacon's estimates.
10. Stock 1 = Lewis and Wilkins $7090 million long-term plus $450 million short-term. Stock 2 = Lewis, *America's Stake*, p. 606. Summed flows includes estimated increases in short-term of $200 million between 1897 and 1914.
11. Stock 1 assumes common stocks were issued at the 1914 market prices rather than at par *and* that one-fourth of railroad bonds and preferred shares were issued before 1890 at 67 percent of par. See Lewis, *America's Stake*, p. 554.

estimate of the flow includes "errors and omissions" and the fact that the $4 million repudiated Florida debt is not included in the stock estimate.

The 1869 figure for foreign investment in the United States, on the other hand, is, as Simon has suggested, quite difficult to accept.[319] If Wells' estimate is correct, it implies that American investments abroad were an astounding $311 million – more than four times the generally accepted figure. If, however, Wells' figures are adjusted downward to reflect the international market's discount on the $1 billion in US government obligations, the adjusted figure of $1116 million turns the + $236 million residual into a –$194 million figure.[320] Moreover, if the discount had been only thirty percent, as Cleona Lewis suggests, the two sets of estimates are believable.[321]

The later estimates, however, are much more difficult to rationalize. As Simon noted, Cleona Lewis' estimates for 1897 ($3395 million in foreign investments in the US and $685 million in American investments abroad) would imply a sum of capital flows of $2710, but the figure from the North–Simon data is $3388, a discrepancy of $677 million.[322] Moreover, since a substantial fraction of the American securities had been issued at not insignificant discounts, the actual discrepancy is almost certainly much larger.[323] The inability to rationalize the 1897 estimates is particularly troubling, since the two stock figures are not the estimates of a contemporary like Wells or Bacon, but are based on Lewis' own extensive research. This problem clearly deserves further academic attention.[324]

Even Nathaniel Bacon's 1899 estimate – an estimate that Simon applauds but that Lewis deplores – although not yielding quite as large an unexplained residual, is still difficult to justify, if Simon's net flow estimates are accurate. Bacon's figure for foreign investment in the United States ($3400 million), when coupled with the summed flow projection, implies a level of American foreign investment of only $291 million – a total well below Bacon's own $500 million and much below Lewis' $685 million for 1897.

Finally, even the well documented stock figures for 1914 are not easily rationalized with the net flow series. If one accepts Wilkins' and Lewis' estimate of $7540 million in foreign investment in the US, Lewis' $3514 million estimate of American investment abroad, and a flow figure that captures the gradual run up of foreign short-term investment, the residual is a very large, and positive, $917 million.[325] In this case, however, there do appear to be adequate explanations of the discrepancy. Lewis herself believes that "many direct investments are probably omitted" from the estimate of American investment abroad.[326] In addition, there is no allowance for any short-term American investment abroad, although that omission is probably not great.[327] Most importantly, however, the portfolio investment is included at par, and some, perhaps a substantial amount, of those securities were sold at significant discounts. If, for example, common stocks are included at their 1914 market prices and if as little as one-fourth of the railroad bonds and preferred shares were issued prior to 1890 when discounts averaged a third of par value, it is possible to account for the entire discrepancy.

What is possible to conclude about the contribution of foreign capital to American growth? Clearly, in the aggregate, foreign capital cannot have played a major role; and, in fact, the flows of financial capital were almost certainly less significant than the flows of human capital that moved across the Atlantic with the nation's voluntary and involuntary immigrants.[328] Overall, between 1790 and 1900 the ratio of foreign capital imports to new national capital formation was almost five percent, and, over the last three decades of the century, it was about four-fifths of that amount.

Despite the small overall relative magnitude, between 1790 and the beginning of 1914 there was a net inflow of some $3.1 billion, and in some times and in some places those transfers were very important. Thus, between 1816 and 1840 capital imports accounted for twenty-two percent of new capital formation. For the years 1861 to 1870 the figure was almost sixteen percent, and between 1880 and 1890 almost nine. It should, of course, be remembered that the first of these periods saw the rapid development of the nation's first man-made inter-regional transportation system; the second encompasses the years of the Civil War and reconstruction as well as the completion of the first inter-continental railroad link; and the third captures the rapid development of the American West and its integration into the national economy.

In the 1830s, the 1860s, and the 1880s foreign capital was important. In 1838, for example, it is estimated that no less than forty percent of foreign long-term capital (almost $45 million) had been directed toward the construction of canals, railroads, and turnpikes. Without those funds it would have taken much longer to develop an integrated market in the East and upper Midwest. In 1869, the record indicates that foreigners had invested very substantial sums in the issues of the federal government and smaller, but still significant, amounts in the bonds of the states, and those funds had been used to relieve the short-run pressures engendered by the War and reconstruction. At the same time European investors had almost certainly made more than $100 million dollars available to the nation's railroads.[329] In the 1880s, while railroads continued to draw the bulk of foreign capital – and the railroad network could not have been completed as quickly without those capital infusions – there were also major transfers to land and land related industries (mines, agriculture, and financial, land, and development companies). These investments played a major role in opening the American West and, taken together with the resources poured into railroad construction, in integrating that sector into the developing eastern industrial economy.

A breakdown of foreign investment in 1914 shows that, although the railroads still commanded almost three in every five dollars of foreign investment, the land related industries drew more than fourteen, the commercial and industrial sector (including breweries and distilleries) received nearly thirteen, and oil and mining ventures almost eight percent of the total. As late as 1900, although Americans had demonstrated a willingness to place their accumulations in government and transport issues, they were still hesitant to risk their savings in less familiar enterprises. Nor was the mobilization problem made easier by the decisions of the managers of the nation's premier securities market – in their attempts to provide signals for the relatively unsophisticated American investors, they had largely ruled out the issues of these new and emerging sectors. As a result, foreign capital played an important role not only during periods of rapid economic growth but also during periods of rapid industrial transformation.

It is hardly a surprise that it was the British saver who proved most willing to risk his resources in the new world. The country had been the first to industrialize, and, although UK savings rates had never been high, the period over which they had been accumulating was long. As a result, the potential pool of investible funds was large, and even as late as 1914 British investments represented the bulk of the foreign commitment to the US. What is, perhaps, more surprising is the erosion of the British position over the postbellum decades, and the increase in importance of the savings of citizens of countries that had only just begun to commercialize and industrialize. Thus, by 1914, although about sixty percent of foreign long-term investment was British, sixteen percent was German, nine percent Dutch, seven percent French, four percent came from the rest of Europe, and an equal amount from our neighbor to the north.

Finally, although in 1914 the US remained a substantial net debtor, it had also become a major creditor. American investments abroad, trivial before the 1890s, had reached almost $700 million in 1897 and stood at an estimated $3.5 billion seventeen years later.[330] While there were American investments scattered across the globe, about a fifth of the total was in Europe, a quarter in Canada, and something more than a third in Mexico, in Central America, and in Cuba and the West Indies. To a large extent, the European commitments reflected the export of the nation's technology and its long-held but no longer dominant position in petroleum production. The questions raised by Canadian, Mexican, Caribbean, and Central American transfers are more interesting.

In the first place, an examination of those investments suggests that the Americans viewed the regions to the north and south as natural extensions of the domestic market – a source of food for its citizens, raw materials for its industrial sector, and a market for its products. No region can, however, be economically integrated until transport links are established. While the British provided the investment needed to integrate the Canadian market, it was largely American capital that financed the railroads that opened the Mexican economy.

It might be easy to conclude that the Americans treated the British dominion to the north differently from the ex-Spanish colonies to the south. Forty percent of American non-railroad direct investment in Canada went to support that nation's manufacturing sector while less than a tenth of that fraction supported the industrial sector to the south. A closer scrutiny, however, indicates that the conclusion is almost certainly false. American manufacturing capital flowed into the developed and urbanized sectors of Ontario and Quebec. It did not go into British Columbia, the Prairies, the Maritimes, or even rural Ontario and Quebec. Those regions, like Mexico, Central America, and the Caribbean – and like the American West – were certainly the recipients of direct investment from the American East, but it was capital directed toward mining and other land related industries. The economic role assigned to all three "western" regions, whether in Canada, the United States, or in the ex-Spanish colonies to the south, was the production of primary products – foodstuff, timber, and minerals – for the rapidly urbanizing and industrializing East.

In the second place, this study raises serious questions about the basis for the charges of "Yankee economic imperialism" and the relevance of the term "Dollar Diplomacy". It is clear that the American government continually interfered – both politically and militarily – in the life of Central America, Cuba, and the other Caribbean nations. It is equally clear that vocal objections were raised to American investment in those regions. It is, however, not clear that there was a close correlation between political interference and the level of American investment, and it is clear that the lot of the average native was much improved by the entrance of American investment into those otherwise largely closed markets.

American investment in Cuba was significant, but, even there, it was not as large as the European component, and, in the rest of the Caribbean and in Cental America, it was trifling. Studies of both Cuba and Mexico have underscored the benefits of American investments to both workers and landlords, and there is no reason to believe the same cannot be said for workers on banana plantations in Costa Rica and the native owners of sugar plantations in Cuba.

Stanley Lebergott has concluded that it was the politically amplified voices of a few native businessmen – businessmen angry when forced to confront foreign competition in what had been their own nearly monopolistic markets – that was primarily responsible for the anti-American rhetoric. Perhaps, then, it was the politically amplified voice of a few native American businessmen who pushed the government into political action to "protect American investments" even when there were, for all intents and purposes, no American investments to protect. That question, however, is best left to the next generation of political economists.

Overall then, given the American, Canadian, Mexican, and Latin American experiences, what can be said about the nature of political response to foreign experiences? First, it is clear that the less the degree of foreign control, the less the domestic resistance. Second, as long as investment was not tied to any guarantees, there appears to have been little domestic resistance to foreign investment in railroads or in government bonds. Third, the more directly competitive the foreign enterprise, the greater the level of complaint. As long as the supply of the public domain appeared limitless, there was little direct competition between foreign and domestic entrepreneurs, and there were few complaints. In a similar vein, if foreign capital was a reasonably close substitute for domestic, there were complaints, but if the two were not so close, domestic entrepreneurs tended to support foreign investment. Fourth, foreign ownership of land and, sometimes, natural resources, tended to generate more anger than ownership of other assets. Finally, if the encouragement of foreign investment was a tenant of political policy and if the political structure was stable, there were few complaints. If, however, the political structure became unstable, there was a tendency to direct anti-government rhetoric at the tenants of those government policies.

Although almost certainly of less importance than the movement of European and African immigrants across the Atlantic, the pace of growth and the evolution of the structure of the American economy were influenced by the availability of foreign capital. In a similar fashion, the pace of growth and the evolution of the structure – to say nothing of the political climate – of the Canadian, Mexican, Central American and Caribbean economies were influenced by the availability of American capital. As Karl Marx and Boris Yeltsin have shown themselves to be fully aware, foreign capital can make a difference.

Endnotes

Chapter 1

1. In 1981, American overseas investments exceeded foreign investments in the United States by more than $140 billion dollars; by 1988 foreign investments in the US exceeded American investments abroad by more than $530 billion. United States Department of Commerce, Bureau of the Census, *Statistical Abstract of the United States, 1990*, (Washington, D.C.: GPO, 1990), Table 1390, p. 793. With the near total collapse of domestic savings, only massive infusions of foreign capital have managed to sustain even the weak productivity growth that has characterized this nation's economy for the past two decades. Over the past decade the rate of growth of output per worker in the US has lagged behind that in Belgium, Italy, Japan, and the United Kingdom to say nothing of Korea and Taiwan. See United States Department of Labor, *News*, (Washington, D.C.: Bureau of Labor Statistics, June 30, 1989), p. 4.
2. Lance Davis and Robert Gallman, "Savings, Investment, and Economic Growth: The United States in the Nineteenth Century", forthcoming in John James and Mark Thomas (eds), *Capitalism in Context*, (Chicago, Ill.: University of Chicago Press, 1993), Table 2 (hereafter cited as Davis and Gallman, "Savings, Investment and Economic Growth").
3. The contribution is reduced somewhat by the substantial export of capital from the US in the 1890s, but even if that decade is excluded, the share is only seven and a half percent. Douglass C. North, "The Balance of Payments of the United States, 1790–1860", (hereafter cited as North, "Balance of Payments", and Matthew Simon, "The Balance of Payments of the United States, 1861–1900", (hereafter cited as Simon, "Balance of Payments") both in William N. Parker (ed.) *Trends in the American Economy in the Nineteenth Century*, Studies in Income and Wealth, Vol. 24 by the Conference on Research in Income and Wealth, National Bureau of Economic Research, (Princeton, N.J.: Princeton University Press, 1960) as reported in US Department of Commerce, Bureau of the Census, *Historical Statistics of the United States, Colonial Times to 1970* (Washington D.C.: GPO, 1970). The capital stock figures for 1840 to 1900 are from Robert E. Gallman, "The United States Capital Stock in the Nineteenth Century", Stanley Engerman and Robert Gallman (eds) *Long Term Factors in Economic Growth*, National Bureau of Economic Research, Studies in Income and Wealth, Vol. 51 (Princeton, N.J.: Princeton University Press, 1986). The figures for 1799–1840 are from Robert E. Gallman, *The Capital Stock of the United States*, mss. Chapter 5, Table 5.1.

115

4. Simon Kuznets, "Foreign Economic Relations of the United States and their Impact upon the Domestic Economy: A Review of Long Term Trends", *Proceedings of the American Philosophical Society*, **92**:4 (1948), p. 233.
5. Jeffrey G. Williamson, *American Growth and the Balance of Payments, 1820–1913: A Study of the Long Swing*, (Chapel Hill, N.C.: The University of North Carolina Press, 1964) pp. 3–5 (hereafter cited as Williamson, *American Growth*). Raymond W. Goldsmith, "The Growth of Reproducible Wealth of the United States of America", in Simon Kuznets (ed.), International Association for Research in Income and Wealth, *Income and Wealth of the United States: Trends and Structures*, Income and Wealth, Series II, (Cambridge, UK: Bowes and Bowes, 1953), pp. 284–286 (hereafter cited as Goldsmith, "Reproducible Wealth").
6. Williamson, *American Growth*, p. 142. Williamson worked with the North–Simon data before they were adjusted by the OBE and with Kuznets' older net capital formation series. His figures, therefore are somewhat different to those based on the OBE–Gallman data. For example, his figure for the 1880s is 9.5 percent.
7. Goldsmith, "Reproducible Wealth", p. 285.
8. The following table provides a comparison between an extension of the "residual based" and the gross long term series.

Years	Residual Based Net	Long Term Gross	Years	Net	Gross
° 1900	−296	−218	Δ 1907	35	+ 71
Δ 1900	−321	−218	Δ 1908	−187	−46
Δ 1901	−273	−245	Δ 1909	143	+ 59
Δ 1902	−82	−135	Δ 1910	229	+ 225
Δ 1903	−154	−21	Δ 1911	40	+ 48
Δ 1904	−117	−50	Δ 1912	36	+ 23
Δ 1905	−94	−83	Δ 1913	−142	°87
Δ 1906	22	+ 68	Δ 1914	+ 14	−522
			∇1914	−72	−72

Note: ° = Simon; Δ = Simon extension; ∇= gross long term.

9. North, "The Balance of Payments" and Simon, "Balance of Payments" pp. 573–628 and 629–716. The estimates of net flows used in this paper are based on those of North and Simon, but are taken from *Historical Statistics*. They have been adjusted by the United States Office of Business Economics. US Department of Commerce, Bureau of the Census, *Historical Statistics of the United States, Colonial Times to 1970* (Washington, D.C.: GPO, 1970) pp. 858–861 and 864–867 (hereafter cited as *Historical Statistics*).
10. Paul D. Dickens, *The Transitional Period in American International Financing: 1897–1914*, Ph.D. dissertation, George Washington University 1933. Charles J. Bullock, John H. Williams and Rufus S. Tucker, "The Balance of

Trade of the United States", *The Review of Economic Statistics*, Preliminary Volume 1 (July 1919) pp. 215–254 (hereafter cited as Bullock *et al.*, "Balance of Trade"). Raymond W. Goldsmith, *A Study of Savings in the United States*, 3 vols. (Princeton, N.J.: Princeton University Press, 1955) (hereafter cited as Goldsmith, *A Study of Savings*), Vol. 1, pp. 1078, 1080, 1084, and 1086.

11. *Historical Statistics*, p. 858.
12. Chronologically, the first was Bullock *et al.*, "The Balance of Trade". Second were the North and Simon pieces, and the last was Williamson's *American Growth*. The discussion in this section is cast in terms of nominal dollars, since that is the measure used in the three major quantitative studies. It should, however, be noted that, because of price changes, the pattern of real transfers differs somewhat from the standard scenario. In particular, if the series are reported in dollars of 1880, the 1815–1819 peak in capital inflows ($25 million per year) is reduced to $17 million and the 1867–1873 reported peak flows of $143 million per year amounted to only $101 million. On the other hand, the $149 million average inflow over the years 1882–1891 is increased by 16 percent to $173 million and the turn of the century peak in capital exports is increased from about $229 to $293 million – 28 percent. The following table compares the nominal and real values of the average flows for each of the six periods used by Bullock and his co-authors.

Annual Average Capital Flow
(Millions of Dollars)

Years	Nominal	Real (1880)
	$	$
1790–1820	6	4
1821–1837	8	8
1838–1849	−2	−4
1850–1873	66	49
1874–1895	69	81
1896–1914	−41	−54

13. Williamson, citing Bogart, reports that of the total of $170,356,187 in bonds issued by 18 states, 31 percent went to banks, 64 percent to transport (35 percent to canals, 25 percent to railroads, and 4 percent to roads), and the remaining 5 percent to various miscellaneous activities. Williamson, *American Growth*, Table 19, p. 102.
14. For example, Cleona Lewis estimates that $23.7 million of the $34 million Pennsylvania, $6 million of the $11.5 million Alabama, and $10.8 of the $26 million New York state debts were held abroad. Cleona Lewis (assisted by Karl T. Schottenbeck), *America's Stake in International Investment*, (Washington, D.C.: The Brookings Institution, 1938) (hereafter cited as Lewis, *America's Stake*). The quotation is from Bullock *et al.* "The Balance of Trade", p. 218.
15. The OBE adjustments to North's capital estimates, for example, include a total of $24 million in defaults in 1841 and 1842. Williamson, citing Imlah, argues

that, of Jenks' estimate of a total of $174 million of American debt held in England in 1838, "almost the whole was in default or repudiated by 1842". Williamson, *American Growth*, p. 106.

16. See Bullock *et al.*, "The Balance of Trade", p. 223 and Lewis, *America's Stake*, pp. 521–522.

17. The source of both Bullock *et al.* and Lewis' estimate is *Hunt's Merchant's Magazine* for October 1868, but the former attribute the assessment to the Secretary of the Treasury, the latter to "currently accepted opinion".

18. David A. Wells, *Report of the Special Commissioner of Revenue, 1869*, 41st Congress, House of Representative, Executive Document #27 (December 29, 1869), p. xxvi (hereafter cited as Wells, *Report*).

19. Bullock *et al.*, "The Balance of Trade", p.223.

20. Lewis, *America's Stake*, pp. 522–523.

21. Simon, "Balance of Payments", p. 706. The $1.216 billion figure is from *Historical Statistics*, series U 40, p. 869. It may be possible to resolve the difference, if one notes that 43% of $700 million is about $300 million and that the difference between $1.5 and $1.2 billion is also about $300 million.

22. Since Kuznets, scholars have viewed American development "as occurring in waves, each dynamic crest . . . followed by an equally stagnant, but shorter period of depression, unemployment, and price deflation". Such "long swings" (or Kuznets cycles) were, typically, about two decades in length, and both the period of expansion and that of stagnation "left their mark on the nation's economic and social history". Williamson, *American Growth*, p. 3.

23. According to Bullock *et al.*, those transfers reflected a delayed European response to the fears engendered by the effects of the Panic of 1873. They report that $300 million of foreign held securities were repatriated between 1876 and 1878, with half of that figure withdrawn in 1878 alone. Bullock *et al.*, "The Balance of Trade", p. 225.

24. Bullock *et al.*, "The Balance of Trade", p. 226.

25. Goldsmith, *A Study of Savings*, Vol. 1, pp. 1078, 1081, 1084 and 1086.

26. An extension of the Simon residual series, however, suggests that the outflow may have totaled more than $1.4 billion.

27. Lewis, *America's Stake*, p. 605.

28. Simon argues that Cleona Lewis' estimates of net indebtedness of $2.710 billion in 1897 are too low, and as a result, she understates the decline in the net indebtedness that occurred between then and 1900. The evidence suggests that he is correct.

The net decline from $3.3 to $2.5 billion comes from *Historical Statistics* series U 40. The difference between the Simon and Goldsmith figures for 1900 account for the two estimates for 1900. In a similar fashion, if Goldsmith's figures for 1900 are correct, the 1905 figure would be $2.1 not $2.0 billion.

29. Between 1908 and 1914 American direct investment abroad increased from $1,638.5 to $2,652.3 million, although portfolio investment declined by $24.8 million. Lewis, *America's Stake*, p. 605.

Chapter 2

30. The 1853 figures are from the Secretary of the Treasury's report to the United
    States Senate, 33 Congress, 1 Session, Senate, executive document 42 (March
    2, 1854). The 1869 estimates are from the report of David A. Wells, *Report*,
    p. xxvi–xxxi. The 1853 figures include investments of $700,000 in Mining,
    $400,000 in insurance, and $100,000 in both manufacturing and utilities. The
    1869 estimate includes $10 million of foreign investment in US mining.
       Lewis' figures for 1843 are largely based on a House of Representatives'
    estimate that state and city bonds held abroad totaled about $150 million (27th
    Cong., 3rd sess., House of Representatives document 296, (March 2, 1843),
    pp. 3 & 7) and on estimates of Andrew Jackson, Martin Van Buren and the
    Comptroller of the state of New York. Her 1914 figures are based on the work
    of (1) George Paish, "Trade Balances of the United States", US Senate, *Na-
    tional Monetary Commission*, 61st Cong., 2nd Sess., 1910 Senate Document
    579, pp. 173–175 and *The Journal of the Royal Statistical Society*, September
    1909 and January 1911; (2) L. E. Loree's railway data as reported in the
    Commercial and Financial Chronicle, March 31, 1917, p. 1217; (3) *Report of
    the Alien Property Custodian* 1932, 1933, 1934 and (4) The *Report of the
    American Dollar Securities Committee*.
       Wilkins' figures for 1803, with the exception of those for the federal debt
    held abroad, are from Samuel Blodget, *Economica, A Statistical Manual for
    the United States of America* (1806: rpt. New York: Augustus M. Kelly, 1964),
    p. 198. Those for 1838 are largely from James Garland as cited in *Niles'
    National Register*, 44 (July 21, 1838), p. 322. For 1880 they are from John
    J. Madden, *British Investment in the United States, 1860–1880*, Ph.D. Disser-
    tation, Cambridge University, 1958, (New York: Garland, 1985) (hereafter
    cited as Madden, *British Investment*). pp. 78–79 and US Census Office, *Report
    on Valuation, Taxation, and Public Indebtedness of the United States – Tenth
    Census*, (Washington, D.C.: 1884), pp. 490 and 518.
       Table 2.3 displays D. C. M. Platt's reports of total foreign indebtedness for
    twenty-nine years between 1820 and 1876. Those estimates are drawn from a
    wide range of sources, and the author has made no attempt to make them
    consistent. Since they do not include any industrial breakdown they are in-
    cluded only to provide a comparison for the more detailed estimates of Lewis
    and Wilkins. D. C. M. Platt, *Foreign Finance in Continental Europe and the
    United States, 1815–1870: Quantities, Origins, Functions and Distributions*,
    (London: George Allen & Unwin, 1984) (hereafter cited as Platt, *Foreign
    Finance*) Appendix I, p. 188.
31. McGrane's examination of the holders of the Pennsylvania loan of 1842 – a loan
    that may not be typical – indicates that, of the total of $34 million, bond holders
    in the UK held $20.0 million, those in Holland $1.8 million, France $600 thousand,
    the West Indies $563, Switzerland $240, Portugal $231, East India and China
    $148, Mexico $41, what is now Canada $34, Italy $31, Denmark $6, and Spain
    $5 thousand for a total of $23.717 million or about 70 percent of the total.
    Reginald C. McGrane, *Foreign Bondholders and American State Debts*, (New
    York: Macmillan, 1935), p. 71 (hereafter cited as McGrane, *Foreign Bondholders*).

Wilkins cites Representative James Garland who told the House that of all state securities outstanding, at least $65 million were held abroad, principally in England. She comments that this figure represents about 38 percent of state securities outstanding. Her total figure is from B. U. Ratchford, *American State Debts*, (Durham, N.C.: Duke University Press, 1941), p. 88. Mira Wilkins, *The History of Foreign Investment in the United States*, Harvard Studies in Business History No. 41, (Cambridge, Mass.: Harvard University Press, 1989), p.59 (hereafter cited as Wilkins, *Foreign Investment*).

32. Leland H. Jenks, *The Migration of British Capital to 1875*, (London: Thomas Nelson & Sons Ltd, 1963) pp. 360–361 (hereafter cited as Jenks, *The Migration of British Capital*).

33. Williamson, *American Growth*, Table 19, p.102; and Lewis, *America's Stake*, p. 21. The 1843 figures do not make adjustment for bonds in default. The OBE estimates those defaults totaled $12 million in both 1841 and 1842. See *Historical Statistics*, p. 869, Series U 40, fn. 1. Platt puts the total for state debt somewhat lower. He cites figures of $50 million in 1836, $80 and $86 million in 1838, $125 million in 1839, and $150 million in 1843. Platt, *Foreign Finance*, Appendix II, p. 191.

34. Twenty-nine percent to banks, 64 percent to canals, railroads, and roads, and 7 percent to everything else.

35. The distributions are made on the basis of the enumerations of state obligations in E. L. Bogart, *The Economic History of the United States*, 2nd edition, (New York: Longmans, Green, and Company, 1913), p. 195.

36. Lewis thinks that foreigners held as much as $20 million of the Bank's stock and had loaned the Bank another $12 million and that these sums were included in the total for 1843. Lewis, *America's Stake*, p. 520. Wilkins' data for 1838 include $20 million of Second Bank stock in the total $24.8 million in bank securities. Her figure for "Other" banks in 1853 is $6.7 million, an increase over 1838 of about 40 percent. Wilkins, *Foreign Investment*, p. 76.

37. Wilkins, *Foreign Investment*, pp. 78–80. Platt, *Foreign Finance* pp. 157 and 163. Platt argues that foreign investors had placed some money privately in US railway issues, but private placements were more common on the continent than in the UK. In the decade of the 1840s the *Economist's* listing of American securities had only two railroads (the Camden–Amboy and the Philadelphia Reading). Overall, in the period before 1876, he concluded that, "foreign finance was far less influential in American railway development that (sic) it is often declared to be".

38. It is assumed that: (1) British investment in 1914 was similar to British investment in 1908; (2) the distribution of the "Industrial and Other" and the direct components of German investments was similar to the distribution of British investments in the non Government, non Railroad, non Utility categories; and (3) that the holdings of other foreign investors were similar to the portfolios of the average of Britain and German investors.

39. Lewis, *America's Stake*, p. 7.

40. Jenks, *The Migration of British Capital*, pp. 65–66.

41. Wilkins, *Foreign Investment*, pp. 53–54.

42. Lewis, *America's Stake*, p. 17. The bonds were issued between 1817 and 1825.

43. Wilkins, *Foreign Investment*, p. 70.
44. Jenks, *The Migration of British Capital*, p. 413. C. K. Hobson, *The Export of Capital*, (New York: Macmillan Co., 1914), p. 128.
45. Wilkins, *Foreign Investment*, p. 89. In terms of the early Dutch commitment, Veenendaal reports that "new federal and state loans for internal improvements were floated in the 1830s. In this way, Dutch money indirectly helped to establish a few early railroads, like the Baltimore and Susquehanna. The Erie and Morris Canal companies also raised loans in Amsterdam . . .". Augustus J. Veenendaal Jr., "The Kansas City Southern Railway and the Dutch Connection", *Business History Review*, **61** (Summer 1987), p. 292 (hereafter cited as Veenendaal, "The Kansas City Southern Railway").
46. Wilkins, *Foreign Investment*, pp. 109 and 120.
47. Lewis, *America's Stake*, p. 45. The quotations are from the *American Railroad Journal*, (1853), p. 370 and the *Commercial and Financial Chronicle*, (July 16, 1870), p. 77. The history of one of the Dutch debacles (their investment in the Kansas City, Pittsburgh, and Gulf railroad) is reported in detail in Venendaal, "The Kansas City Southern Railway".
48. Lewis, *America's Stake*, pp. 49, 93, and 96–97.
49. Herbert Feis, *Europe the World's Banker, 1870–1914: An Account of European Foreign Investment and the Connection of World Finance with Diplomacy before 1914*, (New Haven, Conn.: Yale University Press, 1930), p. 76 (hereafter cited as Feis, *Europe the World's Banker*).
50. Richard Tilly, "International Aspects of the Development of German Banking, 1870–1914" MSS, and "Some Comments on German Foreign Portfolio Investment, 1870–1914", paper delived in Sao Paolo, July 1989. His data from Feis (Feis, *Europe the World's Banker*), suggest that North America received about 29 percent of German foreign portfolio investment in the years 1897 to 1906 and about 12 percent between 1907 and 1914. "International Aspects" Table 3, p. 16.
51. Lewis, *America's Stake*, p 45.
52. John H. Dunning, *Studies in International Investment*, (London: George Allen and Unwin, 1970) (hereafter cited as Dunning, *International Investment*).
53. The British alone appear to have held $3 million of Second Bank Stock in 1820. Jenks, *The Migration of British Capital*, p. 66. Wilkins, *Foreign Investment*, pp. 61–62.
54. John H. Dunning, "British Investment in US Industry", in *Moorgate and Wall Street* **3**, (Autumn, 1961), pp. 5–23.
55. Jenks, *The Migration of British Capital*, pp. 68–69.
56. Lewis, citing C. S. Callender, puts the figure at £17.5 million and Jenks, citing the *Morning Chronicle* (London) places the figure at £20.5 million. Lewis, *America's Stake*, p. 13. Jenks, *The Migration of British Capital*, p. 87. Platt, *Foreign Finance*, Appendix IV, p. 195. The quotation and the estimate for the three "Ws" is from Platt p. 144. On the function of the short-term market, Platt has drawn on Madden, *British Investment*, pp. 150–156. For later years Platt's figures suggest levels of about $150 million from 1853 to 1870 with the total reaching perhaps $200 million between 1871 and 1876. Appendix IV, p. 195.

In the 1820s, for example, James Finley & Company had branches in New York, Charleston and New Orleans, and in 1828 a Baring partner reported no fewer than thirty five European agents in New York alone. The Rothschilds had agents in Philadelphia and New York, and by the mid 1830s the Paris firm of F. de Lizardi and Co. had an office in New Orleans. Wilkins, *Foreign Investment*, pp. 59–60.

57. The other four were the Philadelphia and Reading, the Wilmington and Raleigh, the Harrisburg and Lincoln, and the Richmond Railway.

58. The discussion of private investments in the 1830s is drawn from Lewis, *America's Stake*, pp. 20–22. Wilkins, *Foreign Investment*, pp. 61–66.

59. It is estimated that in 1876, for example, 65 percent of all European held American railroad securities were in default. *Banker's Magazine*, **30** (May 1876), p. 846. Michael Edelstein, *Overseas Investment in the Age of High Imperialism: The United Kingdom, 1850–1914*, (New York: Columbia University Press, 1982), pp. 93–101 (hereafter cited as Edelstein, *Overseas Investment*).

60. Frederick A. Cleveland and Fred Wilbur Powell, *Railroad Promotion and Capitalization in the United States*, (New York: B. Appleton, 1909), pp. 37–38; cited in Lewis, *America's Stake*, p. 30.

61. Wilkins, *Foreign Investment*, pp. 94–97. C. Lewis, *America's Stake*, p. 39. Salomon F. Van Oss, *America's Railroads as Investments*, (New York: Arno Press, 1977), p. 315 (hereafter cited as Van Oss, *America's Railroads*). Ingham lived and grew grapes in Sicily. The McCalmont Brothers first chose a Mr Cullen, but they then decided that he speculated too much on his own account and replaced him with C. E. Smith.

62. The Illinois Central was the first American railroad listed in Amsterdam, but it was quickly followed by the Galveston, Houston and Henderson. In London the seven included the Erie, the Illinois Central, the Michigan Southern & Northern Indiana, the Michigan Central, the New York Central, the Pennsy, and the Reading. Wilkins, *Foreign Investment*, pp. 97–98. Veenendaal, "The Kansas City Southern Railway", p. 293.

63. Wilkins, *Foreign Investment*, p. 105. Lewis, *America's Stake*, p. 105. Paul W. Gates, *The Illinois Central and Its Colonization Work*, (Cambridge, Mass.: Harvard University Press, 1934), p. 76.

64. Wilkins, *Foreign Investment*, p. 114.

65. Jenks, *The Migration of British Capital*, p. 426. Wilkins, *Foreign Investment*, Table 4.8, p. 116. Wilkins however, mistakenly reports the 70 percent figure as "Securities of US railway issued in London, 1866–1874 . . . As [a] percentage of railroad securities issued in London" instead of as the fraction of all foreign and colonial (non Indian) rail securities issued in London. The aggregate estimate is from *Banker's Magazine*, **30** (May 1876), p. 848.

66. Wilkins, *Foreign Investment*, pp. 199–200.

67. William Z. Ripley, *Railroads: Finance and Organization*, (New York: Longman Green, 1915), p. 5.

68. Cited in W. Turrentine Jackson, *The Enterprising Scot: Investors in the American West after 1873*, Edinburgh University Publications: History, Philosophy, Economics, No. 22, (Edinburgh: Edinburgh University Press, 1968), p. 71 (hereafter cited as Jackson, *The Enterprising Scot*).

Mira Wilkins makes the more reasonable point that "it is doubtful that without the foreign capital [mainly British, German, Dutch, French, and Canadian], the US railroad network could have been completed as swiftly or as effectively". Wilkins, *Foreign Investment*, p. 226.

69. Lewis, *America's Stake*, pp. 38–39.
70. Lewis, *America's Stake*, p. 40.
71. Dorothy Adler, *British Investment in American Railways, 1834–1898*, (Charlottesvillet Va.: University of Virginia Press, 1970), pp. 166–168 (hereafter cited as Adler, *British Investment*). George Paish, "Great Britain's Capital Investments in Individual, Colonial and Foreign Countries", *Journal of the Royal Statistical Society*, **74**: Part II (January, 1911), pp. 167–201 (hereafter cited as Paish, "Great Britain's Capital Investments") and "The Export of Capital and the Cost of Living", *Statist. Supplement*, **79** (1914), pp. i–viii. E. Victor Moran and W. A. Thomas, *The Stock Exchange: Its History and Functions*, (London: Etek Books, 1962), pp. 280–281.
72. The list of railroads is taken from the series, "Capital Called on the London Stock Exchange". See Lance E. Davis and Robert Huttenback, *Mammon and the Pursuit of Empire: The Political Economy of British Imperialism 1860–1912*, (Cambridge: Cambridge University Press, 1986), Chapter II (hereafter cited as Davis and Huttenback, *Mammon*). Today, it would be normal to estimate flotations. In nineteenth century Britain, initial flotations frequently did not require that the purchaser pay the full price "up front". Instead, he was often only asked to make an initial payment and agree to make further payments (up to the amount of the face value of the security) when called upon in the future. Thus a "Capital Call" might represent the entire flotation or only some fraction of that total figure. In fact, there are many instances when the purchaser was never asked for the full amount. One caveat: since the penalty for refusing to pay a call was limited to forfeiture of the security, there is no guarantee that all calls were paid. Examination of the records of the stock exchange indicate that such potential distortions were, in fact, small.
73. George Paish, "Great Britain's Capital Investments", p. 174 and "Our New Investments in 1908", *Statist.*, **63** (Jan. 2, 1909), p. 19–21 (hereafter cited as Paish, "Our New Investments"). The 1909 figure is estimated by multiplying the fraction of US rails in all foreign rails for the year 1910 by the total foreign rail placements in 1909.
74. In addition to the Pennsylvania, the Great Northern ($40.8 million), the Northern Pacific ($34.6), the Union Pacific ($36.1), and the Atchison, Topeka, and the Santa Fe ($32.2) all appear to have had more than $30 million of British held equity. *Report of the American Dollar Securities Committee*, cited in Lewis, *America's Stake*, p. 41.
75. Lewis, *America's Stake*, pp. 45–49.
76. Robert E. Riegel, *The Story of the Western Railroads*, (Lincoln, Nebr.: University of Nebraska Press, 1926), p. 139.
77. The Panic of 1873, for example, triggered the suspension of 36 railroad issues listed on the Amsterdam exchange. The Dutch investors held $129 million of those issues. One railroad, the Denver Pacific Railway and Telegraph Company passed completely into the hands of Dutch bondholders. Veenendaal,

"The Kansas City Southern Railway" pp. 245–296. In the case of McHenry, his Atlantic and Great Western railroad, already in default in 1867, is said "during the years 1869–80" to have broken "the record for defaults and reorganizations". Van Oss, *American Railroads*, p. 412.

78. Lewis, *America's Stake*, pp. 41–44.
79. Wilkins, *Foreign Investment*, fn. 58, p. 730. The report puts Dutch holdings of the Kansas City Southern at $17.7 million and of the Kansas and Pacific at $13 million. Lewis, *America's Stake*, pp. 44–45.
80. Just a year before, Fremont had been a candidate for the American presidency. Lewis, *America's Stake*, pp. 49–59.
81. It has been suggested that the French may well have purchased some securities through other financial centers – London or Geneva, to cite two.
82. Lewis, *America's Stake*, pp. 50–51. Wilkins, *Foreign Investment*, p. 196.
83. The eleven included nine from the South (Alabama, Arkansas, Florida, Georgia, Louisiana, North Carolina, South Carolina, Tennessee, and Virginia), Minnesota, and West Virginia (the latter for debt incurred before it was separated from Virginia). The Minnesota debt had been in default since 1859.
84. For example, the bonds issued by North Carolina in 1868 sold in Europe at prices ranging from 10 to 30 cents on the dollar.
85. Lewis, *America's Stake*, pp. 57–63. For a more complete discussion of post-Civil War state debt see McGrane, *Foreign Bondholders*, pp. 239–263.
86. Lewis, *America's Stake*, pp. 53–56. Jenks, *The Migration of British Capital*, p. 280. Platt, citing Madden, argues that the estimate of foreign, particularly British, holdings of US bonds in the 1860s and 1870s are overly inflated. He disputes Cottrell's conclusion that the British investor had a preference for American government issues and he disputes Cairncross' 1870 estimate of £160 million in British held US bonds. He prefers Madden's £33 million estimate. Platt *Foreign Finance*, p. 153.
87. Lewis, *America's Stake*, pp. 66–67. The British portion was oversubscribed ten times. For a more detailed discussion see Frederick Lewis Allen, *The Great Pierpont Morgan*, (New York: Harper and Brothers, 1949), pp. 99–125.
88. Lewis, *America's Stake*, pp. 63–66.
89. Economists often distinguish between direct and portfolio investment. A British investment trust's purchase of the bonds of the Pennsylvania Railroad is unambiguously portfolio investment, and J. & P. Coats' (the Scottish thread maker) decision to open a manufacturing facility in Pawtucket, Rhode Island is equally clearly an example of direct investment. Between these extremes, however, the distinction becomes blurred, and it is often not clear what is gained by making it. If, for example, the focus is on either the quantity or spatial distribution of foreign investments or on the institutional structure that linked foreign investors to American enterprise, it makes no difference if an American company sold its securities in a foreign country or if the American firm was opened or purchased by a group of foreign promoter–investors who then marketed the new or reconstructed enterprise's stocks and bonds in their country. Since these questions are the foci of this study, no attempt is made to distinguish between portfolio and direct investment. Mira Wilkins, for

example, argues that the most common form of British investment in many industries was the "free-standing" company – a hybrid mix of direct and portfolio investment. "Typically, they were included in studies of British portfolio investment, because usually their formation involved capital markets. Yet they were direct investments, since they were designed to conduct business operations abroad, to manage and to direct the specific business". See Mira Wilkins, "The Free-Standing Company, 1870–1914: An Important Type of British Foreign Direct Investment", *Economic History Review*, 2nd Series, **4**: 2 (1988), pp. 259–282.

90. The latter group received 3.5 million acres in New York. The remainder of the land was in northern and western Pennsylvania. The promoters organized the Holland Land Company, a firm that remained moderately profitable until it was dissolved in 1836. See A. M. Sakolski, *The Great American Land Bubble*, (New York: Harper & Bros, 1932), pp. 31–86; Shaw Livermore, *Early American Land Companies*, (New York: The Commonwealth Fund, 1939), pp. 162 and 203; and Paul D. Evans, *The Holland Land Company*, (Buffalo, N.Y.: Buffalo Historical Society, 1924), *passim*.

91. The original company itself went bankrupt in 1875, but in 1879 the Secretary of the Interior issued the company a patent for 1,714,764 acres, and the reorganized Maxwell Land Grant Company (a Dutch corporation) opened for business. Although it had a turbulent history, the Dutch retained their New Mexican lands until 1914. Wilkins, *Foreign Investment*, pp. 122–124 and 232–233.

92. Wilkins, *Foreign Investment*, p. 124.

93. It was not only in land, but also in banks, ranching, real estate and industry, and, to a lesser extent, in mining. Madden concludes that British investment in the first five industries was unimportant in the years 1860–1880, and total investment in mining was only £5.6 million. Platt, *Foreign Finance*, p. 165.

94. Lewis, *America's Stake*, p. 84. Wilkins, *Foreign Investment*, p. 234.

95. Lewis, *America's Stake*, p. 85. *Philadelphia Bulletin*, (December 6, 1909), p. 11 of the postscript edition.

96. A recent study of foreign investment in Nebraska indicates that in 1890 four Scottish, twelve English, and seven American firms had channeled at least $3,419,475 in foreign investment into Nebraska farm mortgages. That figure translates into about 3.8 percent of all farm loans in force in that state. Parallel studies suggest that the comparable figures were 3.7 percent in Minnesota, 9.6 percent in North Dakota, 14.5 percent in South Dakota, 1 percent in Iowa, and 2 percent in Kansas. Larry A. McFarlane, "British Investment and the Land: Nebraska 1877–1946", *Business History Review*, **57** (Summer 1983), pp. 258–292. The figures for Iowa, Kansas, Minnesota and the Dakotas are from Larry A. McFarlane, "British Investment in Minnesota Farm Mortgages and Land, 1875–1900", (unpublished mss); "British Agricultural Investment in the Dakotas, 1877–1953", *Business and Economic History*, 2nd series, **5** (1976), pp. 112–126 and "British Investment in Midwestern Farm Mortgages and Land, 1875–1900, A Comparison of Iowa and Kansas", *Agricultural History*, **48** (January 1974), pp. 179–198.

97. Wilkins, *Foreign Investment*, p. 300.

98. Lewis, *America's Stake*, p. 87. Wilkins, *Foreign Investment*, pp. 304–305. Wilkins actually lists 41 firms but one, the Cattle Ranch Company Ltd, was organized in 1889 to take over the assets of the Cattle Ranch and Land Company Ltd. The latter firm was organized in 1882.

99. The history of British investment in the American range is drawn from Jackson, *The Enterprising Scot*, pp. 73–100 and 114–138, and from Peter J. Buckley and Brian R. Roberts, *European Direct Investment in the USA before World War I*, (New York: St Martin's Press, 1982), pp. 59–63 (hereafter cited as Buckley and Roberts, *European Direct Investment*), and Lewis, *America's Stake*, pp. 87–88.

100. Jackson, *The Enterprising Scot*, p. 137.

101. Wilkins, *Foreign Investments*, p. 234. Buckley and Roberts, *European Direct Investment*, p. 60.

102. Lewis, *America's Stake*, pp. 86–87. Wilkins, *Foreign Investment*, pp. 502–512.

103. Clark C. Spence, "British Investment and the American Mining Frontier, 1860–1914", *New Mexico Historical Review*, **36** (April 1961) p. 121 (hereafter cited as Spence, "The Mining Frontier"). In his previous and better known *British Investments and the American Mining Frontier, 1860–1901*, (Ithaca, N.Y.: Cornell University Press, 1958), pp. 241–260 (hereafter cited as Spence, *British Investments*) he lists only 518. Spence's data exclude firms operating in the Pacific coast states, the Southeast, and Alaska.

104. Edward Ashmead, *Twenty-five Years of Mining, 1880–1904*, (London: Mining Journal, 1909), pp. 81–90.

105. Wilkins, *Foreign Investment*, p. 241.

106. Spence, *British Investments*, p. 127. Lewis, *America's Stake*, p. 89.

107. Wilkins, *Foreign Investment*, p. 239.

108. The Firm was the Société Anonyme des Mines de Lexington. Wilkins, *Foreign Investment*, pp. 242–246.

109. Spence, "The Mining Frontier", p. 84.

110. "The Most Risky of All Investments", *The Economist*, **39** (18 July 1881), p. 756. The reference is not only to the American, but world-wide British mining investments, but the bulk of the investment was in American mines.

111. Jackson, *The Enterprising Scot*, p. 142. The quotation is from "The Speculation in Mining Shares" **46** , *The Economist*, (28 January 1888), pp. 105–106.

112. Lewis, *America's Stake*, pp. 93–94. Wilkins, *Foreign Investment*, pp. 264–283. For a comprehensive examination of the structure of the international copper industry see Christopher Schmidtz, "The Rise of Big Business in the World Copper Industry 1870–1930", *Economic History Review*, 2nd series, **39**: 3 (1986), pp. 302–410 (hereafter cited as Schmidtz, "The World Copper Industry").

113. Buckley and Roberts, *European Direct Investment*, p. 91. Lewis, *America's Stake*, p. 91.

114. Lewis, *America's Stake*, p. 91.

115. Lewis, *America's Stake*, pp. 94–98. Wilkins, *Foreign Investment*, pp. 285–292.

116. Lewis, *America's Stake*, pp. 94–98. Wilkins, *Foreign Investment*, pp. 285–292. The quotation is from Wilkins, p. 292.

117. Wilkins, *Foreign Investment*, p. 325. Lewis, *America's Stake*, p. 89.

118. Wilkins, *Foreign Investment*, p. 325. Lewis, *America's Stake*, p. 99.
119. Lewis, *America's Stake*, p. 100.
120. Paish, "Great Britain's Capital Investments", p. 176. Wilkins calls Paish's estimate "obviously preposterous". Wilkins, *Foreign Investment*, p. 767.
121. Wilkins, *Foreign Investment*, pp. 247, 252, and 263. Lewis, *America's Stake*, p. 101.
122. Wilkins, *Foreign Investment*, pp. 361–368. Lewis, *America's Stake*, pp. 100–101.
123. Of that total, the previous American owners received almost eighty percent. Lewis, *America's Stake*, p. 101. Wilkins, *Foreign Investment*, p. 320.
124. Charles B. Kuhlman, *Development of the Flour Mill Industry in the United States*, (Boston: Houghton Mifflin, 1929), p. 134.
125. Wilkins, *Foreign Investment*, pp. 319–320, 323. Neither milling nor the grain elevators proved a success. Pillsbury–Washburn went into receivership in 1908; the City of Chicago Grain Elevator Company shed its British connection in 1894; and the Chicago and Northwestern Granaries Company went into liquidation in 1910.
126. Lewis, *America's Stake*, pp. 101–102, Wilkins, *Foreign Investment*, p. 340, 352–356, 369, 374, 375, 390 and 434–438. Lewis assigns Siemens & Halske a role in the surgical instrument business, Wilkins is dubious.
127. The data are drawn from *The Investor's Monthly Manual*, a supplement to the *Economist*. This periodical began publication in February 1865, and it regularly carried lists of new publicly floated issues. Included in those lists was not only the name of the issuer; but also the amount of capital that had been "created" or "called". The term capital creation was used to denote a new capital issue that was subscribed to at the "market price" at the time of the issue. Unlike current practice, in the 19th century issues were sometimes sold "on time". That is, a £1000 equity or bond might be sold to an investor on the initial payment of £100 and his agreement to pay for the remainder as the issuing firm demanded. At times there was an agreed schedule of payments; at times the requests were periodic demands at unscheduled intervals. Moreover, in a significant number of cases, the total amount was never demanded. The term "call" was used to describe the announcements of the "periodic installments that were to be paid by the subscribers to the new issue". For purposes of simplicity, in this work, the term "capital called" is used to describe both capital created and capital called. Harvey H. Segal and Matthew Simon, "British Foreign Capital Issues, 1865–1914", *The Journal of Economic History*, **21**: 4 (December 1961) (hereafter cited as Segal and Simon, "British Foreign Capital Issues").

    The reader should bear in mind that the series represents an enumeration of new issues, and it does not include American securities that British investors may have purchased or that may have been traded on the London Exchange and, thus, been available for British investment, unless they were initially floated in London.
128. One word of caution. While it is sometimes possible to unambiguously classify a firm into the appropriate industry – a railroad is usually (but not always) a railroad – there are sometimes questions. In particular, it is sometimes

difficult to distinguish between an agricultural firm that owns several ranches (Agriculture & Extractive Sector), a Financial Land and Development Company (also Agriculture & Extractive Sector) that owns a portfolio of ranches, and a Trust (Finance Sector) that owns a portfolio of ranching securities. When there was any doubt the classification adopted by the *Stock Exchange Annual Year Book* has been employed. Secondly, as Segal and Simon noted more than three decades ago, "one can never be sure that a foreign capital issue floated in the British market actually resulted in a foreign capital transfer". Segal and Simon, "British Foreign Capital Issues". Since many of the foreign issues were made by British owned firms, the issuing firm very likely carried on at least a small fraction of its business in the United Kingdom; and it might even have had a portion of its business located in yet a third country. There is no way of directly estimating the fraction of funds "called" that remained in Britain or that were directed to the third country, but a sampling of firms for which other records exist, suggest that the proportion was, in most cases, not large. In a few cases, it was, however, very significant. For example, Mira Wilkins has called attention to the fact that only a small part of the $21.4 million of new issues that the British–American Tabacco Company floated between 1910 and 1914 were ever actually invested in their American operations. Mira Wilkins, Private Communication, October 4, 1993.

129. Dunning, *International Investment*, pp. 178–181.
130. Davis and Huttenback, *Mammon*, pp. 30–72.
131. Dunning, *International Investment*, Table 2, p. 151. The total UK capital abroad figures are from Imlah, the estimates of UK capital abroad are from Jenks (1854), Cairncross (1870 and 1885), Bacon (1899), and Paish (1908 and 1913). See A. H. Imlah, *Economic Elements of the Pax Britannica*, (Cambridge: Harvard University Press, 1958); Jenks, *The Migration of British Capital*; Alexander Cairncross, *Home and Foreign Investment 1870–1910*, (Cambridge: Cambridge University Press, 1953); Nathaniel T. Bacon, "America's International Indebtedness"; *Yale Review*, 9, Nov. 1900, pp. 265–285 Paish, "Great Britain's Capital Investments".
132. Lewis, *America's Stake*, p. 442.
133. It would, of course, be very useful to examine the industrial and spatial composition of the net series, since that would make it possible to pinpoint industries and regions from which finance was withdrawn as well as those that were the new recipients; but any such analysis would involve disaggregating the series into its export and repatriation components, and, given the existing data, that goal cannot be attained.
134. Measuring British foreign portfolio investment has long been a subject rife with controversy. For example, D. C. M. Platt took exception to estimates from George Paish on the grounds that Paish did not sufficiently account for foreign holdings of securities traded on the London market. Platt offered similar criticisms of estimates derived by Leland Jenks, and he criticized estimates derived by J. Fred Rippy on the grounds that the use of nominal values of loans was improper because often the face value of loans had little relation to the capital actually invested. In general, Platt called for downward revision of all estimates. Charles Feinstein has countered Platt's arguments.

In particular he has offered evidence in support of Paish's conclusions. Fortunately, this chapter is far more concerned with the industrial and spatial distribution of the flows to the US than with their magnitudes, so the question is largely irrelevant. D. C. M. Platt, "British Portfolio Investment Overseas Before 1870: Some Doubts", *The Economic History Review*, 2nd Series, **33**: 1 (February, 1980), pp. 7, 11, 12, 15; Jenks, *The Migration of British Capital*; George Paish, "Great Britain's Capital Investment in Other Lands", *Journal of the Royal Statistical Society*, 72 (1909) (hereafter cited as Paish, "Great Britain's Capital Investment in Other Lands"); J. Fred Rippy, *British Investments in Latin America 1822–1949: A Case Study of the Operations of Private Enterprise in Retarded Regions*, (Minneapolis: University of Minnesota Press 1959). Charles Feinstein, "Britain's Overseas Investments in 1913", *Economic History Review*, 2nd Series, **43**: 2 (May 1990), pp. 288–295.

With regard to the foreign ownership of securities listed on the London exchange, Davis and Huttenback constructed a sample of shareholders of foreign firms traded on the London market between 1883 and 1907 and calculated that only 17 percent of the shareholders were foreign (that is, non-UK residents), while 83 percent were residents of the United Kingdom. Although not all of these firms were American, the assumption that the "Capital Called" series represents flows from British investors appears plausible. Davis and Huttenback, *Mammon*, pp. 195 and 209.

135. A more detailed year-by-year industrial breakdown of those same American flotations and calls appears in Robert Cull and Lance E. Davis, "Un, Deux, Trois, Quatre Marchés? L'Intégration Du Marché Du Etats-Unis et Grande-Bretagne, 1865–1913", in *Annales: Économies Sociétés Civilisations*, No. 3, (May–June 1992), pp. 633–674.

136. Alfred D. Chandler, *The Railroads: The Nation's First Big Business*, (New York: Harcourt, Brace & World, 1965).

137. *Historical Statistics*, Vol. **2**, p. 732. The figures indicate peaks of 7,439 miles in 1872, 5,006 miles in 1879, 6,026 miles in 1902, and 5,523 miles in 1906.

138. Kent T. Healy, "Development of a National Transportation System", in Harold F. Williamson (ed.), *The Growth of the American Economy*, (New York; Prentice-Hall, 1951).

139. For a more detailed description of the United States Rolling Stock Company, see Wilkins, *Foreign Investments*, p. 837.

140. For an excellent discussion of the evolution of the market for industrial securities, see T. Navin and M. Sears, "The Rise of a Market for Industrial Securities", *Business History Review*, **29**: 2 (1955), pp. 105–138.

Navin and Sears report that between 1890 and 1893 thirteen firms formed by the organization of trusts or mergers and eight firms interested in re-capitalization issued investment grade preferred stocks, and of these about one-half *ultimately* found their way onto the New York Stock Exchange. The trusts included the American Cotton Oil Company, the American Sugar Refining Company, and the National Lead Company. The newly merged firms included the American Tobacco Company, the American Soda Fountain Company, the American Type Founders' Company, the General Electric Company, the Hecker–Jones Jewell Company, the Herring–Hall–Marvin Company, the

Michigan Peninsular Car Company, the National Cordage Company, the National Starch Manufacturing Company, the Trenton Potteries Company, the US Leather Company, and the US Rubber Company. The re-capitalizations included the Barney and Smith Car Company, the H.B. Claflin Company, the Henry R. Worthington Company, the P. Lorillard Company, the Proctor and Gamble Company, the R. I. Perkins Horse-Shoe Company, the Thurber, Whyland Company, and the Westinghouse Electric and Manufacturing Company, p. 118.

141. Often, US Agricultural and Extractive firms were listed on smaller, more regionally-oriented American exchanges rather than on the NYSE. For example, the December 31, 1910 listings of the Boston Stock Market include 57 mining operations but only fifteen railroads. Among those mines are the Adventure, the Hancock, the Old Dominion, the Wolverine, and the Wyandotte. The Consolidated Exchange, located in New York, had a special mining stocks section in their December 31, 1910 listings. That list included the El Paso, the Elkron, the Tramps, the Tonopah, and the Yellow Jacket. Although not as extensive as the listings on either the Boston or the Consolidated, mining stocks listed on the Philadelphia Exchange included the Amalgamated Mining Company and Tonopah Mining.

142. The fact that American insurance companies or British insurance companies that we could identify as having predominantly American business floated few new issues does not imply that American investments by British (or other foreign) companies that did American business (particularly fire and marine and casualty companies) were trivial. Mira Wilkins has shown that, in 1913, there were eight–nine foreign fire and marine insurance companies operating in the United States with "admitted American assets" of $184 million. Of those companies, forty-two with $116 million in "assets" were British. Wilkins, *Foreign Investment*, pp. 528–531.

Chapter 3

143. Wilkins, *Foreign Investment*, Chapter 16, "The Reactions to Foreign Investment in the United States".

144. The year was 1907. Cited in Wilkins, *Foreign Investment*, p. 557. Wilkins also cites W. W. Miller, of Hornblower, Miller & Potter, investment bankers, in a 1912 address to the Investment Bankers' Association of America: "We might as well face the situation. We cannot supply all the required capital in the United States. We must look to European countries for assistance, and while this demand for capital continues, we should be most careful not to frighten that capital from our shores", p. 567.

145. Edward P. Crapol, *America for Americans: Economic Nationalism and Anglophobia in the Late Nineteenth Century*, Contributions to American History, No. 8, (Westport, Conn.: Greenwood Press, 1973), pp. 219–220. Hereafter cited as Crapol, *America for Americans*. The quotation is from a speech of James S. Hogg, Governor of Texas, on July 2, 1894. Hogg went on to say, "Why is it that the seat of commerce and finance now in control and dominating the United States and the whole world is located in the little island of England".

146. In 1885 the New Hampshire legislature passed a joint resolution asserting that "American soil is for Americans, and should be owned and controlled by American citizens", and, on January 25th of that year, the editors of the *New York Times* wrote, "an evil of considerable magnitude – the acquisition of vast tracts of land in the Territories by English noblemen . . . the evil demands the attention of Congress . . . We believe that the building up of great estates by Englishmen should be prevented". Wilkins, *Foreign Investment*, p. 569.

147. The fencing controversy resulted in Congress passing a bill that made such fences illegal and authorized the President to remove such obstructions from the public domain by military force. The next year, 1885, the President ordered the removal of fences on public land. *Statutes at Large of the United States*, XXIII (1884), 321–322 and XXIV (1985), 1024–1025.

148. Wilkins, *Foreign Investment*, p. 566.

149. *Statutes at Large of the United States*, XXIV (1887), 476–477. Roger V. Clements, "British Investment and American Legislative Restrictions in the Trans-Mississippi West, 1880–1900", *Mississippi Valley Historical Review*, **42**, (1955), pp. 216–217. (Hereafter cited as Clements, "Legislative Restrictions".) The campaign against British land investment was conducted in the press, in Congress, in state legislatures, and by labor and agrarian groups, p. 212. Since, however, the West still needed capital, the 1887 Act was amended to reassert the right of alien mortgage holders to enforce their contracts by taking possession of the hypothecated real property for a maximum period of ten years. *Statutes at Large of the United States*, XXIX (1897), 618–19.

150. Clements, "Legislative Restrictions" and Crapol, *America for Americans*, p. 117.

151. Clements, "Legislative Restrictions", p. 216.

152. June 3, 1887. Cited in Wilkins, *Foreign Investment*, p. 528.

153. Wilkins, *Foreign Investment*, p. 558. The quotation is from US Senate, *Mining Interests of Aliens*, 50th Congress, 2nd session, 1889. S. Rept. 2690, 2.

154. For a thorough discussion of the position of the mining states and territories see Clements, "Legislative Restrictions". The quotations are from pp. 223 & 226.

155. Roger V. Clements, "The Farmers' Attitude Toward British Investment in American Industry", *The Journal of Economic History*, **15**: 2, 1955, pp. 151–159. Hereafter cited as Clements, "The Farmers' Attitude". The quotation is from the *Girard Herald*, January 26 and June 22, 1889.

156. Crapol, *America for Americans*, p. 109–110. Clement, "The Farmers' Attitude", p. 155.

157. *Northwestern Miller*, **28** (Nov. 8, 1889), p. 578. Cited in Wilkins, *Foreign Investment*, pp. 558–559.

158. Wilkins, *Foreign Investment*, p. 560. Wilkins cites only four examples of state policies designed to further foreign investment, and only two involved specific foreign firms.

159. The first cases involved the British-owned Imperial Tobacco Company and the British–American Tobacco Company and the second the British-owned American Thread and the Coats enterprises. See Wilkins, *Foreign Investment*, pp. 565–566.

160. Wilkins, *Foreign Investment*, pp. 562–563. The quote is from *Banker's Magazine*, New York, Vol. **35** (January 1880), pp. 520–521.

161. Wilkins, *Foreign Investment*, pp. 564–566. The quote is from the *Economist*, **47** (July 27, 1889), p. 965. Cited in Wilkins, *Foreign Investment*, p. 564.

162. Roger V. Clements, "British Controlled Enterprise in the West Between 1870 and 1890, and Some Agrarian Reactions", *Agricultural History*, **27**: 4 (october 1953), p. 133. Hereafter cited as Clements, "British Controlled Enterprise".

163. *The Economist*, **28** (December 3, 1870), p. 1452. Cited in Clements, "British Controlled Enterprise".

164. Clements, "British Controlled Enterprise", p 135.

165. Carl H. Solberg, *The Prairies and the Pampas: Agrarian Policy in Canada and Argentina, 1880–1930*, (Stanford, Ca.: Stanford University Press, 1987), p. 38.

166. Jenks, *The Migration of British Capital*, p 103. McGrane, *Foreign Bondholders*, pp. 265–266.

167. Jenks, *The Migration of British Capital*, p. 106. The editorial is from *The Times*, London, May 5, 1842. The Rothschild quote is from a letter from Duff Green to John C. Calhoun, Jan. 24, 1842, in *The Correspondence of John C. Calhoun*, (Washington, D.C.: 1900), pp. 841–842.

168. *The Times*, London, May 19, 1847 – cited in McGrane, *Foreign Bondholders*, p. 266 – and May 5, 1842. *Times*, October, 31, 1844. Cited in Jenks, *The Migration of British Capital*, p. 104.

169. McGrane, *Foreign Bondholders*, p. 266.

170. McGrane, *Foreign Bondholders*, pp. 270–271.

171. When, in 1851, the state of Georgia sought a railroad loan, the Barings suggested that "the state be directly liable for the bonds and in the case of default in the payment of interest or principle the bondholders should then have a lien on the railroad and its receipts". The Barings employed the services of Captain William H. Swift of the US Army Engineering Corps as their expert on potential railroad offerings. McGrane, *Foreign Bondholders*, pp. 271–275.

172. The Secretary of the Treasury placed the total at $202 million. McGrane, *Foreign Bondholders*, pp. 277–278.

173. Quoted in *American Bankers Magazine*, **14**, p. 435. Cited in McGrane, *Foreign Bondholders*, p. 280.

174. The largely American held railroad bond issue of the state of Minnesota had been in default since the pre-War era, and West Virginia was in default on debts that went back to the time that the state was part of Virginia.

175. McGrane, *Foreign Bondholders*, pp. 284–381.

176. Lewis, *America's Stake*, p. 60–61.

177. Lewis, *America's Stake*, p. 62. McGrane, *Foreign Bondholders*, pp. 384–385.

178. In 1900, *Poor's* estimated that of the $3.1 billion par value in railroad common stock outstanding, $1.25 billion represented only "water". Most of the investment in the construction of a railroad is essentially long term – once contracts were signed building went on, and costs continued to be incurred, independently of the state of the economy. Passenger and freight receipts were, however, closely related to the general level of economic activity.

179. Kent T. Healy, "Transportation", in Harold Williamson (ed.), *The Growth of the American Economy*, (New York: Prentice Hall, 1951), p. 377.
180. Adler, *British Investment*, p. 170.
181. The remainder of this section is based on the work of Dorothy Adler, *British Investment*, Chapter VIII, "Protection of British Investment", pp. 170–189.
182. In one extreme case, McCalmont Bros owned majority control of the Philadelphia and Reading.
183. In the case of the late 80s reorganization of the AT & SF, the bondholders complained bitterly that the restructure favored the stockholders since the "houses" in question held large blocks of equities.
184. The institution, however, dates back to the organization of a Spanish Bondholders Committee in 1827.
185. In the case of the Rio Grande, the preferred shareholders were given the right to select two-thirds of the Board.

Chapter 4

186. The listing of American firms on the London exchange is taken from the end of the year report of the *Investor's Monthly Manual*; the New York issues are those reported in the *New York Times* during the last week in December of each year. The stock, rather than bond issues, were chosen because it was felt that, in the case of New York, the enumeration of stocks traded was more complete than the corresponding enumeration of bond issues.
187. The other two firms were the Mariposa Company and the Canton Company of Baltimore.
188. In 1889 British entrepreneurs purchased the whole of the capital stock and bonds of an American corporation and organized the firm of Fraser and Chalmers (manufacturers of mining machinery). The new firm built a manufacturing works in Britain, but it continued to operate the American properties as a subsidiary company. In 1901, that subsidiary was merged with the Edward P. Allis Company and two other smaller companies to form Allis-Chalmers, Wilkins, *Foreign Investment*, pp. 429–430.

    In 1898, a British incorporated company, Eastman Kodak Company Ltd, "acquired its American namesake, which was by the time the world's leading camera and film producer". The new company was "designed to raise capital in London for the business (and to provide advertising for its products)" and it "had a very short life under British registration". Wilkins, *Foreign Investment*, p. 449.
189. Edelstein, *Overseas Investment*, pp. 233–237. Using Edelstein's data from Table 10.2, a simple regression with the ratio NFI/GNP as the dependent variable and Time and the ratio of GDCF/GNP as the independent variables over all eleven quinquennial shows a strong and significant positive relationship between GDCF/GNP and NFI/GNP.

$$\text{NFI/GNP} = -3.075 - 0.632\,(\text{Time}) + 0.416(\text{GDCF/GNP})$$
$$(-7.62) \quad (-4.72) \qquad\qquad (4.64)$$
$$R^2 = .736$$

190. M. M. Postan, "Some Recent Problems in the Accumulation of Capital", *Economic History Review*, **9**: 1 (October 1935), pp. 1–12. See also Postan, an unpublished series of lectures given at the Johns Hopkins University, 1954–55.

191. Robert B. Zevin, "Are World Financial Markets More Open? If So Why and With What Effects?", in *Financial Openness and National Autonomy*, (New York: 1989).

192. Larry Neal, "The Disintegration and Reintegration of International Capital Markets in the 19th Century", MSS. February 29, 1992. Craig and Fisher, however, have recently suggested that the American market may have been less well integrated than the British, French and German. Lee A. Craig and Douglas Fisher, "Integration of the European Business Cycle: 1871–1910", *Explorations in Economic History*, **29**: 2, (April 1992), pp. 144–168.

193. Somewhat later Alexander Gershenkron made a similar case for Germany and Russia. See his *Economic Backwardness in Historical Perspective*, (Cambridge, Mass.: Harvard University Press, 1962).

194. Lance E. Davis, "Capital Immobilities and Finance Capitalism: A Study of Economic Evolution in the United States, 1820–1920", *Explorations in Entrepreneurial History*, 2nd. Series, **1**: 1 (Fall 1963), pp. 88–105 (hereafter cited as Davis, "Finance Capitalism"). Recently Kerry Odell has found similar evidence for gradual integration *within* the Pacific Coast States even before that region was integrated into the national capital market. Kerry A. Odell, "The Integration of Regional and Interregional Capital Markets: Evidence from the Pacific Coast, 1883–1913", *The Journal of Economic History*, **49**: 2 (June 1989), pp. 297–310.

195. Frank A. Vanderlip was Vice President of the National City Bank. He made the statement in a speech in 1905. He is quoted in G. Edwards, *The Evolution of Finance Capitalism*, (New York: 1908), p. 185 (hereafter cited as Edwards, *The Evolution of Finance Capitalism*).

There were, of course, a set of institutional developments that aided the process of interregional integration. Davis has argued for the role of life insurance companies and the expansion of the commercial paper market, Sylla has looked at changes in the national banking laws, and James at changes made by the states in the legal framework of banking. More recently, and perhaps more appropriately in the light of this paper, Clark and Turner have underscored the role played by the nation's real current account trade balance as an independent factor. Lance E. Davis, "The Investment Market, 1870–1914: The Evolution of a National Market", *The Journal of Economic History*, **25**: 3 (September, 1965), pp. 355–393. Richard Sylla, "Federal Policy, Banking Market Structure, and Capital Mobilization in the United States, 1863–1913", *The Journal of Economic History*, **29**: 4 (December 1969), pp. 657–686. John James, "The Development of the National Money Market, 1893–1911", *The Journal of Economic History*, **36**: 4 (December 1976), pp. 878–897. William Clark and Charlie Turner, "International Trade and the Evolution of the American Capital Market, 1888–1911", *The Journal of Economic History*, **45**: 2 (June, 1985), pp. 405–410.

196. Naomi Lamoreaux, "Banks, Kinship, and Economic Development: The New England Case", *The Journal of Economic History*, **46**: 3 (September 1986), pp. 647–667.

197. Kenneth A. Snowden, "Mortgage Rates and American Capital Market Development in the Late Nineteenth Century", *The Journal of Economic History*, **47**: 3 (September 1987), pp. 671–692.

Recently Hugh Rockoff and Howard Bodenhorn have shown that there was little difference between short term rates in the North and the Old South in the antebellum era. Despite the lack of correlation in the movements, there is evidence of an integrated market between those two sectors, and, given the dependence of southern cotton factors on northern financial markets that result is not surprising. They make a similar argument for the Midwest; however, their evidence is much less compelling, and they find no evidence for any significant integration between the Pacific Coast and any other region. Hugh Rockoff and Howard Bodenhorn, "Regional Interest Rates in Ante Bellum America", in Claudia Goldin and Hugh Rockoff (eds), *Strategic Factors in Nineteenth Century American Economic History, A Volume to Honor Robert W. Fogel*, (Chicago: University of Chicago Press, 1992), pp. 159–188.

198. See Davis, "Finance Capitalism", p. 588–590. G. Edwards, *The Evolution of Finance Capitalism*.

199. Bradford DeLong, "Did Morgan's Men Create Value?", in Peter Temin (ed.) *Inside the Business Enterprise: Historical Perspectives on the Use of Information*, (Chicago: University of Chicago Press, 1991), pp. 205–236.

200. For a more extensive development of this point see Lance Davis, "The Capital Markets and Industrial Concentration: The US and UK, A Comparative Study", *The Economic History Review*, 2nd Series, **19**: 2 (1966).

201. Ranald C. Michie, *The London and New York Stock Exchanges, 1850–1914* (London: Allen & Unwin, 1987), p. 250 (hereafter cited as Michie, *London and New York*).

202. See Michie, *London and New York*, pp. 250–253 on conflicts of interest. Generally, traders were eager to adopt any technological advance that could facilitate increased market activity. Owners resisted many innovations – for instance, ticker tape machines – fearing that their introduction made exchange price quotes readily available to outsiders thus creating a disincentive for non-members to pay fees to join the exchange.

203. See Lee Benham and Phillip Keefer, "Voting in Firms: The Roles of Agenda Control, Size and Voter Homogeneity", *Economic Inquiry*, **39** (October, 1991), on actions taken by collectives (hereafter cited as Benham and Keefer, "Voting in Firms").

204. NYSE: Governing Committee, April 13, 1894. Constitution of the New York Stock Exchange Board, February 21, 1820, Article 10.

205. Michie, *London and New York*, pp. 194–196. Peter Wyckoff, *Wall Street and the Stock Markets: A Chronology (1644–1971)*, 1st Edition, (Philadelphia: Chilton Book Co., 1982) pp. 150–151. Edmund C. Stedman, *The New York Stock Exchange: Its History, its Contribution to National Prosperity, and its Relation to American Finance at the Outset of the Twentieth Century*, (New York: Greenwood Press, 1969 (copyright 1905)), pp. 473–474.

206. See Benham and Keefer, "Voting in Firms", pp. 708–710 on restricting membership in collectives.
207. The term uncertainty is used in the "Knightian" sense. That is, there was a lack of knowledge about the distribution of expected returns.
208. David M. Kreps, *A Course in Microeconomic Theory*, Chapter 17, "Adverse Selection and Market Signaling", (Princeton, N.J.: Princeton University Press, 1990) p. 625–660. The term "quality" appears somewhat pejorative, but in this case it should be taken as a synonym for *either* unable or unwilling (i.e. could find alternative capital sources and, therefore, needed no signal).
209. Kreps defines market screening as a situation in which the party to a contract without information proposes a menu of contracts from which the informed party selects. In this context, the NYSE, as the representative of unsophisticated investors, was the party to the contract at an informational disadvantage because the firms attempting to list their securities were better informed about the distribution of potential returns. The institutional rules imposed costs on those firms. Those firms willing and able to absorb these costs separated themselves from other ventures.
   For a treatment of how promoters of one notorious mining venture, the Emma, used their informational advantage to manipulate investors see Spence, "The Mining Frontier", p. 84. Of course, this firm was listed on the London Stock Exchange; there, screening was far more lax than on the NYSE.
210. Michie, *London and New York*, p. 198.
211. Jonathan Barron Baskin, "The Development of Corporate Financial Markets in Britain and the United States, 1600–1914: Overcoming Asymmetric Information", *Business History Review*, **62**: 2 (Summer, 1988), p. 225.
212. Since most stocks and bonds listed on the NYSE traded near a par value of $100, the value of the smallest allowable transactions was about $10,000, a sum far too large for the typical investor of the day. Michie reports that, of the 131 million shares sold on the exchange in 1912, less than 19 percent were priced at under $50, while 43 percent were over $100. Michie, *London and New York*, p. 199. NYSE: Special Committee on Commissions, 1924. Governing Committee, May 11, 1886, April 13, 1887, November, 1902, May 27, 1903, March 16, 1910, March 30, 1910. Special Joint Committee on Copper Stocks, May 18, 1903.
213. Michie, *London and New York*, pp. 198–199. Sereno S. Pratt, *The Work of Wall Street*, (New York: D. Appleton and Company, 1903) pp. 86, 153.
214. Robert J. Cull, "Capital Market Failure and Institutional Innovation", Ph.D. Dissertation, The California Institute of Technology, 1992. Michie, *London and New York*, pp. 211–212. Joseph G. Martin, *A Century of Finance, Martin's History of the Boston Stock and Money Markets*, (Boston, published by the author, 1898), pp. 196–223.
215. Michie, *London and New York*, pp. 206–207.
216. NYSE: Special Investigation Committee, Continuous Quotations, January 27, 1903; cited in Michie, *London and New York*, p. 210.
217. Arthur M. Johnson and Barry E. Supple, *Boston Capitalists and Western Railroads*, (Cambridge, Mass.: Harvard University Press, 1967), p. 19.
218. Although the London exchange was less likely to shy away from smaller, more volatile issues with low potential trade volumes than its American counter-

part, it has been suggested that the LSE was also unable to serve the full range of financial requirements of the British domestic economy – particularly those of industries characterized by rapid technological innovation and potential economies of scale. "If British capital markets were poor places to buy and sell industrial securities, they, especially London, were very good places to sell government stocks, railroad securities, and municipal and public utility bonds. Substantial markets also existed in London for trading the securities of foreign land, finance, and investment companies – the latter two types generally dedicated to financing international trade – and mining, agricultural, and other extractive activities. Foreign industrial assets, however, were traded in Britain with, in anything, even less success than their domestic counterparts", William P. Kennedy, *Industrial Structure, Capital Markets, and the Origin of British Economic Decline*, (Cambridge: Cambridge University Press, 1987). Regardless, the point here is not that the LSE serviced all American economic sectors sufficiently, but that it serviced more sectors than did the NYSE.

219. Davis and Gallman, "Savings, Investment, and Economic Growth", *passim*.

Chapter 5

220. See Lewis, *America's Stake*, pp. 546 and 606; Nathaniel T. Bacon, "American International Indebtedness", *Yale Review*, 9 (1900), p. 159; and George Paish, "Trade Balances of the United States", US Senate, *National Monetary Commission*, 61st Cong., 2nd sess., 1910, Senate Document 579.

221. Bullock *et al.*, "The Balance of Trade", p. 229. Lewis, *America's Stake*, p. 173.

222. Lewis, *America's Stake*, pp. 175–180. On the basis of very sketchy evidence – a letter from John Forbes, a partner in Russel & Company, to his mother – Carl Remer estimated that the nine American firms listed in the 1836 Canton census may have had as much as three million dollars invested in silver and trade goods. He puts the investment in 1875 at, perhaps, six million, and guesses that the figure might have reached twice that amount by 1898. Carl F. Remer, *American Investments in China*, (Honolulu: Institute of Pacific Relations, 1929), pp. 21–24.

223. Lewis, *America's Stake*, p. 293. John Harry Dunning, *American Investment in British Manufacturing*, (London: Allen & Unwin, 1958), pp. 18–19 (hereafter cited as Dunning, *American Investment*). Colt opened the factory in 1853, but closed it in 1857 because "he could not prevail on his American workmen to remain in England and the English ways of doing things did not suit his ideas of mass production". Charles T. Haven and Frank A. Belden, *A History of the Colt Revolver and Other Arms Made by Colt's Patent Fire Arms Manufacturing Company from 1836 to 1940*, (New York: William Morrow & Company, 1940), pp. 8–89. For a description of the plant drawn from the British weekly, *Household Words*, (Chapter 15 of Volume 9 of 1855), see pp. 345–349.

224. The Great Western received $800,000 of American capital. In addition, the Northern acquired $215,000 and the Buffalo and Brontcord $70,000. Peter Baskerville, "Americans in Britain's Backyard: The Railway Era in Upper Canada, 1850–1880". *Business History Review*, **55**: 3 (Autumn, 1981), p. 317 (hereafter cited as Baskerville, "Americans in Britain's Backyard").

225. Lewis, *America's Stake*, pp. 313–317. The Sonora Railway Company (incorporated in Massachusetts) was launched by Boston capitalists to extend the AT&SF to the Pacific in an attempt to break the Southern Pacific's (that is, Collis P. Huntington's) monopoly. Construction began in Mexico in 1880, and the line was completed to Nogales in 1882. Fred Wilbur Powell, *The Railroads of Mexico*, (Boston: The Stratford Co., 1912), pp. 123–124 (hereafter cited as Powell, *Railroads of Mexico*).

226. This point is explicitly made by Fred Field in his description of American investment patterns in Canada. "The United States citizen, always with an eye to investing money for large returns, is quick to see the opportunities that have been embraced in the Western states, duplicated in British Columbia". Fred W. Field, *Capital Investment in Canada: Some Facts and Figures Respecting One of the Most Attractive Investment Fields in the World*, (Montreal: Monetary Times of Canada, 1914), p. 21 (hereafter cited as Field, *Canada*)

Alfred D. Chandler also attributes the growth of American direct investment to the early innovation of the "large multi-unit industrial firm". That organizational innovation had, by 1914, led to "at least forty-one American companies, clustered in machinery and food industries", having built two or more operating facilities abroad. Alfred D. Chandler, "The Growth of the Transnational Industrial Firm in the United States and the United Kingdom: A Comparative Analysis". *The Economic History Review*, **33**: 3 (August 1980), pp. 396–410.

227. J. H. Dunning, *American Investments*, p. 22.

228. Mira Wilkins, *The Emergence of Multinational Enterprises: American Business Abroad from the Colonial Era to 1914*, Harvard Studies in Business History, Vol. 34, (Cambridge, Mass.: Harvard University Press, 1970), pp. 42–45 (hereafter cited as Wilkins, *Multinational Enterprises*).

229. In 1879 the firm established a shop in Paris to "make brakes", and twelve years later the firm moved to larger quarters in Freinville. Although there had been a sales force and repair shops in the UK since 1872, the first Westinghouse brake factory in the United Kingdom was not established until the Westinghouse Brake Company Ltd, a wholly owned subsidiary, was chartered in 1881. It began production at King's Cross, London, but the firm later built a much larger factory at Trafford Park, Manchester. Dunning, *American Investments*, p. 26. Henry G. Proust, *A Life of George Westinghouse*, (New York: American Society of Mechanical Engineers, 1921), pp. 62 and 269. Wilkins, *Multinational Enterprise*, p. 59.

230. The Edison companies were the predecessors of General Electric. Dunning, *American Investment*, p. 23. John Winthrop Hammond, *Men and Volts, The Story of General Electric*, (New York: J. B. Lippencott, 1941), p. 91. Lewis, *America's Stake*, p. 294. Frank A. Southard Jr., *American Industry in Europe: Origins and Development of the Multinational Corporation*, (Boston: Houghton Mifflin & Co., 1931: reissued Arno Press, 1976), p. 23 (hereafter cited as Southard, *American Industry in Europe*).

231. In France they organized Le Matériel Téléphonique and in the UK the Western Electric Company Ltd, Southard, *American Industry in Europe*, p. 43.

232. As late as 1882 Standard still commanded almost the entire foreign market for kerosene; but, by 1888, the Russians had managed to capture about 22 percent, and by 1891 their share was nearly 30 percent. Standard Oil's new investments in distribution included repair and storage facilities, bulk stations, and pipelines. Ralph W. Hidy and Muriel E. Hidy, *History of the Standard Oil Company (New Jersey), Pioneering in Big Business, 1882–1911*, (New York: Harper & Brothers, 1955), pp. 132 and 153. (Hereafter cited as Hidy and Hidy, *Standard Oil*.) By 1890 the Standard distribution network in Europe included the Compagnie Générale des Pétroles, Paris (1880), the Anglo-American Oil Company, UK (1887), Danish Petroleum (1887), and the Deutsch–Amerikanische Petroleum A.G. (1890). Southard, *American Industry in Europe*, pp. 49–50.

233. Hidy & Hidy, *Standard Oil*, pp. 42, 128, 256, and 497.

234. Among the other investors in Field's New York, Newfoundland, and London Electric Company were Peter Cooper, Moses Taylor, and Chandler White. Robert Luther Thompson, *Wiring a Continent: The History of the Telegraph Industry in the United States, 1832–1866*, (Princeton, N.J.: Princeton University Press, 1947), pp. 300–301. In 1878, the Mexican Telegraph Company and the Central and South American Telegraph Company were incorporated with initial capitalization of $500,000 and $300,000 respectively, but the combined capital of the two companies was soon increased to $6 million. Service began to Mexico in March 1881 and to Peru in October 1882. Lloyd J. Hughlett, *Industrialization in Latin America*, (New York: McGraw Hill Book Company, 1946), pp. 107–110. Wilkins, *Multinational Enterprises*, p. 48.

235. Lewis, *America's Stake*, pp. 316–317. J. Fred Rippy, *The United States and Mexico*, (New York: F. S. Crofts & Co., 1931), p. 312. At the time of nationalization, the Mexican system included the following roads that were included in the program: wide gauge roads, the Mexican Central Railroad (US, UK, and German capital), the National Railway of Mexico (US, UK, and Mexican capital), the Mexican International Railroad (US), the Pan American Railroad (US), and the Vera Cruz and Isthmus (US and Mexican), a total of 6,212 miles, and the narrow gauge roads, the National Railroad of Mexico, Morelico branch (US, UK, and Canadian), the Hidalgo and Northeastern (Mexican), the Michocan and Pacific Railway (UK), the Interoceanic Railway (UK), and the Mexican Southern Railway (UK), a total of 545 miles. Left outside the nationalized system were a number of wide gauge roads: the Southern Pacific of Mexico (US), the Mexico North Western Railway (UK and Canadian), the Mexican Railway (UK), the Kansas City, Mexico, and Orient (US, UK, and Dutch), the Mexican Northern Railway (US), the Nacozan Railway (US), the Paaral and Durango Railroad (US); one part narrow gauge road: the United Railways of Yucatan (Mexican); two mostly narrow gauge roads, and finally, the Coahuila and Zacatecas Railway (UK) an all narrow gauge road. Together these latter roads comprised a total of 3,883 miles that were not nationalized.

236. The estimate on the number of American mines is from David A. Wells, *A Study of Mexico*, (New York: D. Appleton & Company, 1887) p. 161. Isaac Marcosson, *Metal Magic, The Story of the American Smelting and Refining*

Company, (New York: Farrar Straus, 1949), pp. 210–211 (hereafter cited as Marcosson, *Metal Magic*).

237. The later smelter was built to handle both lead and copper; the Monterrey furnace had been built for lead alone. Marcosson, *Metal Magic*, pp. 50, 52–53. Gattenby Williams (a pseudonym for William Guggenheim) in collaboration with Charles Monroe Heath, *William Guggenheim*, (New York: The Lone Voice Publishing Company, 1934), pp. 70, 84, 93, 95, and 100. Lewis, *America's Stake*, pp. 201–202 and 249–250.

It has been argued that while it was Diaz's pro-business policies that first attracted the Guggenheims to Mexico, it was the low wages that kept them there. See Thomas E. O'Brien, "Rich Boy and the Dreams of Avarice: the Guggenheims in Chile", *Business History Review*, **63** (Spring 1989), p. 126 (hereafter cited as O'Brien, "The Guggenheims in Chile").

238. In the words of one observer, ". . . Boston and Philadelphia have indulged in self praise, stating that their enterprise and capital assisted materially in developing Canadian asbestos properties. Notwithstanding that Canadian banks have several million dollars on deposit in New York, Canadian industrial development seemed more naturally attached to Philadelphia and Boston. It was Philadelphia capital which developed the water power and industries around Sault Ste Marie. It was Boston capital and enterprise which developed the Dominion Coal Company, the Dominion Iron and Steel Company and the Shawingan Water and Power Company". Field, *Canada*, p. 24. Lewis, *America's Stake*, pp. 207–208 and 251–252. Herbert Marshall, Frank A. Southard Jr. and Kenneth W. Taylor, *Canadian–American Industry, A Study in International Investment*, (New Haven, Conn.: Yale University Press, 1936), p. 10. (Hereafter cited as Marshall, Southard & Taylor, *Canadian–American Industry*). E. S. Moore, *American Influences on Canadian Mining*, (Toronto: University of Toronto Press, 1941), pp. 16–20, 27–30. The Ritchie enterprises opened the Sudbury Nickel field, the greatest late nineteenth century mining development in Ontario. Although they began as copper mines, the firms soon shifted to nickel; and, in 1902, the two merged forming the International Nickel Company (New Jersey) – a firm launched by Robert M. Thompson and his associates with capital of $36 million.

239. Lewis, *America's Stake*, pp. 229 & 294. Wilkins, *Multinational Enterprises*, pp. 46 & 60.

240. Wilkins, *Multinational Enterprises*, pp. 64–65.

241. Lewis, *America's Stake*, pp. 335–336. The early financing of the Canadian Pacific was made difficult because of the bitter opposition of the owners of the Grand Trunk. As a result, its first bond issue of $10 million was handled by a Montreal–New York syndicate, and its first public stock issue was underwritten by New York and Amsterdam underwriters. Overall, however, the main financial interests of the C.P.R. were, since its completion, overwhelmingly British. In 1906, for example, the Canadians and Americans together owned only slightly more than a quarter of the common stock while British investors held more than 60 percent. Marshall, Southard & Taylor, *Canadian–American Industry*, pp. 16, 114, and 194.

242. So close was the relationship between the American and Cuban governments that in the late 1920s the distinguished economic historian Leland Jenks entitled his study of Cuba, *Our Cuban Colony*. Leland Hamilton Jenks, *Our Cuban Colony: A Study of Sugar*, (New York: Vanguard Press, 1928) (hereafter cited as Jenks, *Our Cuban Colony*).

243. Lewis, *America's Stake*, pp. 265–266. Jenks, *Our Cuban Colony*, p. 35.

244. On his first voyage, Baker carried 160 bunches of bananas from Jamaica to Jersey City. He found the bananas that had cost $0.25 a bunch could be sold for $2.00 – a clear profit of $280. Stacy May and Galo Plaza, *The United Fruit Company in Latin America*, Seventh Case Study in a National Planning Association series on United States Business Performance Abroad (Washington, D.C.: The National Planning Association, 1958), p. 4. (Hereafter cited as May & Plaza, *United Fruit*.)

245. Wilkins, *Multinational Enterprises*, pp. 25–26 and 153.

246. Much of the apparent decline in Mexico's share of direct investment can be explained by the "nationalization" of several railroads and the resulting switch from direct to portfolio investment.

For a discussion of the role of American financiers in China – particularly the role of the House of Morgan – see Clarence B. Davis, "Financing Imperialism: British and American Bankers as Vectors of Imperial Expansion in China, 1908–1920", *Business History Review*, **56**: 2 (Summer, 1982), pp. 236–264.

247. The European share of investment in oil distribution was about 65 percent.

248. In 1911 the Company controlled refineries in seven countries with a combined daily capacity of 16,188 barrels. Hidy & Hidy, *Standard Oil*, pp. 514 and 524–525.

249. Lewis, *America's Stake*, pp. 182–184. Wilkins, *Multinational Enterprises*, pp. 83 and 86. Harold F. Williamson and Arnold R. Daum, *The American Petroleum Industry: The Age of Illumination*, (Evanston, Ill.: Northwestern University Press, 1955), p. 660. Marquis James, *The Texaco Story, the First Fifty Years*, (Houston, Texas: The Texaco Company, 1953), pp. 31 and 102.

250. Lewis, *America's Stake*, p. 184, Wilkins, *Multinational Enterprises*, pp. 91 and 103. M. J. French, "The Emergence of a US Multinational Enterprise: The Goodyear Tire and Rubber Company, 1910–1939", *The Economic History Review*, 2nd series, **40**: 1, 1987, p. 69 and 72 (hereafter cited as French, "The Emergence of a US Multinational Enterprise").

251. Lewis, *America's Stake*, p. 324.

252. Bullock *et al.*, "Balance of Trade", pp. 229–230.

253. 1902, 57th Congress, 1 Session, *Congressional Record*, p. 2201.

254. Robert W. Dunn, *American Foreign Investments*, (New York: B. W. Huebsch & Viking Press, 1926), p. 2 (hereafter cited as Dunn, *American Foreign Investments*). The data are from a New York weekly, the *Annalist*, **16**, p. 452.

255. Lewis, *America's Stake*, pp. 338–345. In 1914, for example, the list of foreign capital issues publicly offered in the United States included $11 million in loans to European governments (Greece, Norway, and Sweden), $5,664,000 to cities and provinces in Canada, $10 million to the government of Cuba, $1.5 million to the government of Panama, $5,796,288 to the National Railways of

Mexico, and $7,775,000 in corporate issues. The latter were all to Canadian firms (the Central Railway of Canada, the Northern Electric Manufacturing Company Ltd, the Dominion Power and Transmission Company (Ltd), the Northern Navigation Company, and the Toronto Railway). Ralph A. Young, *Handbook of American Underwriting of Foreign Securities*, US Department of Commerce, Trade Promotion Series #104, (Washington, D.C.: Government Printing Office, 1930), pp. 58–59.

256. The $180 million in direct investment was converted into $197 million in bonds and preferred stock.

257. Lewis, *America's Stake*, pp. 316–317 and 346.

258. Mexico had passed the US in silver production in 1902.

259. John R. Southworth and Percy C. Homs, *El Directo Oficial Minero de Mexico*, Vol. 9, (Mexico, D. F.: John R. Southworth, 1908), p. 17. John R. Southworth, *El Directo Oficial Minero de Mexico*, Vol. 11, (Mexico, D.F.: John R. Southworth, 1910), p. 6.

260. Lewis, *America's Stake*, pp. 202–203. Wilkins, *Multinational Enterprises*, pp. 116 and 120.

261. The two entrepreneurs behind this venture were Henry H. Rogers, the "piston rod of the Standard Oil Engine and the genius of Amalgamated Copper" and Leonard Lewisohn, a copper entrepreneur. The original firm produced bar gold and silver, pig lead, electrolytic copper, and blue vitriol. It had been organized "to combine all the principal smelting works in the United States with the exception of the Guggenheims", but without the cooperation of the brothers, its position was very fragile. Marcosson, *Metal Magic*, p. 62.

262. ASARCO's initial capitalization was $65 million, but by 1903, after the Guggenheim merger, the figure had increased to $100 million. In the new merged firm both the CEO and the Treasurer were Guggenheims as were five of the twenty-two Directors. The Guggenheims kept their mines, the Tampico–Perth Amboy Steamship Line, and the G.E. Exploration Company out of the merged enterprise. Marcosson, *Metal Magic*, pp. 57–83. John Moody, *The Truth About the Trusts*, (New York: Moody Publishing Company, 1904), pp. 42–48. Henry O'Connor, *The Guggenheims: The Making of an American Dynasty*, (New York: Arno Press, 1976), pp. 104 and 117 (hereafter cited as O'Connor, *The Guggenheims*).

For a discussion of the Guggenheims' ability to take over ASARCO, see O'Brien. "The Guggenheims in Chile", pp. 126–127. As earlier noted, for a general discussion of the organization of the world copper industry, see Schmidtz, "The World Copper Industry", pp. 392–410.

263. Ira B. Joralemon, *Romantic Copper, Its Lure and Lore*, (New York: D. Appleton–Century Company, 1936), pp. 136–165 (hereafter cited as Joralemon, *Romantic Copper*). Harold Underwood Faulkner, *The Decline of Laissez Faire, 1897–1917*, Vol. VII, The Economic History of the United States, (New York: Rinehart & Company, 1951), p. 76. Hereafter cited as Faulkner, *Laissez Faire*. Initially, the Greene Consolidated Copper Company and its operating subsidiary the Greene Cananea Consolidated Copper Company acquired 10,412 acres of partly developed copper mines and

claims located about twenty miles south of the American border and some 486,000 acres of timber land that the two companies leased to others. David M. Pletcher, *Rails, Mines, and Progress: Seven American Promoters in Mexico, 1867–1911*, (Ithaca, N.Y.: Cornell University Press, 1958), pp. 222–225.

264. Transvaal Copper, with its mines in Sonora, was incorporated in Cincinnati, Ohio. Lewis. *America's Stake*, pp. 234–237. Joralemon has the Guggenheims still operating the Nacozari property in 1904. Joralemon, *Romantic Copper*, p. 216.

265. Lewis, *America's Stake*, p. 220. Wilkins, *Multinational Enterprises*, pp. 123–124.

266. For a discussion of the boom in Mexican rubber see William Schell Jr, "American Investment in Tropical Mexico: Rubber Plantations, Fraud, and Dollar Diplomacy, 1897–1913", *Business History Review*, **64** (Summer, 1990), pp. 217–254 (hereafter cited as Schell, "American Investment"). The figure for 1902 is from the "Barlow Report on United States Enterprise in Mexico, 1902". J. Fred Rippy, *The United States and Mexico*, (New York: F. S. Crofts & Co., 1931) pp. 313–315. Wilkins, *Multinational Enterprises*, pp. 120–122. Although, outside of smelting and refining, American investment in Mexico's manufacturing sector was not large, there was some. For example, in 1911, the B. F. Goodrich Company opened a branch in Mexico City to manufacture water-proofed clothing. French, "The Emergence of a US Multinational Enterprise", p. 72.

267. In the words of a contemporary observer, "These [American investments] are principally mining, and lumbering, and timber, with some colonization propositions". Field, *Canada*, p. 21. Lewis, *America's Stake*, p. 288. Wilkins, *Multinational Enterprises*, p. 138.

268. Faulkner, *Laissez Faire*, p. 75. There is some question of the dating. French puts the US Rubber entry in 1907 (rather than Faulkner's 1906) and, more importantly, the B. F. Goodrich entry in Canada in 1923 (thirteen years after Faulkner's dating). Goodrich did, however, open a sales office in March 1910, and seven months later bought the Durham Rubber Company of Bowmanville, a mechanical goods firm. The US firm also owned 80 percent of the initial capital of $250,000 in the Goodyear Tire and Rubber Company of Canada. That firm invested immediately in tire manufacturing capacity. French, "The Emergence of a US Multinational Enterprise", pp. 69 and 71.

269. Lewis, *America's Stake*, pp. 596–597.

270. Lewis, *America's Stake*, p. 595. Wilkins, *Multinational Enterprises*, pp. 138–139. Faulkner, *Laissez Faire*, p. 75. Between 1900 and 1921 Canadian newsprint imports increased from 1.5 to 65 percent of American domestic production. For a complete analysis of the American and Canadian newsprint markets, see Constance Southworth, "The American–Canadian Newsprint Paper Industry and the Tariff", *The Journal of Political Economy*, **30** (October 1922), pp. 681–697.

271. Lewis, *America's Stake*, pp. 208 and 596. Wilkins, *Multinational Enterprises*, pp. 136–137. The expert was John Herbert Curle in *Gold Mines of the World*, (London: Waterlow & Sons Ltd, 1896), p. 264. By the third edition (1905),

however, he reported that the mine "is now low-grade, and probably will not yield a large amount of payable ore", p. 265. "Two prospectors, Joseph Bordeaux and Joseph Morris, working on the Lily May property, went over to Red Mountain and in a single day located the Le Roi, Centre Star, War Eagle, Idaho, and Virginia . . . They gave the Le Roi claim to E. S. Topping, the proprietor of the road house on the Dewaney trail, for providing the $12.50 in fees necessary for recording claims . . ." A group of investors from Spokane and Butte obtained a 53 percent interest in the mine for $16,000; and, in 1898, the mine and a smelter at Northport were sold to the British American Corporation for $4 million. E. S. Moore, *American Influences on Canadian Mining*, (Toronto: University of Toronto Press, 1941), pp. 71–72.

272. Lewis, *America's Stake*, pp. 341, 345, and 348. Jacob Viner, *Canada's Balance of International Indebtedness, 1900–1913*, Harvard Economic Studies Vol. 26 (Cambridge, Mass.: Harvard University Press, 1924), pp. 127–128 (hereafter cited as Viner, *Canada's Balance*).

273. Field, *Canada*, p. 25.

274. For a balanced discussion of the Canadian issue, see Hugh G. J. Aitken, *American Capital and Canadian Resources*, (Cambridge, Mass.: Harvard University Press, 1961) (hereafter cited as Aitken, *American Capital*.) For a less balanced presentation, see Kari Levitt, *Silent Surrender: The American Economic Empire in Canada*, (New York: Liveright, 1970). In the case of Mexico, for a balanced analysis of the strengths and weaknesses of the Porfiriato see Clark W. Reynolds, *The Mexican Economy: Twentieth Century Structure and Growth*, (New Haven, Conn.: Yale University Press, 1970), hereafter cited as Reynolds, *The Mexican Economy*. For a less balanced analysis, see James D. Cockcroft, *Mexico: Class Formation, Capital Accumulation, and the State*, (New York: Monthly Review Press). Hereafter cited as Cockcroft, *Mexico*.

275. Urquhart, M. C., "Canadian Economic Growth 1870–1980", Queens University, Department of Economics, Discussion Paper No. 734 (1988), Tables 2 & 12. The GNP figures are in 1981 prices.

276. Compare the $4.44 per capita figure with transfers of $7.30 to Argentina and $13.08 to Australia over the same three decade period. The data are from the series "Capital Called" on the London market. See Davis and Huttenback, *Mammon*, Chapter 2.

277. Lewis, *America's Stake*, p. 606.

278. The British figure was $1050.1 million and the American $167.9 million. By 1913 the figures were $2793.1 and $779.8 millions.

279. Aitken, *American Capital*, p. 132.

280. Although his evidence is drawn from the years after 1901, his conclusions appear perfectly relevant for the years between 1879 and 1900 as well. K. H. Norrie writes, "the tariff on agricultural implements acted to 'shape, limit, and curtail' Prairie agricultural development. It did this by redistributing income from land to labor and capital, and by delaying the move toward larger, more mechanized operations by some farmers. Fewer homesteads were patented than would have been the case in the absence of the tariff". K. H. Norrie, "Tariffs and the Distribution of Prairie Incomes", *Can-*

adian Journal of Economics, **7** (1974), pp. 449–461. The quotation is from p. 461.

281. The Canadians do not include British born in their count of foreign born.
282. Urquhart, M. C. (ed.), *Historical Statistics of Canada*, (Cambridge: The University Press, 1965), Series A2–A14, p. 14.
283. Lewis, *America's Stake*, p. 606.
284. The fears raised by the threat of an invasion by the Union Army during the Civil War and by the repercussions of the Finian raids in the immediate post-War period (April and June 1866) certainly helped to bring about Confederation in 1867.
285. Between 1876 and 1911 only two men occupied the presidency: Manuel Gonzáles for one term (1880–1884) and Porfirio Díaz for the remainder.
286. Hansen, Roger D., *The Politics of Mexican Development*, (Baltimore, Md.: The Johns Hopkins Press, 1971), p. 14. Hereafter cited as Hansen, *Mexican Development*.
287. Cockcroft, *Mexico*, p. 87.
288. Reynolds, *The Mexican Economy*, p. 22. Hansen, *Mexican Development*, p. 15.
289. Rosenzweig, Fernando, "El desarrollo de Mexico de 1877 a 1911", pp. 405–454. Cited in Reynolds, *The Mexican Economy*, p. 24.
290. In 1911, US investment constituted about 38 percent of all foreign investment, Great Britain about 29, and France about 27 percent. Hansen, *Mexican Development*, p. 16.
291. Schell, "American Investment", *Passim*.
292. It should be noted that the Atkin's refinery was one of those that was amalgamated by Havermeyer to form the Sugar Trust. Jenks, *Cuban Colony*, pp. 35 and 131–132. Lewis, *America's Stake*, pp. 267–268. Wilkins, *Multinational Enterprises*, p. 155. In addition to the firms discussed above the list of American investments in Cuban sugar included by 1914 the Central Cuba (1911), the Francisco (1899), the Guantanamo (1905), the Manati (1912), the New Niquero (1905), the Santa Cecelia (1904), the Stewart Sugar (1907), the Tuinucu (1891), The Central Teresa (1895), the Washington (1910), the Atlantic Fruit (1912), the Cardenas–American (1912), the Cuban Company (1900), Nipe Bay (1900), United Fruit (1899), Warner (1906), and the West India (1913) companies.
293. Jenks, *Our Cuban Colony*, pp. 171–172. "The Havana Electric Railway Light and Power maintained a complete street railway system extending into every section of Havana, and supplies the entire city as well as the surrounding area with electric light and power, and it remains the most important utility in Cuba". Scott Nearing and Joseph Freeman, *Dollar Diplomacy*, (New York: Viking Press, 1925), p. 180 (hereafter cited as Nearing and Freeman, *Dollar Diplomacy*).
294. Lewis, *America's Stake*, 325, 344 and 347. Faulkner, *Laissez Faire*, p. 71.
295. Jenks, *Our Cuban Colony*, pp. 164–165.
296. Railroad investment in South America was largely a British preserve. The largest American financed railroad investment in South America was almost certainly four sections of the Bolivian Railway (416 miles across the

Altoplano). The contract, negotiated by the New York banking house Speyer & Company, called for an investment of more than $16 million in construction costs (the road cost $38,752 a mile to build). Margaret A. Marsh, *The Bankers in Bolivia: A Study of American Foreign Investment*, (New York: Vanguard Press, 1928), pp. 73–74.

297. The Hearst–Haggin group controlled the Homestake Mining Company with its gold mines in South Dakota.

298. Before the mine was able to operate it was necessary to build 80 miles of railroad through the mountains, to locate and develop coal deposits for fuel, and to construct a large and technically complex filter. Because of the remote location it also proved difficult to recruit skilled labor. H. Foster Bain and Read Thomas Thornton, *Ores and Industry in South America*, (New York: Harper & Brothers, 1934), pp. 282–283 and 296 (hereafter cited as Bain and Thornton, *Ores and Industry in South America*). Joralemon, *Romantic Copper*, pp. 234–238. Lewis, *America's Stake*, 237–238. The mine produced 22,415 tons of copper in 1913.

299. O'Brien dates the Braden Copper Company from 1908, and he puts the initial capitalization at $23 million. O'Brien, "The Guggenheims in Chile", p. 130. O'Briens's dating probably refers to the date that the Guggenheims took over the Braden Copper Company. They initially retained the original name. Wilkins, *Multinational Enterprises*, pp. 178–181.

300. Bain and Thornton, *Ores and Industry in South America*, pp. 219–221. Kennecott Copper had been organized by the Guggenheims in 1907 to develop Alaskan copper. Its initial financing had come partly from the brothers' Mexican operations and partly from J. P. Morgan's efforts on Wall Street. It might be noted that Kennecott was forced to invest an additional $22.5 million in its Chilean operations before the enterprise was a success. The new mine required very heavy capitalization because of the cost of the technology required to treat the low-yield ores. "El Trente, the principal Braden mine, was the first in the world to apply the flotation process in concentrated low-grade ores . . .". O'Brien, "The Guggenheims in Chile", p. 131.

301. Burrage took a minority interest in Chile Exploration. Bain and Thornton, *Ores and Industry in South America*, pp. 221–222. Joralemon, *Romantic Copper*, pp. 238–247. Lewis, *America's Stake*, pp. 238–240. O'Brien, "The Guggenheims in Chile", p. 131. The Guggenheims received $2.8 million in stock and $15 million in cash for their $12 million investment in the Chile Exploration Company's Chuquicamata holdings. O'Connor, "The Guggenheims", pp. 346–349.

302. Lewis, *America's Stake*, pp. 257–259. Wilkins, *Multinational Enterprises*, pp. 183 and 185.

303. In the initial organization Boston Fruit and its associated firms received $5.2 million and Keith and his associates $4 million. Zemurray's initial success was, in part, postulated on his support for the revolution led by Manuel Bonilla against the then president Miguel Davila. Charles David Kepner and Henry Soothill Jay, *The Banana Empire: A Case Study of Economic Imperialism*, (New York: Vanguard Press, 1935), pp. 35–36, 34, 70, and 101. May & Plaza,

United Fruit, pp. 6–7, 13, and 15–16. Charles Morrow Wilson, *Empire in Gold and Green: The Story of the American Banana Trade*, (New York: Henry Holt & Co., 1947), pp. 91, 107–110, and 118.

304. May & Plaza, *United Fruit*, pp. 10–11. Lewis, *America's Stake*, pp. 280 and 602. Wilkins, *Multinational Enterprises*, p. 159.

305. Lewis, *America's Stake*, pp. 343 and 347. In the case of the coffee valorization loan, bankers in Europe initially refused to provide the required financial aid, but Herman Sielcken, who represented the National City Bank of New York, did manage to raise $90 million – most in the US but some in Europe. Later Sielcken and some participating bankers were indicted under the American anti trust laws; however, the charges were later dropped because of Brazilian diplomatic pressure, but the valorization committee was forced to sell its coffee holdings. Benjamin H. Williams, *Economic Foreign Policy of the United States*, (New York: McGraw Hill Book Co., 1929), pp. 400–402 (hereafter cited as Williams, *Economic Foreign Policy*).

306. Although the American government had sent troops to Panama six times between 1856 and 1901, each time it had been at the request of the Colombian government. In 1902, however, there had been no such request, and the Americans prevented the movement of Colombian troops on the Panama Railroad as they attempted to suppress the rebellion. In a speech at Berkeley, California, seven years after the Panamanian revolution, Theodore Roosevelt is quoted as saying, "I am interested in the Panama Canal because I started it. If I had followed traditional conservative methods I should have submitted a dignified state paper of probably two hundred pages to Congress and the debate on it would have probably been going on yet, but I took the Canal Zone and let the Congress debate, and while the debate goes on, the canal does also". The speech was reported in the *Washington Post* on March 24, 1911. Howard C. Hill, *Roosevelt and the Caribbean*, (Chicago, University of Chicago Press, 1927), pp. 44 and 68. Nearing and Freeman, *Dollar Diplomacy*, p. 83.

307. William M. Malloy (ed.), *Treaties, Conventions, International Acts, Protocols and Agreements between the United States and Other Powers*, (Washington: GPO, 4 vols, 1910–1938), Vol. 1, pp. 362–364.

308. In 1912 alone, for example, they objected no less than three times: they objected to a contract with the Cuban Ports Company (a UK firm) because the tied revenues might be needed for other purposes; they objected to a concession to drain the Zapata swamp because it was "improvident and a reckless waste of revenues and natural resources"; and they objected to a contract to build the Caibarien–Nuevitas Railway because it represented an "improvident strain on the Cuban Treasury". It might be noted that, in the case of the railway, when it was discovered that it was American interests that were involved, the objection was withdrawn. Williams, *Economic Foreign Policy*, pp. 202–203. The first military intervention was designed to protect American loans made for public improvements. "Among the bloated contracts that led to the American intervention in 1906 was one for 'paving and sewage' in Havana to the McGivney and Rokely Construction Company. The richest, however, was to Frank Steinhart's Havana Electric Railway,

Light, and Power Company". Nearing and Freeman, *Dollar Diplomacy*, p. 180.

309. As a result of a treaty signed between the US and Cuban governments (passed and ratified in 1903), Cuba received a preferential 20 percent reduction in US tariffs and American products and the US a 20 to 40 percent reduction in Cuban tariffs. The Cuban share of the American sugar market increased from 18 percent in 1900 to 50 percent in 1913, and American exports to Cuba increased from $27 million in 1897 to $200 million in 1914. By the latter date, Cuba had become the sixth best American customer. Robert F. Smith, "The United States and Cuba", in Marvin Berstein (ed.), *Foreign Investment in Latin America: Cases and Attitudes*, (New York: Alfred A. Knopf, 1966), pp. 147–148.

310. The original loans had been made in 1888 and 1890 by a Dutch firm, and the right to take over the customs houses was included in the initial contract. The bonds went into default in 1892, and the Santo Domingo Improvement Company was chartered in New Jersey to buy the Dutch claims. Melvin M. Knight, *The Americans in Santo Domingo*, (New York. Vanguard Press, 1928), pp. 18–23. Nearing and Freeman, *Dollar Diplomacy*, pp. 125–128.

311. Initially, Haiti's national bank was to be reorganized in connection with a new loan to be taken by French bankers. The American Secretary of State, Philander Knox, argued that some American banking interest ought to be represented. He called a conference of those bankers, and as a result the National City Bank, Speyer and Company, Hallgarten and Company, and Ladenburg, Thalmann and Company each agreed to subscribe to two thousand shares of the new bank. US Government, Select Committee on an Inquiry into the Occupation and Administration of Haiti and Santo Domingo, *Hearings*, 67th Congress, 1st and 2nd sessions, (Washington, D.C.: GPO, 1922) 2 vols, p. 105. Cited in Nearing and Freeman, *Dollar Diplomacy*, pp. 133–135.

312. Faulkner, *Laissez Faire*, pp. 70–73. Lewis, *America's Stake*, pp. 343–344. The loan agreements called for the bankers to improve (and control) the National Railway and to build a new railway (on their own terms) and to reorganize the National Bank – taking over 51 percent of the equity in the process. Nearing and Freeman, *Dollar Diplomacy*, pp. 151–152.

313. Jenks, *Our Cuban Colony*. Josefina Zaraida Vasquez and Lorenzo Meyer, *The United States and Mexico* (Chicago, Ill.: University of Chicago Press, 1985), p. 91. Schell, "American Investment", p. 252.

314. Stanley Lebergott, "The Returns to US Imperialism, 1890–1929", *The Journal of Economic History*, **40**: 2 (June 1980), pp. 229–252. The quotations are from p. 249.

Chapter 6

315. The theoretical relationship between the three is simply:

Σ Net Flows = Stock of Foreign Investment in the US − Stock of US Investment Abroad, or
Stock of Foreign Investment in the US − Σ Net Flows = Stock of US Investment Abroad.

The problem is, however, made more complex because, among a myriad of problems: (1) the portfolio components of the stock estimates are included at par; but, if the issues are sold at a discount, the flow figure captures only the discounted value; and (2) repudiated debt is subtracted from the stock estimates but there is no offsetting adjustment to the flows. These problems are discussed in great detail in Mira Wilkins unpublished paper, "Flows Do Not Stock Make: Guidelines for Determining the Level of Long Term Foreign Investments in the United States – Methodological Quandaries in Handling Pre-1914 Data", Florida International University, 1986.

316. The estimate of the sum of the net capital flows assumes that there was $19 million in foreign investment in the US and no American investment abroad in 1790. That figure is based on the known foreign held US debt of $12.1 million and an estimated $6.9 million of short term credit.

317. Office of Business Economics puts those reductions at $24 million in 1841 and 1842 alone, and some sources suggest it may have been more.

318. North's concern centers on Lewis' use of an 1857 estimate of the balance of short-term capital. He feels the 1857 figure is too high, but any reduction makes the two sets of estimates even more difficult to rationalize. North, "Balance of Payments", p. 626.

319. Simon, "Balance of Payments", p. 706

320. The 43 percent discount is from Hunt's *Merchant's Magazine*, **59** (October 1868), pp. 241–248.

321. Lewis, *America's Stake*, p. 158.

322. Simon, "Balance of Payments", p. 707.

323. Lewis, for example, puts the average discount on railroad bonds issued before 1890 at 33 percent and the discount on railroad equities at 90 percent. Lewis, *America's Stake*, p. 160.

324. The problem could, of course, be solved if some of the capital outflow that Simon places in the years 1898 to 1901 had actually taken place in earlier years.

325. The stock estimates are all for July 1914, and, since most of the large capital repatriation that occurred in that year happened after the outbreak of the War in August, the summed flow figures used in these calculations are those for the end of 1913 not for 1914. The summed flow figures are, for the years after 1900, Goldsmith's long-term estimates adjusted for (by extrapolation) the increase in short-term from Lewis' $250 million figure in 1897 to the "official" $450 million figure in 1914.

326. Lewis, *America's Stake*, p. 606.

327. It averaged only $79 million for the first three years that data are available, and those years (1923–1925) followed a decade of very large American investments abroad.

328. For example, Neal and Uselding find that in 1912, *at minimum*, 13 percent of the capital stock of the American economy could be attributed to the social savings arising from immigration (their maximum estimate was 42 percent). Larry Neal and Paul Uselding, "Immigration, a Neglected Source of American Economic Growth: 1790 to 1912", *Oxford Economic Papers*, Vol. 24, NS, 1972.

329. Wells' estimates puts the holdings of federal government issues at $1 billion and those of states at one-tenth that amount. He also places the increase in railroad issues at just less that $200 million. Those figures are, however, par values, the actual transfers were almost certainly less.

330. Since the bulk of the investment was direct not portfolio (over 90 percent in 1897 and still more than 75 percent in 1914), the question of discounted issues is much less important than it was for foreign investment in the United States.

Bibliography

Adler, Dorothy. *British Investment in American Railways, 1834–1898*. Charlottesville: University of Virginia Press, 1970.

Aitken, Hugh G. J. *American Capital and Canadian Resources*. Cambridge: Harvard University Press, 1961.

Allen, Frederick Lewis. *The Great Pierpont Morgan*. New York: Harper & Brothers, 1949.

Ashmead, Edward. *Twenty-five Years of Mining, 1880–1904*. London: Mining Journal, January 1909.

Bacon, Nathaniel T. "America's International Indebtedness", *Yale Review*, 9, November 1900, pp. 265–28

Bain, H. Foster, and Thornton, Read Thomas. *Ores and Industry in South America*. New York: Harper & Brothers, 1934.

Baskerville, Peter. "Americans in Britain's Backyard: The Railway Era in Upper Canada, 1850–1880", *Business History Review*, **55**: 3 (Autumn 1981).

Baskin, Jonathan Barron. "The Development of Corporate Financial Markets in Britain and the United States, 1600–1914: Overcoming Asymmetric Information", *Business History Review*, **62**: 2 (Summer 1988).

Blodget, Samuel. *Economica: A Statistical Manual for the United States of America, 1806*. New York: Augustus M. Kelly, 1964.

Bogart, E. L. *The Economic History of the United States*, 2nd edition. New York: Longmans, Green and Company, 1913.

Buckley, Peter J., and Roberts, Brian R. *European Direct Investment in the USA before World War I*. New York: St Martin's Press, 1982.

Bullock, Charles J., Williams, John H., and Tucker, Rufus S. "The Balance of Trade of the United States", *The Review of Economic Statistics*, Preliminary Volume 1 (July 1919).

Cairncross, Alexander. *Home and Foreign Investment 1870–1910*. Cambridge: Cambridge University Press, 1953.

Chandler, Alfred D. "The Growth of the Transnational Industrial Firm in the United States and the United Kingdom: A Comparative Analysis", *The Economic History Review*, **33**: 3 (August 1980).

Chandler, Alfred D. *The Railroads: The Nation's First Big Business*. New York: Harcourt, Brace & World, 1965.

Clark, William, and Turner, Charlie. "International Trade and the Evolution of the American Capital Market, 1888–1911", *The Journal of Economic History*, **65**: 2, (June 1985).

Clements, Roger V. "British Controlled Enterprise in the West Between 1870 and 1890, and Some Agrarian Reactions", *Agricultural History*, **27**: 4 (1953).

Clements, Roger V. "British Investment and American Legislative Restrictions in the Trans-Mississippi West, 1880–1900", *Mississippi Valley Historical Review*, **42** (October 1953).

Clements, Roger V. "The Farmers' Attitude Toward British Investment in American Industry", *The Journal of Economic History*, **15**: 2 (1955).

Cleveland, Frederick A., and Powell, Fred W. *Railroad Promotion and Capitalization in the United States*. New York: B. Appleton, 1909.

Cockcroft, James D. *Mexico: Class Formation, Capital Accumulation, and the State*. New York: Monthly Review Press, 1983.

Craig, Lee A., and Fisher, Douglas. "Integration of the European Business Cycle: 1871–1910", *Explorations in Economic History*, **29**: 2 (April 1992).

Crapol, Edward P. *America for Americans: Economic Nationalism and Anglophobia in the Late Nineteenth Century*. Contributions to American History, No. 28, Westport, CT: Greenwood Press, 1973.

Cull, Robert J. "Capital Market Failure and Institutional Innovation", Ph.D. dissertation, The California Institute of Technology, 1992.

Cull, Robert J., and Davis, Lance E. "Un, Deux, Trois, Quatre Marchés? L'Intégration Du Marché Du États-Unis et Grande-Bretagne, 1865–1913", *Annales: Économies Sociétiés Civilisations*, No. 3, Mai–Jun 1992.

Curle, John Herbert. *Gold Mines of the World*. London: Waterlow & Sons Ltd, 1896.

Davis, Clarence B. "Financing Imperialism: British and American Bankers as Vectors of Imperial Expansion in China, 1908–1920", *Business History Review*, **56**: 2 (Summer 1982).

Davis, Lance E. "Capital Immobilities and Finance Capitalism: A Study of Economic Evolution in the United States, 1820–1920", *Explorations in Entrepreneurial History*, 2nd Series, **1**: 1, (Fall 1963).

Davis, Lance E. "The Capital Markets and Industrial Concentration: The US and UK, A Comparative Study", *The Economic History Review*, 2nd Series, **19**: 2, (1966).

Davis, Lance E. "The Investment Market, 1870–1914: The Evolution of a National Market", *The Journal of Economic History*, **25**: 3 (September 1965).

Davis, Lance E., and Gallman, Robert E. *Savings, Investment, and Economic Growth: The United States in the Nineteenth Century*, in John James and Mark Thomas (eds) *Capitalism in Context*. Chicago: University of Chicago Press, 1994.

Davis, Lance E., and Huttenback, Robert. *Mammon and the Pursuit of Empire: The Political Economy of British Imperialism, 1860–1912*. Cambridge: Cambridge University Press, 1986.

DeLong, Bradford. "Did Morgan's Men Add Value?" An Economist's Perspective on Finance Capitalism, in Peter Temin (ed.) *Inside the Business Enterprise: Historical Perspectives on the Use of Information*. Chicago: University of Chicago Press, 1991.

Dickens, Paul D. *The Transitional Period in American International Financing: 1897–1914*, Ph.D. dissertation, George Washington University, 1933.

Dunn, Robert W. *American Foreign Investments*. New York: B. W. Huebsch & Viking Press, 1926.

Dunning, John H. *American Investment in British Manufacturing*. London: Allen & Unwin, 1958.

Dunning, John H. "British Investment in US Industry" in *Moorgate and Wall Street*, 3, Autumn, 1961.

Dunning, John H. *Studies in International Investment*. London: George Allen & Unwin, 1970.

Edelstein, Michael. *Overseas Investment in the Age of High Imperialism: The United Kingdom, 1850–1914*. New York: Columbia University Press, 1982.

Edwards, G. *The Evolution of Finance Capitalism*. New York: 1908.

Evans, Paul D. *The Holland Land Company*. Buffalo Historical Society, 1924.

Faulkner, Harold U. *The Decline of Laissez Faire, 1897–1917*, Vol. 7, The Economic History of the United States. New York: Rinehart & Company, 1951.

Feinstein, Charles. "Britain's Overseas Investments in 1913", *The Economic History Review*, 2nd Series, **43**: 2 (May 1990).

Feis, Herbert. *Europe the World's Banker, 1870–1914: An Account of European Foreign Investment and the Connection of World Finance with Diplomacy before 1914*. New Haven: Yale University Press, 1930.

Field, Fred W. *Capital Investment in Canada: Some Facts and Figures Respecting One of the Most Attractive Investment Fields in the World*. Montreal: Monetary Times of Canada, 1911 and 1914.

French, M. J. "The Emergence of a US Multinational Enterprise: The Goodyear Tire and Rubber Company, 1910–1939", *The Economic History Review*, 2nd series, **40**: 1 (1987).

Gallman, Robert E. *The Capital Stock of the United States*, mss.

Gallman, Robert E. *The United States Capital Stock in the Nineteenth Century*, in Stanley Engerman and Robert Gallman (eds) *Long Term Factors in Economic Growth*. National Bureau of Economic Research, Studies in Income and Wealth, Vol. 51. Princeton: Princeton University Press, 1986.

Gates, Paul W. *The Illinois Central and Its Colonization Work*. Cambridge: Harvard University Press, 1934.

Gershenkron, Alexander. *Economic Backwardness in Historical Perspective*. Cambridge: Harvard University Press, 1962.

Goldsmith, Raymond W. *A Study of Savings in the United States*, 3 vols. Princeton: Princeton University Press, 1955.

Goldsmith, Raymond W. "The Growth of Reproducible Wealth of the United States of America", in Simon Kuznets (ed.) International Association for Research in Income and Wealth, *Income and Wealth of the United States: Trends and Structures, Income and Wealth*, Series II. Cambridge, UK: Bowes and Bowes, 1953.

Hammond, John Winthrop. *Men and Volts, The Story of General Electric*. New York: J. B. Lippencott, 1941.

Hansen, Roger D. *The Politics of Mexican Development*. Baltimore: The Johns Hopkins Press, 1971.

Haven, Charles T., and Belden Frank A. *A History of the Colt Revolver and Other Arms Made by Colt's Patent Fire Arms Manufacturing Company from 1836–1940*. New York: William Morrow & Company, 1940.

Healy, Kent T. "Development of a Natural Transportation System", in Harold Williamson (ed.), *The Growth of the American Economy*. New York: Prentice Hall, 1951.

Hidy, Ralph W., and Hidy, Muriel E. *History of the Standard Oil Company (New Jersey), Pioneering in Big Business, 1882–1911*. New York: Harper & Brothers, 1955.

Hill, Howard C. *Roosevelt and the Caribbean*. Chicago: University of Chicago Press, 1927.

Hobson, C. K. *The Export of Capital*. New York: Macmillan Company, 1914.

Hughlett, Lloyd J. *Industrialization in Latin America*. New York: McGraw Hill Book Company, 1946.

Imlah, A. H. *Economic Elements of the Pax Britannica*. Cambridge: Harvard University Press, 1958.

Jackson, W. Turrentine. *The Enterprising Scot: Investors in the American West after 1873*. Edinburgh University Publications: History, Philosophy, Economics, No. 22. Edinburgh: Edinburgh University Press, 1968.

James, John. "The Development of the National Money Market, 1893–1911", *The Journal of Economic History*, **36**: 4 (December 1976).

James, Marquis. *The Texaco Story, the First Fifty Years*. Houston: The Texaco Company, 1953.

Jenks, Leland H. *The Migration of British Capital to 1875*. London: Thomas Nelson & Sons Ltd, 1963.

Jenks, Leland H. *Our Cuban Colony: A Study of Sugar*. New York: Vanguard Press, 1928.

Johnson, Arthur M., and Supple, Barry E. *Boston Capitalists and Western Railroads*. Cambridge: Harvard University Press, 1967.

Joralemon, Ira B. *Romantic Copper, Its Lure and Lore*. New York: D. Appleton–Century Company, 1936.

Kennedy, William P. *Industrial Structure, Capital Markets, and the Origin of British Economic Decline*. Cambridge: Cambridge University Press, 1987.

Kepner, Charles David, and Jay, Henry Soothill. *The Banana Empire: A Case Study of Economic Imperialism*. New York: Vanguard Press, 1935.

Knight, Melvin M. *The Americans in Santo Domingo*. New York: Vanguard Press, 1928.

Kuhlman, Charles B. *Development of the Flour Mill Industry in the United States*. Boston: Houghton Mifflin, 1929.

Kuznets, Simon. "Foreign Economic Relations of the United States and their Impact upon the Domestic Economy: A Review of Long Term Trends", in *Proceedings of the American Philosophical Society*, **92**: 4 (1948).

Lamoreaux, Naomi. "Banks, Kinship, and Economic Development: The New England Case", *The Journal of Economic History*, vol. 46, 3 (September 1986).

Lebergott, Stanley. "The Returns to US Imperialism, 1890–1929", *The Journal of Economic History*, **60** (June 1980).

Lewis, Cleona (assisted by Karl T. Schottenbeck). *America's Stake in International Investment*. Washington, D.C.: The Brookings Institution, 1938.

Levitt, Kari. *Silent Surrender: The American Economic Empire in Canada*. New York: Liveright, 1970.

Bibliography 155

Livermore, Shaw. *Early American Land Companies*. New York: The Commonwealth Fund, 1939.

Madden, John J. *British Investment in the United States, 1860–1880*, Ph.D. dissertation, Cambridge University, 1958. New York: Garland, 1985.

Malloy, William M. (ed.). *Treaties, Conventions, International Acts, Protocols and Agreements between the United States and Other Powers*. Washington: GPO 4 vols, 1910–1938.

Marcosson, Isaac. *Metal Magic, The Story of the American Smelting and Refining Company*. New York: Farrar Straus, 1949.

Marsh, Margaret A. *The Bankers in Bolivia: A Study of American Foreign Investment*. New York: Vanguard Press, 1928.

Marshall, Herbert, Southard, Frank A., and Taylor, Kenneth W. *Canadian–American Industry, A Study in International Investment*. New Haven: Yale University Press, 1936.

Martin, Joseph G. *A Century of Finance, Martin's History of the Boston Stock and Money Markets*. Boston, published by the author, 1898.

May, Stacy, and Plaza, Galo. *The United Fruit Company in Latin America*. Seventh Case Study in a National Planning Association series on United States Business Performance Abroad. Washington, D.C.: The National Planning Association, 1958.

McFarlane, Larry A. "British Agricultural Investment in the Dakotas, 1877–1953", *Business and Economic History*, 2nd series, **5** (1976), pp. 112–126.

McFarlane, Larry A. "British Investment and the Land: Nebraska 1877–1946", *Business History Review*, **57** (Summer 1983).

McFarlane, Larry A. "British Investment in Midwestern Farm Mortgages and Land, 1875–1900, A Comparison of Iowa and Kansas", *Agricultural History*, **48** (January 1974).

McFarlane, Larry A. "British Investment in Minnesota Farm Mortgages and Land, 1875–1900". Mimeographed.

McGrane, Reginald C. *Foreign Bondholders and American State Debts*. New York: Macmillan, 1935.

Michie, Ranald C. *The London and New York Stock Exchanges, 1850–1914*. London: Allen & Unwin, 1987.

Moody, John. *The Truth About the Trusts*. New York: Moody Publishing Company, 1904.

Moore, E. S. *American Influences on Canadian Mining*. Toronto: University of Toronto Press, 1941.

Morgan, E. Victor, and Thomas, W. A. *The Stock Exchange: Its History and Functions*. London: Etek Books, 1962.

Navin, T., and Sears, M. "The Rise of a Market for Industrial Securities", *Business History Review*, **29**: 2 (June 1955).

Neal, Larry. "The Disintegration and Reintegration of International Capital Markets in the 19th Century". Mimeographed, February 29, 1992.

Neal, Larry, and Uselding Paul. "Immigration, a Neglected Source of American Economic Growth: 1790 to 1912", *Oxford Economic Papers*, **24**, NS, 1972.

Nearing, Scott, and Freeman, Joseph. *Dollar Diplomacy*. New York: Viking Press, 1925.

North, Douglass C. "The Balance of Payments of the United States, 1790–1860", in William N. Parker (ed.) *Trends in the American Economy in the Nineteenth Century*, Studies in Income and Wealth, Vol. 24, by the Conference on Research in Income and Wealth, National Bureau of Economic Research. Princeton: Princeton University Press, 1960.

Norrie, K. H. "Tariffs and the Distribution of Prairie Incomes", *Canadian Journal of Economics*, **7** (1974).

O'Brien, Thomas E. "Rich Boy and the Dreams of Avarice: the Guggenheims in Chile", *Business History Review*, **63** (Spring 1989).

O'Connor, Henry. *The Guggenheims: The Making of an American Dynasty*. New York: Arno Press, 1976.

Odell, Kerry A. "The Integration of Regional and Interregional Capital Markets: Evidence from the Pacific Coast, 1883–1913" *The Journal of Economic History*, **49**: 2 (June 1989).

Paish, George. "Great Britain's Capital Investments in Individual, Colonial and Foreign Countries", *Journal of the Royal Statistical Society*, **74**, Part II (January 1911).

Paish, George. "Great Britain's Capital Investment in Other Lands", *Journal of the Royal Statistical Society*, **72** (1909).

Paish, George. "Our New Investments in 1908", *Statist.*, **63** (January 1909).

Paish, George. "The Export of Capital and the Cost of Living", *Statist. Supplement*, **79** (1914).

Paish, George. "Trade Balances of the United States", US Senate, *National Monetary Commission*, 61st Cong., 2nd sess., 1910, Senate Document 579.

Platt, D. C. M. "British Portfolio Investment Overseas Before 1870: Some Doubts", *The Economic History Review*, 2nd Series, **33**: 1 (February 1980).

Platt, D. C. M. *Foreign Finance in Continental Europe and the United States 1815–1870: Quantities, Origins, Functions and Distributions*. London: George Allen & Unwin, 1984.

Pletcher, David M. *Rails, Mines, and Progress: Seven American Promoters in Mexico, 1867–1911*. Ithaca, N.Y.: Cornell University Press, 1958.

Postan, M. M. "Some Recent Problems in the Accumulation of Capital", *Economic History Review*, **9**:1 (October 1935), pp. 1–12.

Powell, Fred Wilbur. *The Railroads of Mexico*. Boston: The Stratford Company, 1912.

Pratt, Sereno S. *The Work of Wall Street*. New York: D. Appleton and Company, 1903.

Proust, Henry G. *A Life of George Westinghouse*. New York: American Society of Mechanical Engineers, 1921.

Ratchford, B.U. *American State Debts*. Durham: Duke University Press, 1941.

Remer, Carl F. *American Investments in China*. Honolulu: Institute of Pacific Relations, 1929.

Reynolds, Clark W. *The Mexican Economy: Twentieth Century Structure and Growth*. New Haven: Yale University Press, 1970.

Riegel, Robert E. *The Story of the Western Railroads*. Lincoln: University of Nebraska Press, 1926.

Ripley, William Z. *Railroads: Finance and Organization*. New York: Longman Green, 1915.

Rippy, J. Fred. *British Investments in Latin America, 1822–1949: A Case Study of the Operations of Private Enterprise in Retarded Regions.* Minnesota: University of Minnesota Press, 1959.

Rippy, J. Fred. *The United States and Mexico.* New York: F. S. Crofts & Co., 1931.

Robert, W. Dunn, American Foreign Investments (New York: B. W. Huebsch & Viking Press, 1926).

Rockoff, Hugh and Bodenhorn, Howard. "Regional Interest Rates in Antebellum America", in Claudia Goldin and Hugh Rockoff (eds) *Strategic Factors in Nineteenth Century American Economic History.* Chicago: The University of Chicago Press, 1992.

Sakolski, A. M. *The Great American Land Bubble.* New York: Harper and Brothers, 1932.

Schell, William Jr. "American Investment in Tropical Mexico: Rubber Plantations, Fraud, and Dollar Diplomacy, 1897–1913", *Business History Review*, **64** (Summer 1990).

Schmidtz, Christopher. "The Rise of Big Business in the World Copper Industry 1870–1930", *The Economic History Review*, 2nd series, **39**: 3 (1986).

Simon, Matthew. "The Balance of Payments of the United States, 1861–1900", in William B. Parker (ed.) *Trends in the American Economy in the Nineteenth Century*, Studies in Income and Wealth, Vol. 24 by the Conference on Research in Income and Wealth, National Bureau of Economic Research. Princeton: Princeton University Press, 1960.

Smith, Robert F. "The United States and Cuba", in Marvin Berstein (ed.), *Foreign Investment in Latin America: Cases and Attitudes.* New York: Alfred A. Knopf, 1966.

Snowden, Kenneth A. "Mortgage Rates and American Capital Market Development in the Late Nineteenth Century", *The Journal of Economic History*, **47**: 3 (September 1987).

Solberg, Carl H. *The Prairies and the Pampas: Agrarian Policy in Canada and Argentina, 1880–1930.* Stanford: Stanford University Press, 1987.

Southard, Jr. Frank A. *American Industry in Europe*, Ph.D. dissertation, U. C. Berkeley, 1930.

Southard, Jr. Frank A. *American Industry in Europe: Origins and Development of the Multinational Corporation.* Boston: Houghton Mifflin & Co., 1931.

Southworth, Constance. "The American–Canadian Newsprint Paper Industry and the Tariff", *The Journal of Political Economy*, **30** (October 1922).

Southworth, John R., and Homs, Percy C. *El Directo Oficial Minero de Mexico*, **9**. Mexico, D.F.: John R. Southworth, 1908.

Southworth, John R. *El Directo Oficial Minero de Mexico*, **11**. Mexico, D.F.: John R. Southworth, 1910.

Spence, Clark C. *British Investment and the American Mining Frontier, 1860–1901.* Ithaca: Cornell University Press, 1958.

Spence, Clark C. "British Investment and the American Mining Frontier, 1860–1914", *New Mexico Historical Review*, **36**, (April 1961).

Stedman, Edmund C. *The New York Stock Exchange: Its History, its Contribution to National Prosperity, and its Relation to American Finance at the*

Outset of the Twentieth Century. New York: Greenwood Press, 1969, copyright 1905.

Sylla, Richard. "Federal Policy, Banking Market Structure, and Capital Mobilization in the United States, 1863–1913", *The Journal of Economic History*, **29**: 4 (December 1969).

Thompson, Robert Luther. *Wiring a Continent: The History of the Telegraph in the United States, 1832–1866*. Princeton: Princeton University Press, 1947.

Tilly, Richard. "International Aspects of the Development of German Banking, 1870–1914". Mimeographed.

Tilly, Richard. "Some Comments on German Foreign Portfolio Investment, 1870–1914", paper delivered in Sao Paolo, July 1989.

Urquhart, M. C. "Canadian Economic Growth 1870–1980", Queens University, Department of Economics, Discussion Paper 734, 1988.

Urquhart, M. C. (ed.) *Historical Statistics of Canada*. Cambridge: The University Press, 1965.

US, Census Office, *Report on Valuation, Taxation, and Public Indebtedness of the United States, Tenth Census*, Washington, D.C., 1884.

US, Congress, House, 27th Cong., 3rd sess., 1843, H. Document 296.

US, Congress, Senate, 33rd Cong., 1 sess., Secretary of the Treasury report to the United States Senate, Executive Document 42, March 2, 1854.

US, Congress, Senate, 50th Cong., 2nd sess., 1889, S. Document 2690.2.

US, Congress, Senate, 61st Cong., 2nd sess., 1910, S. Document 579.

US, Department of Commerce, Bureau of the Census. *Historical Statistics of the United States, Colonial Times to 1970*, V. 1 and 2. Washington, D.C.: GPO, 1970.

US, Department of Commerce, Bureau of the Census. *Statistical Abstract of the United States, Historical Statistics, 1990* . Washington, D.C.: GPO, 1990.

US, Department of Labor. *News*. Washington, D.C.: Bureau of Labor Statistics, June 30, 1989.

US Government, Select Committee on an Inquiry into the Occupation and Administration of Haiti and Santo Domingo, *Hearings*, 67th Cong., 1st and 2nd sessions. Washington, D.C.: GPO, 2 vols, 1922.

Van Oss, Salomon F. *America's Railroads as Investments*. New York: Arno Press, 1977.

Vasquez, Josefina Zaraida, and Meyer, Lorenzo. *The United States and Mexico*. Chicago: University of Chicago Press, 1985.

Veenendaal, Jr. Augustus J. "The Kansas City Southern Railway and the Dutch Connection", *Business History Review*, **61**: 2 (Summer 1987).

Viner, Jacob. *Canada's Balance of International Indebtedness, 1900–1913*, Harvard Economic Studies, **26**. Cambridge, Mass.: Harvard University Press, 1924.

Wells, David A. *A Study of Mexico*. New York: D. Appleton & Company, 1887.

Wells, David A. *Report of the Special Commissioner of Revenue, 1869*, 41st Congress, House of Representative, Executive Document 27, December 29, 1869.

Wilkins, Mira. "The Free-Standing Company, 1870–1914: An Important Type of British Foreign Direct Investment", *Economic History Review*, 2nd Series, **41**: 2 (1988).

Wilkins, Mira. *The Emergence of Multinational Enterprise: American Business Abroad from the Colonial Era to 1914*, Harvard Studies in Business History, 34. Cambridge: Harvard University Press, 1970.

Wilkins, Mira. *The History of Foreign Investment in the United States to 1914*, Harvard Studies in Business History, Vol. 41. Cambridge: Harvard University Press, 1989.

Williams, Benjamin. *Economic Foreign Policy of the United States*. New York: McGraw Hill Book Co., 1929.

Williams, Gattenby [William Guggenheim], and Heath, Charles Monroe. *William Guggenheim*. New York: The Lone Voice Publishing Company, 1934.

Williamson, Jeffrey G. *American Growth and the Balance of Payments, 1820–1913: A Study of the Long Swing*. Chapel Hill: The University of North Carolina Press, 1964.

Williamson, Harold F., and Daum, Arnold R. *The American Petroleum Industry: The Age of Illumination*. Evanston, Ill.: Northwestern University Press, 1955.

Wilson, Charles Morrow. *Empire in Gold and Green: The Story of the American Banana Trade*. New York: Henry Holt & Co., 1947.

Wyckoff, Peter. *Wall Street and the Stock Markets: A Chronology (1644–1971)*, 1st Edition. Philadelphia: Chilton Book Co., 1982.

Young, Ralph A. *Handbook of American Underwriting of Foreign Securities*. US Department of Commerce, Trade Promotion Series # 104, Government Printing Office, 1930.

Zevin, Robert B. "Are World Financial Markets More Open? If So Why and With What Effects", *Financial Openness and National Autonomy*. New York: 1989.

Index

161